THE BOOK OF
MULBARTON
'A Village that has No History'?

JILL AND DAVID WRIGHT

HALSGROVE

First published in Great Britain in 2006

British Library Cataloguing-in-Publication Data
A CIP record for this title is available from the British Library

ISBN 1 84114 503 3
ISBN 978 1 84114 503 7

HALSGROVE

Halsgrove House
Lower Moor Way
Tiverton, Devon EX16 6SS
Tel: 01884 243242
Fax: 01884 243325
Email: sales@halsgrove.com
Website: www.halsgrove.com

Frontispiece photograph: *Adam delving – a panel of
fifteenth-century stained glass in the east window
of Mulbarton Church. Adam is shown as a
barefoot medieval gardener with a spade. Other
panels of the east window can be seen on page 70.*
(PHOTO TAKEN FOR THIS BOOK BY JILL WRIGHT)

Printed and bound in Great Britain by CPI Bath

CONTENTS

Acknowledgements

First and foremost, thanks must go to the many present and past residents of Mulbarton and nearby villages who have lent photographs and other documents or the fruits of their research, and to those who have written memories for inclusion in this book. They include:

Bill Alborough; Clifford Allison; Bernard Ambrose; Juliet Amos (née Lofty); Betty Anderson; Lawrence Bailey; Rodney Barker; Ronnie Barrett; Mavis Bastin; John Betts; Sue Bird; Patrick Bobbin; Barry Brooks; Elizabeth Brown; Rachel Burchell; Terry Burchell; Jane Burgess; Jane Burrell; Rene Carlton; Marina Carter; Robin and Elizabeth Clayton; Elizabeth Cliffe; Daphne Collins; Malcolm and Dale Court; Robert Court; John Cranston; Anne Dack (née Barclay); Jo Daynes; Irene Eagle; Judith Fairclough; Ingrid Fairman; Nick Farthing; Phyllis Feltham; Sue Filmer; Enid Fox; Iris Frost; Barbara Gent; Joan Goffin; Jean Goodrum; Anne Gotts (née Bridgeman); Jack Grady; Vic Gray; Mary Guttridge; Valerie Hanson; John Hardman; Tony Harrod; Peter Haverson; Margaret Hedges (née Sparke); Pam Hemming; John Hewitt; Bridget Jackson (née Finch); Malcolm and Valerie Jones; Tony Kent; David and Cynthia Ladbrooke; Lynn and Roger Lambert; Michael Lambert; Alice Lince; Peter Lincoln; Stanley Lincoln; Peter and Sheila Lockhart; Sidney Mason; David and Mary Mellor; Chris Mickleburgh; Norma Mickleburgh; Peter Mickleburgh; George Moore; John and Kathryn Moore; Maurice Norman; Liz Newbery; Rachel Noonan (née Wright); Richard Pilch; Clive Potter; Olive Riches; Peter Riches; Clifford and Rosalind Robinson; Diane Robinson; John Rumball; James and Patricia Rump; Howard Scotter; Russell Scotter; Rosemary Shaw; Daphne Skeet; Evelyn Smith (née Stackyard); Kathleen Smith; Philip Standley; Mr and Mrs A. Stevens; Alan and Linda Steynor; Revd Jess Stubenbord; Brenda Swingler; Mrs J. Swift; Pam Tancock; David Thomas; Muriel Tooke (née Lincoln); Mrs Trafford; John Tuddenham; Bryan Tungate; Dorothy Tungate; Elizabeth Valiant; Evelyn Vincent; Queenie Wasey; Harry Walsh; Rosemary Watkinson (née Steward); Lindsay Watson; John and Jil Wheeler; Susie Whitehouse; Barbara Wick; David Wick; Julie Wilkins; Rosemary Wright; Steven Wright; Charlie and Brenda Yallop.

The pond with pump, cottages and church in about 1910. The little girl in the middle of the group is thought to be Vera ('Babs') Middleton, daughter of the postmaster. (CONTRIBUTED BY ANNE DACK)

Sadly, some of these contributors are no longer with us, which is a reminder of the need to collect people's memories while we can – and we hope this serves as a tribute to them.

Mulbarton Church and the First and Middle Schools have made their resources available. Many hours have been spent in the Norfolk Records Office and the Norfolk Heritage Centre, guided by their helpful staff. The Norfolk Museums and Archaeological Service, in particular the Bridewell Museum, Norwich, the Gressenhall Farm and Workhouse Museum of Norfolk Life, Norfolk Landscape Archaeology and the Wymondham Heritage Museum have allowed us to photograph artefacts or have advised on local 'finds'. The Ordnance Survey and the Norfolk County Council Planning Department have allowed us to reproduce old maps, and Archant Photographic Norfolk has kindly allowed us to reproduce those photos that people lent us which originally appeared in the *Eastern Daily Press* and *Evening News*. And thanks to Dr Kim Fleet, who was the mastermind and inspiration behind the creation of the website: www.norfolkheritage.org.uk/mulbarton.

If we have omitted to acknowledge anyone correctly, we apologise and hope to make amends in any future edition. Modern photographs not otherwise acknowledged were taken by Jill Wright especially for this book.

Last but not least, we must acknowledge a debt to one photographer in particular: Tom Nokes (1872–1944) who was selling his photographs in Norwich from the age of 11. He took a particular interest in the villages south of Norwich – including Mulbarton – and rode around on his bike with his camera, a case of glass negatives and his tripod strapped to the crossbar. He photographed families and rural life, then returned to Norwich to develop his prints onto postcards in a shed at the bottom of his garden. Then he would return to take more photos and sell his cards through village shops. Look out for the distinctive 'T. Nokes' signature on many old photos in this book.

Full details and references for all items about Mulbarton and Kenningham held by the Norfolk Record Office and Norfolk Museums Service are listed on http://www.noah.norfolk.gov.uk/ and can be searched for under 'Mulbarton' and 'Kenningham'.

Extracts from the following sources have been quoted:
Victorian History of the Counties of England, Norfolk, Vol. 2, p.153 (first published 1906; reprinted 1975 for the University of London).
Blomefield, Francis, *History of Norfolk* (published 1802), Vol. 5. pp.74–83.
Mackie, Charles (ed.), Norfolk Annals, Vol. 2, 1851–1900 (Norwich: Norwich Chronicle, 1901) – available in Norfolk Records Office.
Within Living Memory – a collection of Norfolk Reminiscences (written and compiled by members of the Norfolk Federation of Women's Institutes, 1971). All anonymous.
Priestley, Ursula (ed.) *The Letters of Philip Stannard, Norwich Textile Manufacturer (1751–1763)* Norfolk Record Society, Vol. LVII for 1992.
Norfolk Chronicle
Norfolk News

Mulbarton even had its own Christmas card, showing the frozen pond and the church tower. The photo of the pond was probably taken in the hard winter of early 1929.

(CONTRIBUTED BY TERRY BURCHELL, FROM PHILIP STANDLEY'S COLLECTION)

A Mulbarton Heritage Group visit to the Norfolk Records Office in 2005, where Education Officer Frank Mears (left) introduces them to some Mulbarton records. He is pointing to the 1841 Tithe Map. Also on display are the 1724 Manor map; a Manor Court book; and Registers of Births and Deaths. Listening to Mr Mears are (left to right) Jill Wright and Chris Carter (partly hidden), Jil Wheeler, Evelyn Smith, Charlie Yallop, Cynthia and David Ladbrooke, Bryan Tungate, Irene Eagle, Michael Lambert, Peter Riches, Peter Mickleburgh.

(PHOTO: TERRY BURCHELL)

Money, Weights and Measures

For those who have forgotten – or who never knew – the prices, weights and measures used in some of the text and illustrations in *The Book of Mulbarton*, here is a brief guide:

Money
2 ha'pennies or 4 farthings = 1 (old) penny (written 1d.); 12 pence = 1 shilling (written 1s. or 1/-); 20 shillings = £1; 21 shillings = 1 guinea.

Weights
16 ounces (16oz) = 1 pound (1lb); 14lbs = 1 stone; 112lbs = 1 hundredweight (1cwt); 20cwt = 1ton (BUT a quarter loaf = just over 4lbs; 56lbs of flour = 1 bushel)

Measures
2 pints (4 pts) = 1 quart; 4 quarts = 1 gallon (1 gal); 8 gals = 1 bushel; 4 bushels = 1 coomb

Distance
12 inches (12″) = 1 foot (1ft or 1′); 3 feet = 1 yard (1yd); 22 yards = 1 chain; 10 chains = 1 furlong; 8 furlongs (1,760yds) = 1 mile

Area
1,210 square yards = 1 rood = 40 square rods, poles or perches; 4 roods (4,840sq.yds) = 1 acre; 640 acres = 1 square mile

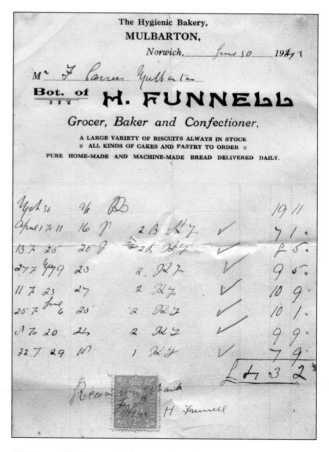

H. Funnell, Grocer, Baker and Confectioner, The Hygienic Bakery, Mulbarton – bill for items purchased 30 June 1943, amounting to £4.3s.2d., therefore receipted over a 2d. stamp. (CONTRIBUTED BY VIC GRAY)

Introduction

'Mulbarton has NO history…'. These were the words of a former Rector, Revd 'Sandy' Sanderson, when the village sign was unveiled in July 1979. In one sense he was right: Mulbarton has had NO battles, NO revolution and NO national headlines. And yet… Mulbarton is FULL of history: the ordinary, everyday history of ordinary people. And it is ordinary people, determined to preserve their history, who led to the creation first of the website, www.norfolkheritage.org.uk/mulbarton, then to the Mulbarton Heritage Group and then to more and more people asking for a 'Book of Mulbarton'.

Over 100 past and present residents of the village have hunted out photographs, programmes, magazines, receipts and many other archives; they have written their memories and found memories recorded by earlier generations. There have been some exciting 'finds', such as the Poor Rate Book for 1851, which matches the census of that year; the 'Penny Book' of the Oddfellows Benevolence Lodge listing local names; a Practical Farmer's Account Book with details of work and payments in 1865–66, including an account of the harvest; and even the Darts Cup from a demolished pub! The school logbooks, church archives, and resources in the Norfolk Records Office have been invaluable sources of information, too.

We are the inheritors of at least 3,500 years of history, yet this book concentrates on the past 200 years. Even so, there is too much for one book and some material has been added to the heritage website. Villagers have rediscovered their history, yet this is not a blow-by-blow chronological account – we hope readers will dip into different topics. Every chapter links with all the other chapters, which makes Mulbarton a delight to explore, but it's impossible to create a perfect plan for this book! There is so much more to discover – hopefully this book will stimulate more 'finds', more research, and yet more articles about Mulbarton past and present.

The unveiling of the village sign, July 1979: Revd C.J.H. Sanderson ('Sandy'), retired Rector of Mulbarton, blesses the village sign after it has been unveiled by his wife Mary (seated left). Among those in the audience are Peter Lockhart, Chairman of the Parish Council (standing left of sign); Sandra Phillips of the Young Wives (behind Revd Sanderson) and Miss Ireland of the Women's Institute (seated behind Mary Sanderson). (Photo: Evening News, reproduced courtesy of Archant Photographic Norfolk)

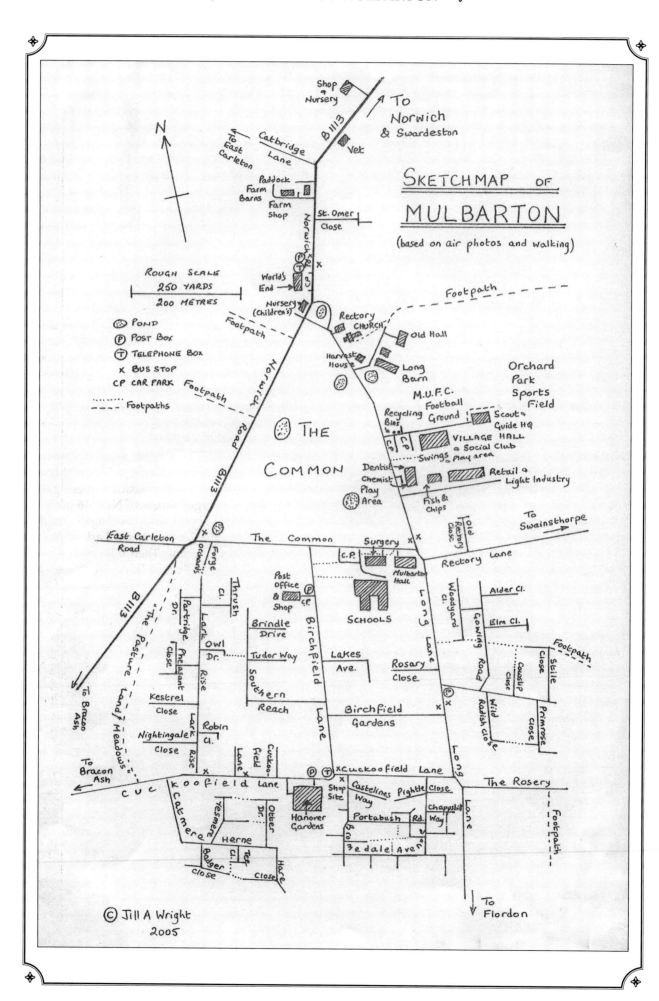

CHAPTER 1

Setting the Scene

Mulbarton may be 'at the World's End' but the milepost by the corner of the pub car park shows it is five miles south of Norwich. The old village was always concentrated in this area, with pockets of housing near the other two corners of the triangular Common. There were two other hamlets: The Rosery, near which the early council-houses were built, and The Wood, at the southernmost end of Wood Lane, Swardeston, which was never linked to the rest of Mulbarton by a 'paved' road. Kenningham, a 'lost' village to the east, was joined to Mulbarton in 1452. This is the parish which is the subject of this book, and the scene is set with the ups and downs of its geography and history.

The Lie of the Land

The acquisition of 'The Meadows' enables Mulbarton folk to walk beside the pleasant stream that forms the main outlet for most of Mulbarton's water. Some would like it named the River Mul on maps; in fact it is rather prosaically labelled 'Mulbarton Stream –

Western Branch'! This stream begins near Mulbarton's highest point on Flordon Long Lane (51 metres above sea level) and flows along part of the parish boundary. It is usually a feeble trickle, but it can become a torrent after heavy rain. Mrs Goodrum clearly remembers one night in 1968 when boys had been demolishing a haystack and some of it blocked the pipe under Cuckoofield Lane. Her husband rescued the family by boat from the resultant flood. Today, water from the new Mulberry Gardens estate drains from a special holding tank designed to prevent flooding to an outlet beside the Cuckoofield Lane bridge (Chapter 11).

Pipes have replaced the ditches that once separated the fields where Lark Rise and Southern Reach were built, and these also flow into the stream by The Meadows. A stream from The Rosery/Long Lane junction once flowed across the field that is now Birchfield Gardens and across Mr Emms's land near the present-day Post Office (Chapter 11). Today it is in ditches and pipes behind the back gardens of the bungalows, to emerge between Nos 16 and 18 Birchfield Lane – only to disappear again until it flows between Forge Orchards and Lark Rise and into the Mulbarton stream. Then this stream flows under the B1113 at 'Mulbarton Bridge', not far from the south-west corner of the Common and East

This milestone by the former Methodist Chapel and World's End dates from road improvements to create the Norwich to New Buckenham Turnpike, soon after 1772. It shows that the old centre of the village is only 5 miles from Norwich.

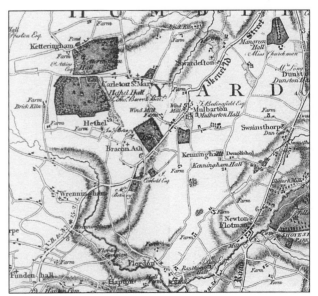

Extract from Faden's Map of Norfolk, 1797, showing the Mulbarton area. The whole county was surveyed in 1790–94 by Thomas Donald and Thomas Milne, and the maps were published at approximately 1 inch to 1 mile by William Faden, Geographer to His Majesty.

The village from the air looking north, from Cuckoofield Lane to the Common and further north towards Norwich, 1975.
(PHOTO: DAVID WRIGHT)

Mulbarton Bridge over the Mulbarton stream (called the 'River Mul' by some), looking north along what is now the B1113 towards the Tradesman's Arms (Chapter 3). The thatched Forge Cottage (right) still stands.
(PHOTO CONTRIBUTED BY IRIS FROST)

The water-splash: the so-called 'River Mul' when it crossed Catbridge Lane, looking towards East Carleton.
(PHOTO CONTRIBUTED BY CLIFFORD ROBINSON)

Carleton Road. In wet winters, water pours from the waterlogged Common towards this low point. Another ditch flows from the pond by Birchfield Lane, down the south side of the Common, to the same point.

Having collected all this water, the stream flows to and through the lake in the Cheshire Home grounds. It once crossed Catbridge Lane at a ford, but there is now a bridge. Soon it is joined by water from another shallow Mulbarton valley. This begins near The Rosery and crosses fields to a pond in Rectory Lane. The valley that continues northwards can be seen from the track east of the church. It crosses the B1113 in the valley near the vet's surgery and then to the 'River Mul'. An important job on Old Hall Farm (Chapter 6) was to clear out the ditches that channelled this stream from near The Rosery to the Norwich Road, but today some ditches hardly exist, leaving the higher land waterlogged. The 'River Mul' then flows northwards through Swardeston and Intwood, and joins the River Yare upstream of Keswick Mill.

Beneath our Feet

The full story of Mulbarton starts many millions of years ago, when a warm sea covered our area. Onto the sea floor fell the remains of tiny shellfish – and all the waste they produced – until there were hundreds of metres of deposits. These deposits were compressed: we now call them CHALK – a soft white limestone with FLINTS – hard silica nodules.

It is hidden now, but this chalk is important to Mulbarton people every day. The water we drink is pumped from deep in the chalk – pure but 'hard' water. Look in your kettle for proof of its origin! Look westwards from Mulbarton Common to see the water-tower at East Carleton which supplies our water.

Fast-forward about 130 million years. The next thing that matters is the ICE AGE – the most important event in Mulbarton's prehistory – that still affects all of us every day. The ice sheets came across the North Sea (though there was no sea then). As they came they scraped up mud and rocks and, when they melted, everything was dumped where the ice had been. Mulbarton's BOULDER CLAY is 100 feet or so thick. That's why the Common is so muddy – the clay holds rainwater for weeks.

In the clay are boulders: mostly flints, brought from where the North Sea now is, plus lumps of chalk. Hundreds of these lumps of chalk and flint were visible during the deep excavation south of Cuckoofield Lane in 2004. This helps to explain why our fields and gardens can grow such good crops: the clay is acid, but the chalk is alkaline; the clay retains the water, but the chalk is porous. Mix them together and you have a very fertile soil.

The old houses were built from the boulder clay, with 'clay lump' (large clay blocks that were not fired) or local red bricks and pantiles. Brick Kiln Lane leads to the site of an old brick pit and kiln between the railway and the A140. Almost all the 40 ponds of Mulbarton parish have been dug in the boulder clay. Flints from the fields were used to build Mulbarton Church (the limestone cornerstones came from over 100 miles away – west of the Fens). So when we rejoice at the flowers in Mulbarton, or grumble at the sticky mud, we are praising – or blaming – the ice sheets that brought us their gifts.

Digging up the Past

The oldest archaeological find to come to light in Mulbarton is some potboilers dated to 1500BC: they were left behind 3,500 years ago! Nothing else so old has ever been found to suggest when the area was first settled. Casual finds have emerged within the parish, thanks to the fact that our ancestors were as careless or forgetful as we are. Among the most interesting are a piece of a Bronze-Age axe-head found west of the Norwich Road; a fragment of a late-Bronze-Age spear-head found behind the church; an Iron-Age Icenian silver coin and a Romano-British key handle. Were people living here when the Romans built Pye Street from Colchester (now the A140) to *Venta Icenorum* (now Caister-by-Norwich) and fortified *Ad Taum* (Tasburgh camp)? Were they forced to work on any of these projects? Did they take advantage of new trading opportunities? Or did some people from Caister first come and settle here?

We know little about Mulbarton in the so-called 'Dark Ages', yet there have been several amazing discoveries in this area. A number of Saxon items

The crazed surface of these flints shows they were heated in a fire and dropped into a pot to heat liquid. There is no record of exactly where in the parish they were found, but they can be seen in Wymondham Museum.

(PHOTOGRAPHED WITH KIND PERMISSION
OF WYMONDHAM HERITAGE MUSEUM)

Bill for bricks from Swainsthorpe, 1887. Robert Carpenter's Swainsthorpe works is presumably the origin of the name Brick Kiln Lane. Receipted 31 January 1888.

(CONTRIBUTED BY MULBARTON MIDDLE SCHOOL)

have been found in Mulbarton parish, including three early-Saxon (pagan) brooches; a piece of a cross-shaped Saxon brooch; a brooch and a box mount from late-Saxon times; and a Viking five-lobed sword pommel decorated with interlaced animal designs. Some finds from nearby parishes featured in the Castle Museum's 'Buried Treasure' exhibition (2005–06), including the end of a second-century finger ring found at Keswick; a Carolingian denier coin (the European equivalent of the English penny) from the time of King Louis the Pious (814–40) found at Shotesham; and, most fascinating, 'a silver Arab dirham coin issued by Caliph al-Mu'tadid (892–902) from the mint at al-Shash', which was probably carried by a Viking trader. This was found at Swainsthorpe.

Most Mulbarton items have been found near the church or between the main road and the river – which may have more to do with who looks where today, than who lived where in the past! It is likely that Angles (closely related to the Saxons) explored the river valley and then cleared farmland above the marshes.

What's in a Name?

'Mulbarton' is given as *Molkebartuna* and *Molkebetstuna* in the Domesday Book. '-ton' or '-tone' is an Anglo-Saxon place-name ending meaning 'enclosure' or 'farmstead'. 'Barton' means 'an outlying farm' where barley or other corn was grown (from the Old English *beretun*). Francis Blomefield considered 'Mulbarton' to mean '*MOLKE, MYKIL, MUCHE* or *GREAT-BARTON*'. 'Molke' could mean 'milk', indicating 'an outlying dairy farm'. 'The outlying dairy farm on the hill' may be the extended meaning of the name Mulbarton – but outlying from where? Presumably there were a number of Saxon settlements in the area – at Carle-ton and Swardes-ton. 'Ham' (homestead) and 'inga' (group of people under a leader), as at Kenn-ing-ham and Wren-ing-ham, also indicate Anglo-Saxon place-names. 'Thorpe' is a Danish word, so perhaps Vikings settled in nearby Swains-thorpe, Gow-thorpe and Ashwell-thorpe.

Domesday Mulbarton

The 'Little' Domesday Book of 1086 has two entries for Mulbarton:

Land of Ralf de Bellofago
Hundred of Humbleyard. MOLKEB[AR]TUNA [Mulbarton] is held by Richard, which Ordinc, a theign held in the time of King Edward [as] 2 plough-lands. Then and afterwards [there were] 10 villeins, now [there are] 7. Then [there were] 7 bordars, now [there are] 16. Then [there were] 2 serfs, now 1. Then as now 2 ploughs on the demesne, and 2 ploughs

belonging to the men; 10 acres of meadow. Woodland for 16 swine. Then as now 1 mill, now 1 rouncey. Then 1 beast, now 6 swine. And sokemen [with] 60 acres. Then as now [they had] 1½ ploughs. [Richard also holds land in Carleton and Swardeston – in total 56 acres.] Then and afterwards [Mulbarton] was worth 60 shillings, now 100. And the freemen are worth 6 shillings. It is 6 furlongs in length and 5 in breadth, and [renders] 6 pence of geld. [There is] 1 church [with] 15 [acres], and it is worth 2 shillings. In MOLKEB[AR]TUNA He [also holds] 1 freeman, under Stigand by commendation only [with] 30 acres. Then [he had] 2 ploughs and 1 acre of meadow. Then as now he was worth 20 shillings.

Land of Roger Bigot
In Molkebetstuna [Mulbarton] 1 freeman with 30 acres under Godric's predecessor in patronage [before 1066]. Always 2 smallholders. Then half a plough now 1. In the same 1 freewoman under Godric's predecessor in patronage, 30 acres of land. Godric had possession of this when R[alf] forfeited and she duly paid him 5 shillings. A certain man of Roger's in patronage only, the son of this woman, dwelt on the same land with his mother and so Roger claims half the land. The father of this man had other free land in another place under R[oger's] predecessor in patronage only. Roger holds all that 1 land. On the above 30 acres, then 1½ plough, now one. 4 smallholders. Meadow, 2 acres. Under these 2 freemen and a half in patronage only, at 17½ acres; always 1½ plough. Value of all these free men before 1066 £8; later 10; now £15.5 shillings 1½ pence.

The Domesday Survey gives us the names of the pre-Norman landowners: Ordinc and Godric, and also Stigand, one-time Bishop of Elmham, who became Archbishop of Canterbury and died in 1072. For ordinary village people the Conquest probably meant little: a system already in place was fixed more firmly as 'the Manorial System'; a new king theoretically owned all the land; new French-speaking overlords with different names, Ralf and Roger, pocketed the revenue but probably took little interest in the village. Roger Bigot was one of the

Domesday Book entry for Mulbarton – Molkebtuna (from a copy of the 'Domesday Book – Part Relating to Norfolk' photozincographed at the Ordnance Survey, Southampton, 1862). (CONTRIBUTED BY DAVID AND JILL WRIGHT)

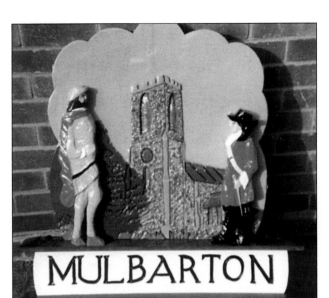

The Mulbarton village sign in detail in 1985, repaired and repainted and awaiting erection on the refurbished post. The sign shows Baron de St Omer (left) *and Sir Edwin Rich on either side of Mulbarton Church.*

(PHOTO: IRENE EAGLE)

'Great Servants' of William the Conqueror, and his son, bailiff of all the king's holdings after 1077, was made Earl of Norfolk, Constable of Norwich Castle and held no fewer than 187 manors!

The unnamed people are just as interesting: the six smallholders, seven villeins (NOT villains!), 16 bordars, one serf, three freemen plus further freemen and an uncertain number of sokemen, and 1 free-woman and her family equal at least 40 people. Double the number, assuming as many women as men; double again, assuming as many children as adults, to give a population of at least 160 – a quarter the size of the village in 1900. They would plough the land, cut the meadow, and their pigs would graze the woodland – which also provided fuel for their fires. As the centuries passed, the woodland disappeared and the farmland increased.

The Medieval Manor

Mulbarton's village sign shows the church and two men. The medieval man on the left is Baron de St Omer, a lord of the manor. St Omer Close takes its name from this same person. It is NOT St Omer (or Audomarus) himself – this French Christian was a monk for 20 years, became bishop in 637 and was a missionary among the pagan Morini in what is now the Pas de Calais. He was a renowned preacher and founded an abbey at Sithiu – now the site of the town of St Omer in northern France. He died in around 699 and, should the residents of St Omer Close wish to celebrate, his saint's day is 9 September!

St Omer (the town) was in the heartland of the Normans and presumably people from there were 'surnamed' *de* (from) St Omer. There is no record of

anyone associated with St Omer having links with Mulbarton until 160 years after the Norman Conquest. According to Francis Blomefield's 'History of Norfolk' at some time in the early 1200s, 'Sir Bartholomew de St Omer had lands here but was not Lord'. It was his son, 'William de Sancto Audomaro, Omero – or St Omer...' who became lord of the manor of Mulbarton '... in the time of Henry III (1216–72). The king granted him entitlement to a 'free-warren' and fair here and at Brundale (Brundall) in 1253.'

The manor then passed to his son, Thomas de St Omer – infamous for wrongly hanging a man from East Carleton in 1285 and possibly (re)building the church as a penance (Chapter 5). 'Thomas de St Omer, married Petronella... daughter and co-heir of Thomas Malmain' (= left-handed!) and then 'widow of Ralf de Tony...' Each wife had one daughter, and these half-sisters, Elizabeth and Alice, were his heiresses. Presumably this is the man who is pictured on our village sign, for after him the manor passes to another line and a very different relationship with France.

It was Alice, daughter of Thomas and Petronella, who took the manor of Mulbarton into her marriage, and her husband, Sir William de Hoo, knight, became lord of the manor from 1367. Sir William was a well-known warrior in his day, who fought against the French and probably visited the Holy Land. In Mulbarton he is reputed to have built the present church tower and nave, where he and his wife, Alice, were buried (Chapter 5). The manor passed to their son, Thomas Hoo, who became Sir Thomas around 1434 and was sent to Normandy to suppress a rebellion around Caux. Elected a Knight of the Garter in 1445, he returned to France and was honoured for his efforts by being made a baron, Lord Hoo of Hastings, and thus a Member of Parliament. He married three times – (1) Elizabeth Felton bore him a son, Thomas, who died before his father; (2) Elizabeth Wichingham bore him a daughter, Anne; and (3) Eleanor Wells bore him three daughters. In his will, dated 1454, he bequeathed Mulbarton Manor to Anne, the daughter of his second wife, Elizabeth.

Anne de Hoo became the second wife of Sir Jeffrey Boleyn, who was Lord Mayor of London in 1457 and a wealthy cloth merchant who bought Blickling Hall. Thus, through Anne de Hoo's marriage, the manor of Mulbarton came into the hands of the Boleyn family. Anne's grandson was Thomas Boleyn, who became Earl of Wiltshire and Viscount Rochford and married Lady Elizabeth Howard (eldest daughter of the Duke of Norfolk), and their daughter was Anne Boleyn, second wife of Henry VIII. Thomas Boleyn moved in loftier circles than Mulbarton, and in 1535 he sold the manor to John Gresham, who also acquired next-door Kenningham.

In the hands of the Gresham family, both manors

A Kenningham Interlude

Kenningham Hall in the 'lost' village of Kenningham. The farmhouse has kept some of its original character, although it has been considerably extended at the back.
(PHOTO CONTRIBUTED BY TERRY BURCHELL, FROM PHILIP STANDLEY'S COLLECTION)

Kenningham was a little settlement east of Mulbarton – now reduced to Kenningham Hall Farm and a row of cottages in Brick Kiln Lane. It is one of Norfolk's 'lost villages' – perhaps a victim of the Black Death (1348–49) and the epidemics that followed. Kenningham is listed in the Domesday Book:

Land of Godric the Sewer (Sower)
In Kenincham Ancholfus held 1 sokeman with 30 acres, ½ a plough and worth 5 shillings.

Land of Tovi
In Kenincham there are 3 freemen with 75 acres and 5 freemen under them with 18½ acres and 2 bordars and 2 ploughs.

In Domesday times Kenningham was paying 11d. Danegeld – nearly twice as much as Mulbarton. A total of 11 men are listed, so there were possibly around 50 people in this hamlet. The humps and bumps in the field south of the farmhouse probably mark the site of the medieval village, and the church was in the woodland next to the cottages. From 1309 13 Rectors are listed, the last one resigning when old and lame in 1452. The parish of Kenningham, with its 50 acres of glebe land, was united with Mulbarton, and the church building was a ruin by the time of the Reformation.

Up to the time of Queen Elizabeth I, the Dukes of Norfolk were lords of the manor of Kenningham, but it was sold to Sir Thomas Gresham, who also acquired Mulbarton Manor. It is likely that the Turner family was already living there: 'Wylliam Turner of Kenyngham' made his will just before his death in 1547, leaving 25s. for mending the highway in Mulbarton, land and a cow 'to Richard my belchild [grandchild]. My son Thomas to occupy same till Richard be 20 years old.' He also left money and a cow for other grandsons when they reached 20, gifts to godchildren, 'to every priest at my burying, and praying for my soul, gift and their dinners…Residue to Johane my wife and Thomas my son, Executors'. This son, Thomas Turner, bought the 500-acre manor from Sir Richard Gresham in 1570 as a farm. The inventory taken at the death of one of Thomas Turner's sons, Richard, in 1601 shows that Kenningham Hall was a two-storey house with hall, parlour, dining-room and bedroom on the ground floor, two bedrooms upstairs, plus buttery and outhouse. Possessions considered of value were cupboard, tables, chairs, a pair of 'dogirons', three beds (one worth 40s.), blankets, coverlet, pillows and 'apparel' worth £4.6s.8d. His crops and livestock are not listed, but the total value of all his possessions (excluding money and land) was £54.11s.4d.

Over the years the Turners added a new front to the house with rooms on either side of the central hall and their land extended into neighbouring parishes. Other family members owned what is now Paddock Farm in Mulbarton (Chapter 6). John Turner, 'owner and yeoman', sold the Kenningham estate to James Muskett of Surlingham in 1861, but John Hotblack, husband of Mary Turner (and Mayor of Norwich in 1884), bought it back in 1886 after Mr Muskett died. Their son, John Turner Hotblack, inherited it, but the farm seems to have been leased to tenants most of the time. In 1931 Kenningham Hall Farm was put up for sale by auction by the executors of the late Mrs L.E. Hotblack and was bought by Joseph Burfield, a surgeon at the Norwich and Norfolk Hospital. His daughter, Eileen, married Eric Gowing, who farmed at Kenningham Hall. He was a parish councillor for 27 years until 1983, and a district councillor with Forehoe and Henstead, the Rural District Council before local government reorganisation in 1974. The house is still in the family.

Kenningham Cottages from the air, June 1986. The woodland beside the cottages is the site of Kenningham Church.
(PHOTO: DAVID AND JILL WRIGHT)

passed to Sir Richard Gresham (Lord Mayor of London in 1537), who sold Kenningham to Thomas Turner (see above). In 1575 the manor of Mulbarton passed to Sir Thomas Gresham, a financier and founder of the Royal Exchange, who founded Gresham's School, near Holt, in 1555. When he died, the manor passed to his son, William Gresham, of London, who almost certainly never lived here. He mortgaged or leased the hall to Francis Cuddon.

We know little about the 'ordinary' people of Mulbarton in medieval and Elizabethan times. The Norfolk Lay Subsidies of 1327 and 1332 (before the Black Death) list those people owning personal property 'surplus to those regarded as necessities' on which they had to pay a tax of one-fifteenth of the value. Those whose payments would have been under 6d. (1327) or 8d. (1332) were excused. The Villat de Mulkberton had only 14 taxpayers, of whom five were assessed in shillings – the rest paid between 12d. and 18d. First in the list is Will-o de s-ce Omero, presumably a member of the St Omer family. The names of other taxpayers are delightful, including Nich-o Yimme; Will-o Smale; Rad-o Birch and Rad-o Batte; Godefr' Shephirde.

A few wills and inventories survive for Mulbarton. They record possessions of people who had something to possess, not the average villager. The inventory for Richard Pritchard, 'Husbandman', shows he lived in a single-storey house and left 'apparel' worth 13s., blankets, bed-coverings, pillows, a feather bed and bedhead and a coffer when he died in 1591. His crops were wood, barley, rye, peas, apples and fruit and he left two bullocks (worth 32s.), a calf and two pigs. William Bircham Senior, 'Husbandman', died a few years later, in 1597, leaving table, chairs, bedstead and blankets in his single-storey house. It would be good to know if Henry Burcham, a far richer 'husbandman' in a two-storey house, who left many possessions in 1642, was a descendant. These people were almost certainly tenants, but we do not know where they lived or how much money they left. Mulbarton seems to have been an 'average' village, with no very rich or famous people living here; a few people who might be described as 'comfortable', and a large number of humble poor with no security in this life.

Rich and the Poor

In 1599 the manor of Mulbarton was sold to Sir Edwin Rich, a descendant of Richard Rich, who was Lord High Chancellor of England under Henry VIII and Edward VI. According to the Rich monument at the back of Mulbarton Church [in the corner above the door, where it was moved from the north wall in 1875], Sir Edwin was knighted at the 'Cadiz voyage'. This was an expedition to seize Cadiz and its treasure from Philip II of Spain in 1596 and included Sir Walter Raleigh among its members. His four sons

Monument in Mulbarton Church (moved to south wall, near door) to Sir Edwin Rich senr. The monument lists 'the fruits of the Spirit' – love, joy, peace, etc., and includes a sculptured skull.

Monument in Mulbarton Church (west wall) to Sir Edwin Rich (the younger). It was formerly topped by an hour-glass sculpture made of wood and stone.

each inherited the manor of Mulbarton in turn.

First Robert Rich, eldest son of Sir Edwin, inherited the manor. He died in 1651, was buried in Swardeston and, according to the monument, his brother Edwin arranged for him to be reinterred in a family vault at Mulbarton. This Sir Edwin Rich (son of the elder Sir Edwin, brother of Robert) is the one who 'lov'd the poor', as his own monument on the west wall of the church says. It also tells us that: 'Thetfoord gave me Breath and Norwich breeding...'. He died in 1675, aged 81, and the inscription begins, 'Our Lyef is like an Hower Glasse, and our Riches are like Sand...': there was a large stone hour-glass above the monument until recently. A poem he wrote himself included the wise advice:

Soe speake to God as if men heard you talke,
Soe lyve with men as if God saw you walke...

Sir Edwin left money to benefit the poor of Mulbarton and of Thetford, and to repair the road between Wymondham and Attleborough (the 'old' A11, now the B1172), where a monument to him exists today. The manor passed to the remaining two brothers, then a niece's husband, who sold it to a gentleman of Norwich around 1700. Thus ended the association of Mulbarton with the Rich family – apart from the Rich Charity.

The Rich Charity

Sir Edwin Rich (1594–1675) is the other gentleman on the Mulbarton village sign. In his will (dated 1670) he gave the (then) large sum of £100 to be invested by trustees and the proceeds distributed to the poor each year. The sum of £90 was used to buy:

... a close of pasture, containing by estimation 10 acres, and a piece of pasture land, containing by estimation one acre... upon trust to pay the clear yearly rents and profits to the overseers of the poor of Mulbarton who... should distribute the same... at a public meeting in the church.

The larger area of land, in Long Lane near the boundary with Bracon Ash parish, had trees on it at some stage. The smaller piece was a strip beside The Rosery which is still rented out as allotment land – in 1828, the annual income from rents was £20.10s.0d. The remaining £10 was invested with interest. In 1783, timber sold from the charity land raised £22.10s.0d., and more was sold in 1828 for £29.2s.0d. These profits were added to the investment, which was taken out in 1829 to help pay for a house to be built (at a cost of £124.9s.1d. and 'worth at least £5 a year') on part of the land by The Rosery. This later became a school (Chapter 4).

On New Year's Day, the rent income was '... divided amongst the poor persons belonging to

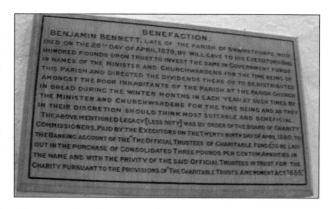

Plaque stating the terms of the Benjamin Bennett's Bread Charity, on the west wall inside Mulbarton Church. This was another charity to benefit the poor of Mulbarton and nearby villages, but today the annual income does not even buy one bread roll! (PHOTO: JILL WRIGHT)

the parish, in sums varying from 4s. to 8s. according to their age and infirmities, and the number in each family...'. Reports to the annual parish meeting are sporadic but show that in 1911 £12.19s.9d. had been distributed to 58 parishioners, and in 1938 £13.9s.6d. was distributed to 60 people. After postwar periods of disuse, the administration was tightened up and rents raised, and in 1992 £500 was shared among 40 elderly residents to help with winter fuel bills. Today, government payments far exceed the amount that the charity can give, so the trustees now help to meet other needs. Recipients have to be residents of the parish but there is no age barrier. The trustees meet twice a year, and consist of the Rector, two members appointed by the Parish Council and two co-opted members; a secretary and almoner are appointed.

Later Lords

James Balls's monument in the chancel of Mulbarton Church tells us (in Latin) that 'James Balls, Lord of the Manor and Patron of this Church died in 1748 aged 70.' He commissioned the map of the manor (believed to date from 1724) that is referred to several times in this book. The survey must have been quite an expensive undertaking, but it indicates a business-like approach to the family domain as the map shows exactly who owns or rents every piece of land. This map may have been a prelude to consolidating the different strips into fields, for land enclosure was a private matter in Mulbarton. His son, John, is described on his monument in church as 'citizen of Norwich' – he was an alderman. John Balls died in 1755, and the monument put up by his wife Susannah (née Spendlove) describes him as 'best of husbands'. Above the monument are the arms of Balls impaling Spendlove. A 'John Bowles' is listed in the 1768 Norfolk Poll Book as an elector of Mulbarton. James Balls of Norwich (son of John?) is given as 'the

Past and present Chairmen of Mulbarton Parish Council gather in December 1983 for the retirement party of Mr E.A. Marlow, Clerk to the Council for 10 years. Left to right: *Peter Lockhart, Peter Mickleburgh, Mr E.A. Marlow, John Wheeler, Valerie Grogutt.* (Photo contributed by Irene Eagle)

present lord and patron' when Blomefield was writing in 1802.

Managing a country estate was a complicated task, with fields and cottages let and sub-let; copy-hold, leasehold and freehold tenures; common and other rights. The Manor Court had lost most of its powers by 1600 and met largely to sort out rents, land rights, boundaries and other legal matters which were dealt with by the chief officer, the steward. In our area, at some point soon after 1800 the steward (small 's', the office-holder) was Steward (capital 'S', a Norwich solicitor and notary public) who took opportunities as and when they arose to acquire country estates and the titles that went with them.

We know John Steward (1766–1829) was involved in the administration of the East Carleton Estate after Margaret Dod died in 1793 without making a will. Margaret's sister, Elizabeth, personally renounced her right to administer the estate 'in the office of John Steward... situate in the parish of Saint Stephen in the City of Norwich...' allowing John Cowcher Dod to administer his inheritance. John Dod held a Manor Court in East Carleton in 1795 with John Steward as his steward, and he was still the owner and occupier in 1802. By 1803 John Steward was lord of the manor of East Carleton, and the Dod family had disappeared from all records by 1804. It is likely he acquired the manor of Mulbarton around this time, too. John Steward continued to live in Norwich, where he became an Alderman in 1807, Sheriff in 1808 and Mayor in 1810. In 1813 he was

living in Upper King Street whilst East Carleton manor house was being built. Around 1823 he bought Gowthorpe Manor, Swardeston. He was also lord of the manors of Peveralls, Saxlingham, Netherhall, Verdons and Thorpe Hall and patron of three livings. His grandson, another John Steward, allowed the school to be built on common land (Chapter 4).

Under successive generations of the Steward family, the Old Hall and many other properties, plus large areas of farmland in Mulbarton parish, were part of the East Carleton Manor estate. It was after the death of Major John Geoffrey Steward in 1915 that his widow, Eleanor Mary, took over the lordship and put the East Carleton estate up for sale in 1920. This had important results for land ownership in Mulbarton (Chapter 6). She moved to Gowthorpe Hall, where she died in 1952 and where her grand-daughter, the current lord of the manor, still lives. Mrs Elizabeth Watkinson (née Steward) is still consulted about management of the Common and, like previous lords of the manor, is also patron of Mulbarton Church. It is the Steward coat of arms – a lion rampant debruised with a ragged staff – which appears under the village sign.

A Parish and its Council

The lord of the manor might own land in many different parishes and the Manor Court became increasingly irrelevant for local administration.

Swainsthorpe Station looking towards Norwich, with the level-crossing gates and siding with cattle pens and loading gauge. In 1889 trains took only nine minutes from Norwich Victoria (on Queen's Road) to Swainsthorpe. Mr Middleton, postmaster, cycled to Swainsthorpe Station to take the Post Office takings to Norwich for banking. Coal and other freight was carted from here until it closed in 1952. (CONTRIBUTED BY TERRY BURCHELL, FROM PHILIP STANDLEY'S COLLECTION)

Parishes as a unit of local government were recognised under Elizabeth I when they became responsible for looking after the poor, and an overseer was appointed in each. Administration became the responsibility of the Vestry Meeting, whose concerns included rates, the poor, local law and order, and the upkeep of roads. From 1834 responsibility for the poor passed to the Poor Law Unions, and Mulbarton was part of Henstead Union. Their workhouse was built in neighbouring Swainsthorpe in 1835 – now The Vale. Mulbarton was one of the many villages where a Parish Council was formed for the first time in 1894 – the year of Gladstone's Local Government Act, which finally took local secular matters out of the hands of the church.

Parish Meeting held on 4th December 1894 to form Parish Council

Mr Clay elected (30 votes) Chairman of the meeting. [The Rector was also proposed, but only received 4 votes.] *Twelve parishioners nominated, of whom the seven who received the highest number of votes at the meeting were elected: Arthur Meade (43); William Church (40); George Nelson (37); William Huggins (36); William Towler (31); William Randall (30); James Barrett (29).*

At the first council meeting, held a few days later, in public, in the schoolroom, William Church was elected Chairman and Mr Peake was appointed Parish Clerk – at a 'salary of £9 (payable twice yearly)

agreed on 17th April 1895'. The council agreed to meet on the first Monday of every month, and this decision still stands, over 100 years later.

Until 1949, parish councillors were elected at the annual parish meeting which was – and still is – held every year. Annual elections meant that parishioners came to the annual meeting to have their say and their vote. But apathy is nothing new – sometimes only one person and the clerk turned up. At first councillors held office for one year, but later this became every three years, and now it is four years. Men have dominated the council but the first woman councillor (Mrs Mary Hill) was elected in 1922 and the first woman chairperson (Miss Larter) in 1949.

Business items in the past were not so very different from today. Problems over road repairs and footpaths were high on the list. Litter in the pond and on the Common was a regular complaint – then as now. It took from 1935 to 1993 to get a speed limit in the village, and from 1946 to 2005 to get a safe path from north of the village to the school. An entry in 1911 despairs of getting various parish problems solved – it could have been written this year!

Widening Horizons

With Norwich only a couple of hours away on foot – and less on horseback – the city has always been accessible from Mulbarton. The main road (now the B1113) was improved considerably after the Act of Parliament 'for Repairing and Widening the Road

An alternative station was Hethersett, which gave access to the Midlands, Manchester and Liverpool via Ely.
(CONTRIBUTED BY TERRY BURCHELL, FROM PHILIP STANDLEY'S COLLECTION)

Jimmy Thurston (left) *and Clifford Allison beside a Spratts coach. Their coaches were hired for outings and 'away' matches, and for a number of years provided a bus service between Mulbarton and Norwich.*
(PHOTO CONTRIBUTED BY CLIFFORD ALLISON)

from Ber Street Gates, *[Norwich]* to New Buckenham' was passed in 1772. It was the coming of the railways that made more distant places accessible. The railway through Swainsthorpe opened in 1849, after which local directories stated that Mulbarton is '… one mile and a half from Swainsthorpe Station, 5 miles south-west from Norwich, 6 from Wymondham, and 109 from London…'. Fares were not cheap: in 1889, a single from Norwich to Swainsthorpe was 10d. (first class), 8d. (second class) and 4½d. (third class) at a time when a farm labourer's wage was around 13s. a week. But by then another invention was making road travel quicker and easier – the 'safety bicycle'.

The Mulbarton entry in *Kelly's Directory* of 1933 notes 'frequent motor omnibus services to Norwich, New Buckenham, East Harling and Thetford, and a daily coach service to London', making travel far easier. Miss Burrell remembers the 1930s:

I travelled by bus from Norwich – it was a fairly frequent service then, with the last bus from Norwich, Mon–Fri, being 9.20p.m., Sat 10.20, Sun 9.20 (I think). The fare, I cannot be certain, but 9d. rings a bell.

After the war there were fewer bus companies, fewer buses, and buses only along the B1113, of course. Maurice Norman remembers walking to the Tradesman's Arms twice a week in the 1950s to go to Norwich for football training. 'I walked home many

a time from Norwich, and almost every Friday night.' In the 1960s, Jane Burgess recalls:

The local bus to Norwich ran about four times daily – but only on the main road (B1113). It was a long trek to either the Tradesman's Arms corner or the World's End with a pushchair.

By then car ownership was on the increase and newcomers who moved here looked to Norwich for work, shops and leisure. But Mulbarton's attraction continues to be that it is a true village, with a life and heritage of its own.

Mulbarton Common, 1907 or earlier, when the windmill and church towered over the well-grazed grass.

(PHOTO CONTRIBUTED BY JULIET AMOS)

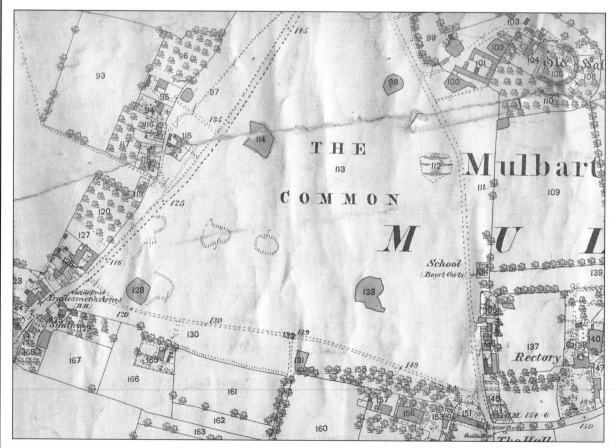

Most of Mulbarton Common with its pits and ponds, as shown on the Ordnance Survey 1:2500 County Series, 1881.

(REPRODUCED WITH PERMISSION OF THE ORDNANCE SURVEY)

CHAPTER 2

An Uncommon Common

The Common is the glory of Mulbarton: over 45 acres of open land, mostly within a triangle of roads. Today, the Common is a conservation area and a playground for the people of the village – and their dogs. Its football pitches are used by all ages; it has been used for cricket and hockey; for fêtes and fundays. But in the past, the Common and its pits and ponds were a vital part of an agricultural economy, and villagers guarded their common rights jealously enough for it not to have been enclosed.

Dorothy Tungate remembers:

The main part of the Common is triangular in shape with at least five ponds on it. It was used for cricket matches during the summer, and football later in the year. In the 1930s, Mulbarton Common was used for grazing cattle, and at times for sheep, and a man – or a young lad in the school holidays – used to 'walk the green', as one old chap called it. But in the winter it was mostly used by children. When the snow lay thick and deep in those days, Charlie [Tungate] and Jack Cooper (who lived by the Tradesman's Arms) used to cut 2 ft wide pathways down one side of the Common so the children and others could get to the school and to the butcher's shop.

Mulbarton Common has three main exits, each of which was once narrow and could be blocked with 'hurdles' to discourage grazing animals from wandering away. On the 1724 map of the parish there are gates marked across the road in the south-east and south-west corners of the Common. Two exits, at the north end (near World's End) and in the south-east corner (near Mulbarton Hall) are still noticeably narrow. The other exit was widened in the early 1970s when the Tradesman's Arms was demolished. On the south side of the Common a ditch, known as a 'ha-ha', which divided the Common from cultivated land, can still be seen.

Preserving Common Rights

The Common was important for grazing – and villagers fought doggedly to keep their grazing rights. There is some evidence of encroachment onto the Common: the mill seems to have been built on common land. Quite why the house named 'Carpenters' is on former common land is a mystery, but several tenants applied to enclose small areas for a shed, sawpit and a larger yard. The old school and the butcher's shop (once only a wooden hut – now the Humbleyard Centre) are the other buildings sited on former common land. In 1865 people vigorously opposed enclosing the Common and 125 years later villagers were invoking regulations about common land to fight a new development for a chemist's shop (Chapter 8)! In the minutes of Vestry Meetings, 1865 (the predecessor of the Parish Council), there is a proposal that the Common be enclosed:

At a Vestry Meeting held on Thursday 4th May, 1865, Captain Bellairs in the chair, it was proposed by W. Todd and seconded by W. King that a Committee composed of the following Ratepayers, viz: Capt. E. Bellairs; Mr Jas Turner; Mr Wm Riches be hereby appointed to enquire into the right of depasturage on the Common Mulbarton with power to apply to the Lord of the Manor as to his views thereon, and as to whether he would be a party to the Enclosure of the said Common provided it were wished by the majority of persons interested, and to obtain a legal opinion relative to these matters, if necessary, and give in a report of their proceedings herein to this meeting which stands adjourned for the purposes of receiving the same to the 29th Inst. at 11 am at the World's End Mulbarton.

But on 27 May 1865:

Considerable opposition was manifested, not only by the villagers, but by the citizens of Norwich, to an attempt made by Capt. Bellairs to enclose Mulbarton Common. A meeting was held in the village at which a strong protest was made against the proposal, and it was asserted that if ever the ancestors of Capt. Bellairs had possessed the power to effect the enclosure, they had allowed their rights to lapse.

The Commons Act of 1899 and bye-laws of 1909 are still in force. But, as Parish Council minutes show, villagers continued to be vigilant about their rights to graze the common. In 1910 a Parish Council amendment to the bye-laws proposed:

That horses and sheep be allowed on the Common only during the hours between one hour before sunrise and one hour after sunset... That no one person be allowed to turn more than 35 sheep on the Common at one time.

The pinder was responsible for rounding up stray animals and seeing that the rules were kept. Billy Goward (blacksmith) is remembered as a pinder of Mulbarton Common. According to Parish Council

Looking north from near the old school towards the church and what is now Harvest House (then the farm foreman's house, with sheds). Date uncertain.

(PHOTO CONTRIBUTED BY BRYAN TUNGATE)

Children looking at the cattle and ducks in the pond. One version of this card was sent from Mulbarton on 12 September 1906 to Wymondham with the message: 'How do you like this card Jack!'. Postage: a halfpenny!

(PHOTO CONTRIBUTED BY MALCOLM AND VALERIE JONES)

The caption on this card reads: '27 September 1911. The ponds have not been dry for 46 years.' In the background is the Parish (Wingfield) Hall, the Methodist Chapel, the World's End and the bakery.

(PHOTO FROM VILLAGE ARCHIVE)

The pond almost dried out in 1990, and an attempt was made to dig out some of the mud. The mechanical digger, driven by Roy Frost, got well and truly stuck!

(PHOTO: ROSEMARY SHAW)

Looking south along Norwich Road between Frost's garage (right) and 'Todd's Pit' (the pond, left), early 1950s. Beyond is the Common, with no trees, and in the distance only Mulbarton Hall and Birchfield House.

(PHOTO CONTRIBUTED BY IRIS FROST)

Left: Looking at the water lilies in Mulbarton pond, 1976.

(PHOTO: BRENDA YALLOP)

minutes, he retired in July 1952 and was succeeded by Len Dack, who seems to have been the last in a long line.

Cattle on the Common

Tony Kent wrote:

In the 1930s, Les Smith was a 'keeper' on the Common. When sheep were kept there, the shepherd would have his wooden hut on the Common. Various villagers kept cows on the Common – the Lincolns at Dairy Farm had cows there. John Stackyard, who lived in Holly Cottage in The Rosery, would drive four or five cows up to Mulbarton Common to graze and fetch them back to the cowhouse by his house to milk them... Animals grazed right up to the door of cottages around the Common and wandered to the pond for a drink. There was no traffic to worry about in those days.

I remember... H.E. Cross employed a shepherd who looked after the sheep on the Common. He used a horse to set the fold at night, or for the shearing. The fold consisted of iron hurdles ('haddles' in Norfolk). Each hurdle was ten feet long and 3½ feet high and they had two axles on the bottom which contained iron wheels and if they were not oiled, 'blast bor they shrick!' They were pulled into position in a square then supported by wooden stakes. When the children in Sunday School were asked 'Who is the Good Shepherd?' they replied 'Mr Adams!' (I know, I was there).

Margaret Hedges (née Sparke) remembered being nearly late for school when she skirted the Common in order to avoid walking past the herd of cows! And in a Radio Norfolk interview in 1998, Bob Jackson described his father having cows on the Common when he lived at Paddock Farm. 'I would be sent to fetch them at the end of the day, and often they'd be walking down the road to meet me. No problems with traffic then!' It may have been one of his cows that was X-rayed and operated on in the 1940s by a vet who discovered that its problems had been caused by swallowing a brass-edged and clasped Bible or Prayer Book dropped on the Common. So litter is not a new problem!

The ponds (locally known as 'pits') on the Common were important for the grazing animals. The 'village pond' – Todd's Pit, named after a World's End landlord – was carefully watched for both the amount and the quality of water. In a Parish Council minute of July 1899 it was noted: '... Clerk To write to Doctor Burton and complain of bad smells from the pit on the common near the World's End'.

A similar complaint in 1911, when the water level was very low, resulted in the pond being cleaned out – but not without a wrangle over who should pay. History repeated itself 80 years later, but this time heavy mechanical equipment was used and got stuck in the mud!

Mulbarton pond is even listed on a national website as a fishing venue! The story goes that fish were first put in the pond during the Second World War. Chris Mickleburgh recalls local lads getting hold of old jerry-cans from the garage opposite, cutting off the tops and taking them to 'Scott's Lake' (now the Cheshire Home lake) with sticks with hooks on the end. 'One evening we caught 77 fish and brought them back and put them in Mulbarton pond!'

Cattle Go: Trees Grow

'The Common was a large empty space in my time with one or two ponds but almost empty grassland', says Brenda Ford (née Collins) of the 1940s. An aerial photo taken in 1946 shows no trees on the main part of the Common, and very few near where the schools now are. But the increasing amount of traffic caused problems in the 1950s, and grazing dwindled. Once the cattle were taken off, the Common grew wild and it was no longer possible to play cricket there. Complaints at the annual parish meetings are recorded in the minutes and show how quickly the grassland reverted to rough land:

1953 July: No stock now feeding on the Common so thistles are growing and have become a problem. Rural District Council should cut the thistles, but do not get it done when it is needed – would pay Parish Council to get Common cut at most appropriate time.

1956 July 5th: Mr Dack asked if anything could be done to the Common which had got into a very rough state.

1957 April 18th: A complaint was brought forward in reference to the rough state the Common had got into and it was suggested that something should be done to remove the small trees and bushes etc that had grown up.

People soon discovered that this 'natural open space' was not strictly natural – left to itself it would return to being woodland. It takes hard work and careful management to keep this 'open space' open!

Clearing the Common

In the 1960s a Commons Committee was formed to work on clearing the Common of trees and undergrowth, to create new football pitches and make the Common more 'user-friendly' for leisure pursuits. As reported in the *Eastern Daily Press*, 25 August 1967:

Volunteers saving Mulbarton's pride and joy – the Common
... the Common, once the pride and joy of the village, has for some time been overgrown and neglected. This year, at the annual parish meeting, it was agreed that this state could be tolerated no longer. Following the

The True Legend of Mulbarton Common

The story runs that many, many years ago, an old couple, Billy Grimms (or Grimes) and Mary, his wife, lived in a small cottage on the edge of the Common. It was winter and there had been a heavy snowfall and blizzards which kept people indoors. The old couple had been in the habit of trotting across the Common to the World's End every evening for a glass of beer, but the weather had prevented them for the best part of a week.

One evening the old man said, 'Mary, maw, I can't go wi'out my sup o' beer no longer. The snow ha' stopped, I kin git across the Common to the World's End.'

'No! No! Bill – yew ain't tew good. I'll go for yer and fetch a pint back.'

'That yer don't, mawther. Yew bide here. I'll have my stick an' 'tis munelight.'

The old man went off. His wife waited. An hour passed: two hours – and he wasn't home. Frantic with worry, Mary put on her hood and cloak and went to look for him.

The next day, a neighbour called at the cottage and, getting no answer to her knock, tried the door, found it unfastened and went in. No one there!

Some six weeks later, when a rapid thaw set in and the snow cleared from the Common, they were found, each in a separate hollow. The 'holes'

Sledging in 'Mary Grimms's Hole' on Mulbarton Common in early 1991. (PHOTO: JILL WRIGHT)

had been filled with snowdrifts six feet or more deep and it was evident that first Billy and then Mary had blundered into each hole separately and had been suffocated by the snow. In their feeble old age they would have had no strength to struggle.

(The 'holes' can still be seen in the south-west part of the Common: Billy Grimms's Hole is a deep, dry pit once popular for sledging in winter but now very overgrown with trees. Mary Grimms's Hole is a shallower dry pit a little further up the hill.)

election of the new Parish Council, a Common Committee was formed, to be responsible to the Parish Council, to organise the restoration of Mulbarton Common. Its object is to organise the clearance of the rubbish growing there, with regular cutting of grass and general maintenance, so that it will finally be restored to the pleasant sight it once was.

An area of 47 acres may seem a formidable task for a band of volunteers to tackle, but an excellent start has been made... Mr Ted Ellis, the well-known Norfolk naturalist and vice-chairman of the Norfolk Planning Committee, has met members of the Common Committee after carrying out an inspection lasting two hours. He warmly approved the scheme for clearing the Common and the plan which has been prepared and wished the clock could be put back twenty years so that he could have a hand in the work...

Brigadier Harris instigated the cutting of paths and football pitch with a tractor and swipe and offered the use of his equipment to experienced volunteers. Now much of the rough grass has been cut... Trees near the Hall Corner, which were a danger to the traffic, have been pulled up. These and the raked grass were deposited in Mary Grimm's Hollow for burning.

The Young Wives have a plan and some money already available for children's playground equipment and it is hoped the football team will be encouraged to use the football pitch once again...

Quite a correspondence followed, but one person with a long memory appreciated what was done and had a letter published in the *EDP* in January 1968:

Crouch End, London, 31st December 1967

Sir – A friend of mine has just sent me a cutting from the EDP about the restoration of Mulbarton Common and it has given me a real joy and satisfaction as the great-granddaughter of the Rev. Richard Spurgeon who was Rector of Mulbarton from 1812 to 1842. I well remember riding over there with my father to see the splendid Common, sheep trimmed, aided by horses, ducks, fowls and a couple of goats.

The last time I saw the common, about seven years ago, it was a desolation indeed. I cannot say how grateful I am to the parishioners and those who have

Foot and mouth disease closed Mulbarton Common to all-comers for the first time ever in 2001. (PHOTO: JILL WRIGHT)

helped them to restore this, one of the few commons existing, relics of a more peaceful age, when that juggernaut, the motor car, was undreamed of!

... as an old lady of 96, I cannot hope to see Mulbarton Common again, but I am glad to think that I can imagine it as it was in my childhood days, trimmed and enjoyed by its rightful possessors, the animals and the fowls.

Yours etc., ELLA COLLIER (Mrs)

Common Conservation

The original Scheme of Management for Mulbarton Common (1899) was drawn up with both animal grazing and recreation in mind. Grazing has ceased, and 'recreation' is the main use, but it does not have to conflict with conservation. 'I can remember snipe whizzing across the Common on a summer evening, and skylarks nesting,' commented John Rumball of the immediate post-war years. The famous Norfolk naturalist Ted Ellis discovered a rare ergot fungus on spike-rush in the pond near the Malthouse corner which led to newspaper headlines: 'MULBARTON POND HOLDS HOPE FOR MANKIND'. Apparently biochemists in Britain and Germany were studying this ergot fungus for its medicinal properties and were excited about a possible new source. No one seems sure if it is still there, but it relied on heavy frosts to trigger the spores so it may be a victim of climate change rather than neglect.

The advice of other experts has led to a management plan which seeks to preserve a variety of habitats on Mulbarton Common with a programme for clearing ponds and trimming trees in rotation and a careful cutting regime. This enables both people and wildlife to benefit. Part of the southern end is kept short for sport, the rest of the grass is left to grow and is then cut in summer as a hay crop. The time of cutting is important if particular species are to reseed. In August 1989 54 flowering plants and seven species of grass were listed. A survey of the flora in June 2000 by Dr Roy Baker and Alec Bull identified 169 different species, some of which are rare, such as adder's tongue fern and marsh watercress. The variety of plants is important to insects, including

Opposite page: Aerial view of Mulbarton Common looking north-east, May 1974. The Common has far fewer trees and bushes than now. Just visible in the foreground (the south-west corner) is the small pond where Ted Ellis found the ergot fungus. Beyond that is Billy Grimms's Hole and above right of that is the shallower Mary Grimms's Hole. To the left are the remnants of the cycle speedway track. The B1113 is on the left (with 'Carpenters' in front of other cottages), leading to 'Todd's Pit' (the village pond, top left) and in front of the church is 'Church Pit'. The football pitch and Village Hall have not yet taken over the field at the top of the picture, but the schoolhouse, old school and industrial area are visible. The clear circle beside the football pitch (centre) is an unsolved mystery! (PHOTO: DAVID WRIGHT)

Mulbarton Common, 1975, with small trees recently planted around 'Blake's Pit' (the pond near the play area) to improve the habitat. (PHOTO: DAVID WRIGHT)

Planting a tree on Mulbarton Common to celebrate the Queen Mother's 80th birthday, December 1980. Arthur Cook, chairman of South Norfolk District Council's housing committee, plants the first of eight trees. Looking on are (left to right) Mr D. Riley, South Norfolk Forestry Officer; Mike Haslam, Chief Planning Officer, SNDC; Peter Mickleburgh, Parish and District Councillor; Mr E.A. Marlow, Parish Clerk.

(PHOTO: EVENING NEWS, REPRODUCED WITH PERMISSION)

several species of butterfly and moth, and both seeds and insects are important for the bird life and animals.

Fun and Games

'Throngs of people assemble on the village green, in Whitsun week, to witness pony and donkey races, and other sports and amusements' (*White's Directory of Norfolk*, 1845). Through the nineteenth century there were day-trips from Norwich to Mulbarton for games on the Common and liquid refreshment at the World's End. Over 60 years later, a Parish Council minute in April 1907 suggests problems with such use: 'Mr E. Eke called attention to the disgraceful way in which parties of showfolks and others of a like character treated the Common, to the annoyance of the inhabitants near at hand...'

Every year, children (and adults) spent weeks building a huge bonfire for 5 November:

We would cut your fence, clear your rubbish and take anything to burn. The garage gave old spoiled oil and grease and shops had a clear-out for us. A number of grown-ups used to help us on the night, it was a big thing and very well organised, the village turned out in strength for the occasion...

Other annual events included rallies for agricultural workers (Chapter 6) and the Bank Holiday fêtes. Brenda Ford (née Collins) remembers:

There used to be a fête on the Common on August Bank Holiday Monday, the first Monday in August in those days. We used to have all sorts of races and competitions and I used to take part in a wild flower competition seeing how many different varieties of wild flowers we could collect. This would not of course be allowed nowadays.

A rally of the Union of Agricultural Labourers & Rural Workers arrives on Mulbarton Common with the county banner, July 1917. This event was held on our Common most summers until the Second World War, and occasional marches were organised until the 1960s (Chapter 6). (PHOTO CONTRIBUTED BY CLIFFORD ROBINSON)

George VI coronation celebrations, 1937, in Mulbarton: George Martin, photographed outside the cottages south of Scott's Terrace, won second prize with this decorated bicycle. (PHOTO CONTRIBUTED BY CLIFFORD ROBINSON)

The Whit Monday village fête to celebrate the restoration of Mulbarton Common in May 1968. Shown here is the Territorial Army caravan; the Medical Corps gave demonstrations during the afternoon. The Common Committee worked regularly each Sunday to clear tangled growth and rubbish from the whole 47 acres, trim worthwhile trees, and mow four acres for sporting and village events. Donations came from villagers and the District and Parish Councils. (PHOTO: PETER MICKLEBURGH)

The three-legged race on the well-cleared Mulbarton Common, Whit Monday 1969. (PHOTO: PETER MICKLEBURGH)

Prize-giving at the end of the Whitsun funday on the newly-restored Common. The prizes are being presented by Brigadier Harris, watched by John Wheeler (right), both of whom were very involved in the restoration of the Common. (PHOTO: PETER MICKLEBURGH)

Special events were celebrated, too – for the coronation of King George VI in May 1937, there were 'sports for the children commencing at 3p.m... [and] by permission a copper beech tree will be planted on the Common in commemoration of The Coronation.' (Obviously the Parish Council was being very careful, as Mrs Steward had complained that the tree for the jubilee in 1935 had been planted without her permission!) A sports day and bonfire were organised for the 'Annual Meeting Victory Celebrations planned for

8th June 1946' and, despite the rain on Coronation Day 1953, another sports afternoon took place.

The efforts of the Commons Committee to clear the Common were marked with a grand fête and children's sports day, Whit Monday, 3 June 1968. In the front of the programme (price 6d.), Major J.G. Steward, lord of the manor, wrote:

The Mulbarton Sports were held on the Common regularly until recent years when the ever-increasing traffic on the roads around the Common made cattle and sheep grazing without a 'pinder' impossible and consequently grazing stopped. As a result the Common became overgrown and it was not until the Parish formed a Mulbarton Common Committee to administer and maintain the cutting of the grass etc. that it has been possible to hope for the Common being used for recreation and sport. It is hoped that this afternoon's event will help the funds of the Common Fund and village organisations besides giving all those attending the chance to enjoy themselves.

The 1969 fête paid for a tree-planting programme and celebrated the new play equipment organised by the Young Wives, who had raised money with jumble sales and carol singing supplemented with a grant from the National Playing Fields Association. In the programme, Major J.G. Steward announced that:

The transfer of the rights of the Lord of The Manor relating to the Common, to the Parish of Mulbarton, is in the hands of solicitors and when the transfer has been completed I believe the Parish will be unique in this respect.

Further trees were planted for the Queen Mother's 80th birthday and for the Millennium. The Common continued to be used for fêtes and fundays, many of which raised funds to purchase the old school as a Village Hall (Chapter 4). Once the present Village Hall and the adjacent Orchard Park playing-field were available, these events moved to a more enclosed venue.

Football on the Common

The 'Mulbarton Village Festival Programme, 4th & 5th July' 1992, included this article about football:

When Mulbarton first sported a football team is now lost in the mists of village history. However, when work was being done a few years ago on one of the old cottages in the village, a newspaper cutting dated 1904 was found with reference to a Mulbarton football side travelling to Yarmouth for a cup game in the rain...

Records between the two World Wars are little less sketchy. In those days the Club was known as the Mulbarton & Swardeston Football Club, and although little is known of the Club's achievements during this

Mulbarton & Swardeston United football team, 1913. Left to right, back row: *Harry Bobbin, Dr Nicholls, Reg Burgess, F. Oakley, Bob Loveday, Sam Parfitt, B. Davey, William Lake (Club Sec.);* front row: *Harry Bayfield, Ed Davey, ?, John Stowe, Herbert Vincent;* sitting with ball: *A. ('Tabs') Oakley.*   (PHOTO CONTRIBUTED BY TERRY BURCHELL, FROM PHILIP STANDLEY'S COLLECTION)

Mulbarton & Swardeston football team in 1920. Left to right back row: *Jack Williams, Sid Funnell, Cliff Allison, Herbert Lake (goalie), Wally Chubick, Jack Wharton, Billy Burgess;* front row: *Chris Davy, Fred Hall, Albert Rix (captain), Tom Smith, Jack Pettigrew.*

(PHOTO CONTRIBUTED BY SUE BIRD)

period, photographs still remain as a permanent reminder of that period in the Club's long history...

Like many other villages, the War in 1939 brought an end to village football. Although some football was played in the village in those early years following the War, the real re-formation of Mulbarton football did not occur until around 1960 when the Club was re-formed under the name MULBARTON UNITED FOOTBALL CLUB. The re-formation was in great part due to the efforts of Bryan Tungate, retiring as Club secretary [in 1992] after thirty two years.

As they say 'Mighty Oaks from Little Acorns Grow'. From that humble rebirth in 1960 the Club has grown to be one of the most powerful Club sides in the County. In 1987 the Club decided that following many years of playing on the common, the time had come for the Club to have a home pitch of its own...

Mulbarton & Swardeston football team, winners of Wymondham & District league cup, 1922 and 1923. Left to right, back row: Peter Thomas, Albert Rix, Harry Bayfield; middle row: A. ('Tabs') Oakley, Chris Davey, Fred Waters, Harry Hall, Charlie Alborough; front row: Hubert Davey, Harry Bobbin, Jack Pettigrew, Arthur King. (PHOTO CONTRIBUTED BY TERRY BURCHELL, FROM PHILIP STANDLEY'S COLLECTION)

Mulbarton football team on the Common in the goal mouth (looking north), mid-1950s. Left to right, back row: Chris Mickleburgh, Dennis Mickleburgh, Peter Lincoln, Rex Bulcock, Tony Lincoln, George Parfitt, Mr Allen (linesman); front row: Terry Adcock, Mike Parfitt, Peter Haverson, Peter Parfitt, Pat Parfitt. (PHOTO CONTRIBUTED BY PETER HAVERSON)

The victorious Mulbarton football squad on the green behind the World's End, 1954–55, when they were the Norwich & District League championship winners. Left to right, back row: Tony Smith, Tony Lincoln, Billy Burrett, Peter Tooke, David Postle, Jimmy Abendroth; middle row: Peter Parfitt; Terry Adcock, Peter Lincoln, Peter Haverson, George Parfitt; front row: Mike Parfitt, Pat Parfitt. (PHOTO CONTRIBUTED BY PETER HAVERSON)

Mulbarton United Football Club team on the hallowed turf of the Norwich City Football Ground for the Norfolk Junior Cup Final, 1984. Mulbarton United beat Tottenhill by two goals to one. The team, left to right, is: G. Henderson, Mark Hindle, Michael Lincoln, Andrew Lincoln, Phil Wheeler, Stuart Cooper, David Thomas, John Thompson, Ross Collard, David Parfitt, Martin Robinson, David Robinson (mascot), Mike Webb (captain). (PHOTO: BRYAN TUNGATE)

The successes of Mulbarton United from 1983 to 1993 are certainly impressive:

1983–84 Mulbarton won the Norfolk Junior Cup at Carrow Road and top of Anglian Combination Division 4.

1984–85 Anglian Combination Division 3 runners-up.

1989–90 Anglian Combination Division 2 winners.

1990 After a £25,000 fund-raising drive, they moved to the impressive Mulberry Park ground north of the Village Hall.

1990–91 Anglian Combination Division 1 runners-up.

1991–92 Anglian Combination Premier Division runners-up.

1992–93 Anglian Combination champions: 'retiring manager Dave Bedson has guided United to the league's ultimate prize – the Sterry Cup.' MUFC won the Cup again in 1997.

Players were paid from 1993, but fortunes changed and the club was relegated to Division 1. At the time of writing (2006) MUFC has left the league and the club is being wound up.

A Mulbarton United Youth Football Club was started by Chris Carter in 1989, but split from the

Maurice ('Monty') Norman
by Bryan Tungate

Maurice (Monty) Norman, aged six or seven, in his first suit – pictured here against the backdrop of the thatched church cottages and the church fence in 1940. He was born and spent his childhood in the last brick cottage by the pond, next to the thatched cottages (now named 'The Buffs').

(ALL PHOTOS ON THIS PAGE CONTRIBUTED BY MAURICE NORMAN)

Maurice Norman's place in the history of football came through his transfer from Norwich City to Tottenham Hotspur who were, at that time, one of Europe's top teams. He was born and bred in Mulbarton and lived with dad Billy, mum Trixie, and sister Maureen in his young days in a cottage by the village pond [next to what is now the Rectory entry]. It was rumoured that when he was sent to bed for some misdemeanour he shinned down the drainpipe to join the rest of us on the Common for a game of football.

In the early 1950s, the family moved to a new council-house in Birchfield Lane, and Maurice was a farmhand on Mr White's farm at Bracon Ash. He had a trial at Norwich City who signed him on. In time he made it into the League team and came under the scrutiny of the big-time teams. Jimmy Adamson of Spurs was the man who was to arrange Monty's transfer in 1955. Within a year, Monty had won three International Caps for England at Under 23 level. Despite being continually mentioned for full International Honours, it was not until 1962 that the breakthrough came. What a break that was! Monty was picked for the South American tour taking in the 1962 World Cup. His first match was beside another debut-maker, Bobby Moore, against Peru. In 1962, 1963 and in 1964 Monty played 23 times for England. For Spurs, Monty Norman started as a full back in November 1955 and totalled 357 League matches, scoring 16 goals before his injury left him unable to continue as a footballer. In the FA Cup he played 37 games, netting twice. Monty played 17 games in European competitions (getting 1 goal) and also appeared in 42 other matches for Tottenham. Monty had been a member of the illustrious team that achieved the League and FA Cup double in 1960–61 and was in the 1961–62 Cup winning team. In 1963 he was a player in a 5–1 winning Spurs team against Athletico Madrid in the European Cup Winners Cup.

In November 1965, just 11 years after joining Spurs, a friendly match was arranged between Tottenham and a Hungarian XI – it was Monty's last match. He broke his left leg and never played football again. It is interesting to record that in 1955, from the transfer fee of £18,000, Norwich City gave Mulbarton & Swardeston Football Club a set of red and black quartered shirts and four new footballs. It is said that the transfer fee paid for floodlighting at Norwich City football ground.

Mulbarton Junior Team on the Common, Autumn 1946 – including Maurice (Monty) Norman, then aged 13, who went on the play for the Senior team, Norwich City, Spurs and England. Left to right, back row: Bryant Mickleburgh, Dennis Dawson, Maurice Norman, Bernard Rayner, Guy Lambert; front row: Gordon Clements (from Hethel), Clifford Robinson, Bob Kedge, Dennis Mickleburgh, Lionel Robinson, Gerald Collins.

Mulbarton's senior football team, 1948–49, including 15-year-old Maurice (Monty) Norman (standing, left). The following season he joined Norwich City Football Club as a junior player, and later in his career played for Tottenham Hotspur and England. With him, back row, left to right, are Jimmy Abendroth, Rex Bulcock, Charlie Oakley, Ben Cook, George Parfitt; front row: Tony Smith, Pat Parfitt, Cliff Allison, Michael Parfitt, Peter Parfitt (twin of Pat).

Below: *Maurice (Monty) Norman at home in Bush Hill Park, Enfield, with some of his 23 England caps and flags from the countries and cities in which he played.*

(BOTH PHOTOS CONTRIBUTED BY MAURICE NORMAN)

The wedding of Maurice (Monty) Norman to Jacqueline Knight, a student nurse, at Northaw, Cuffley, Hertfordshire, 27 March 1961. The happy couple are surrounded by Monty's Tottenham Hotspur team-mates. Left to right, back: William Brown, John Ryden, Tony Marchie, Danny Blanchflower, Robert Smith, John White *(behind the bride),* Terry Medwin, Ron Hollowbread, Peter Baker, Bill Nicholson *(manager),* front: *Mel Hopkins, Terry Dyson, Cliff Jones, Dave Mackay, Ronnie Henry.*

senior club in 1998 to become the Mulbarton Wanderers Youth Football Club. Three years later, a girls' club, Harford Belles, moved to Mulbarton to join the Wanderers, and together they formed one of the largest football clubs in Norfolk. Also in 2001, the Wanderers and Belles received the FA National Football Grass Roots award from Kevin Keegan at a special ceremony later shown on national TV. Since then, both Belles and Wanderers have formed women's and men's senior teams and have achieved further awards – including Charter Standard Community Club of the Year for Norfolk in 2005.

Mulbarton Wanderers Youth Football Club Under 9s in the 1998–99 season. Left to right, back row: *John Farrow (coach), Bradley, Josh, Luke, Phil, Louis, Robert, Dale, Ryan, Jamie, Roy George (manager);* front: *Lewis, Sam, Michael, Owen, April, ?, Chris, Anthony, Edward.* (PHOTO CONTRIBUTED BY RUSSELL SCOTTER)

Cricket on the Common, early 1930s. Bill Alborough (in the middle) *is with two members of the Hall family from Swardeston. In the distance is the Long Barn, with trees to the north* (left) *where Harvest House and Elm House now stand.* (PHOTO CONTRIBUTED BY BILL ALBOROUGH)

The Bracon Ash cricket team, playing at 'Woodlands', relied on a number of Mulbarton men. Left to right, standing: *George Evans, Freddy Davy, Roger King, Ray Martin, Brian Bird, Kenneth Feltham, 'Gussy' Martin* (with cap, umpire), *Roy Hemming, Norman ?;* sitting on bench: *Peter Finch of Woodlands, Derek Gent, Tony Smith, Col Jewson of Mergate Hall. Late 1950s.*

(PHOTO CONTRIBUTED BY JOHN BETTS)

Maurice (Monty) Norman was an all-round sportsman – pictured here (back left) *with the Bracon Ash cricket team of 1951–52, in which there were a number of Mulbarton men.* Left to right, back row: *Maurice Norman, Derek Gent, Ray Martin, Johnny Martin, George Evans, Graham Martin;* front: *Dicky White, Tim Finch (of 'Woodlands'), Tony Martin, Tony Smith, Roy Hemming (of Swardeston).* (PHOTO CONTRIBUTED BY MAURICE NORMAN)

Cricket on Mulbarton Common, a timeless scene – this photo was taken in the 1990s. (PHOTO: TERRY BURCHELL)

Cricket and Other Games

Mulbarton is possibly one of the oldest cricket clubs in Norfolk. In 1811 the Mulbarton Club played a special match against Ashwellthorpe: the sides played for 22 bottles of cider and 22lbs of cherries! Mulbarton Cricket Club is mentioned in some directories: Secretary, 1883, Mr Jeffries; 1896, Herbert Hubbard; 1904, J.H. Vincent. The parish magazine records that 'East Carleton Cricket Club played its first match on July 8th 1914 against Mulbarton on Mulbarton Common. East Carleton made 38 runs; Mulbarton 84 for 6 wickets.'

The cricket club and the football club were known as 'Mulbarton and Swardeston', but in the 1960s the football club became Mulbarton FC and the cricketers

Swardeston CC. Mulbarton men also played with Bracon Ash cricket club at nearby Woodlands and Bracon Lodge. Following the clearance of Mulbarton Common, the 1969 fête programme announced:

At present work is in hand in preparing a first class cricket square on the Common. In three of the past four years the Club has won the 'R.G. Carter Cup' and earlier had won the Norfolk Junior Cup. Both Clubs [Football and Cricket] *are running sideshows today and would like to thank you in advance for your support.*

The present Mulbarton Village Cricket Club started life playing at Dunston Hall, but when the pitch was lost to make way for a golf course the club moved to Mulbarton, thanks to George Henderson (later Club

Ladies' Hockey Team – reputed to be on Mulbarton Common about 1907. Only known members are Beatrice (Trixie) Corbould-Warren (born 1887), who carved the eagle lectern in Bracon Ash Church (seated middle row, far left) and her sister, Winifred Alice Corbould-Warren, born 1885, (seated middle row, far right), both of Bracon Lodge, off what is now Cuckoofield Lane.

(PHOTO CONTRIBUTED BY BRIDGET TYLER)

Mulbarton Cycle Speedway Team, 1961. Left to right, back: *Robin Tungate, Mike Tkozca, Bryan Tungate (manager), Keith Sparkes;* front: *Michael Cook, Ron Barrett (captain), Roger Skipper.* (PHOTO: BRYAN TUNGATE)

President) and Bryan Tungate. The Parish Council accepted the proposal to play on the Common and the club played there for three seasons. The setting for village cricket was ideal, but sharing a playing area with a football club and the Common's rabbit population made the upkeep of the square a nightmare for the long-suffering groundsman, Neil Warner.

When the Parish Council purchased a field behind the Village Hall a cricket square was laid down. Following much hard work and many laborious hours of stone picking, the move from the Common to Orchard Park was finally achieved when Mulbarton Village Cricket Club played East Harling in the inaugural match in June 1997. Youth Cricket was added in 1999, the brainchild of Joe Harris. After hours of work from Secretary Mike Savory and Groundsman Bob McKenzie, men's league cricket returned to Mulbarton in 2003. In only their third season the club came top of the league by one point.

Football and cricket are not the only games to have been played on the Common. Ladies' hockey is definitely before living memory. Cycle Speedway attracted a good crowd at its track on a Sunday afternoon. At the 1959 annual parish meeting: 'Mulbarton Cycle Speedway Club asked to improve its existing track on the Common. Only sport in the Parish; Council agreed as long as lord of the manor informed.' Mulbarton's team went on to give some impressive performances. Their track was revamped decades later for BMX bikes, and the overgrown site can still be found on the Common.

Perhaps most impressive of all is Mulbarton's record in the inter-village sports contests of the 1980s. Led first by Peter Mickleburgh and then by Jane Stevenson, a team of nearly 50 people took part in a variety of junior and senior team sports and a relay race in the 'Medium Villages' section. Mulbarton won the district round for three successive years from 1982 to 1984, and in 1983 was the champion of the whole Eastern Region in the Medium Villages competition held at Shotley.

Mulbarton's inter-village sports team show off their shields after winning the South Norfolk round at Harleston in 1982. They went on to win the County finals. Holding the shield is team manager Peter Mickleburgh (centre). In the following year Jane Stevenson (standing third from right) took over as team manager. Among the team members pictured are Barry and Vivienne Edwards, Graham and Tracey Coleman, Philip Wheeler, Louise Dean, Amanda Harper, Fern Grogutt, Glyn Baker, Philip Smith, Fiona Lambert.

(PHOTO CONTRIBUTED BY IRENE EAGLE)

Right: *Bowling on the green at the back of the Tradesman's Arms, c.1910.*
(PHOTO CONTRIBUTED BY BRYAN TUNGATE)

Below: *The view north along the turnpike (now B1113) over Mulbarton Bridge to the creeper-covered Tradesman's Arms and neighbouring cottages. On the right is 'Forge Cottage', home of the blacksmith. 1907 or earlier.*
(PHOTO CONTRIBUTED BY C. POTTER)

The Bowls Club at the Tradesmen's Arms, about 1950. The bowls teams and the darts teams competed against other clubs and were locally well known. For the members, trips away to play other teams were welcome outings. Left to right, back row: W. Cook, Frederick Middleton (Mulbarton postmaster), ?, ?, ?; middle row: Percy Stackyard, ?, ?, ?, W. Bell, George Tungate, ?, ?, ?, ?; front row (seated): Jimmy Larwood, 'Moat' Cunningham, ?, Sid Funnell, William Towler (Swardeston postmaster), ?, ?. Also present are: A. Edwards, Loftus Watling (Bracon Ash postmaster), Mr Warman, J. Futter, Billy Lake.
(PHOTO CONTRIBUTED BY PHYLLIS FELTHAM)

✦ CHAPTER 3 ✦

Pubs, Clubs and Places to Meet

Mulbarton had two public houses until the end of the 1960s: the World's End (which still exists) and the Tradesman's Arms. Both hosted a variety of clubs and organisations. From the early years of the twentieth century, Mulbarton has had a succession of village halls – venues for many other activities. The present Village Hall also has a Social Club, so once again villagers have a choice of 'watering holes'.

The Tradesman's Arms

'A nice little old pub where people used to gather to play cards and dominoes,' recalled Bob Jackson in a radio interview. It was next to the Malthouse, almost on the corner of Norwich Road (B1113) and East Carleton Road – a site now occupied by modern houses. For most of its existence it was described as a 'beer house': the proprietor was a 'beer retailer' who did other work as well, and his wife often ran the premises. Usually it was in the hands of wheel-wrights – it was very conveniently placed opposite the forge (Chapter 7). In 1950 a wine licence was applied for. Now the pub has gone, people remember it with considerable affection.

Dorothy Tungate lived in a cottage adjoining the pub in the 1930s and 1940s: 'The old Tradesman's Arms was owned by Bullard's Brewery of Norwich, and was managed by Frank Swain and his wife Blanche. An 8ft wall separated the pub from Malthouse Farm.' Dorothy's son, Bryan, remembers certain advantages to being so near:

The bedroom I shared with my brother was overlooking the bowling-green at the back of the pub. As we grew up we were able to shout out of the bedroom window on Sundays to father that it was time for dinner and he would bring us a 'Vimto' drink and one for my sister as well. He'd be playing bowls on the green with my grandfather or darts in the back room.

Village characters gathered there:

This was the workers' pub – a real 'spit and sawdust' place. Sunday lunchtime, those that worked with live-stock dropped in for a pint or three and the humidity rose as did the good agricultural smells. Jack Howard from Lodge Farm would engage in a wind-up with Jimmy Mackerell from Kenningham Hall Farm about straight furrows and 'ringes' (rows of crops). Charlie Elvin would be busy boasting how his tractor ploughed straighter and deeper than the other two's hosses...

The Tradesman's Arms was at the southern end of a terrace of three brick houses (the central one being the landlord's), but at the back it extended further with a 'smoking room' overlooking the bowling-green. The entry to the beer garden and bowling-green was along the passageway. In the distance is the Malthouse. The lorry belonged to Mr Baxter of Wood Lane, a carrier for local farms.   (PHOTO CONTRIBUTED BY DAPHNE SKEET)

The Tradesman's Arms c.1970, when it was no longer a pub and about to be demolished for housing. The large doors in the building on the left used to lead into the wheelwright's yard. Note the bus timetable on the wall – the stop was known as 'the Tradesman's Arms' long after the pub had disappeared!   (PHOTO: CLIVE POTTER)

Rosemary Wright (née Morris) moved to the Tradesman's Arms when her parents took over from her grandfather. Her bedroom, on the first floor, was 'as big as a ballroom – and freezing cold in winter.' She remembers the bowling-green which her mother cut with a hand mower almost every day – it was said to be the best green in the Bullard's League. The pub had no cellar – barrels were kept in a cool place below the bar. On hot days, wet towels were

The view north along the B1113 from Mulbarton Bridge in 1975. The site of the Tradesman's Arms and adjacent cottages is now modern housing, and the Malthouse is clearly visible. The thatched Forge Cottage and frontage of the old forge still stand on the right. (PHOTO: ROBERT COURT)

wrapped round the barrels to keep the beer cool. Water came from a pump fitted over the well out the back. In the bitterly cold winter of 1947, the family had to boil kettles and pour hot water over the pump to unfreeze it to get more water! Rosemary Wright and her husband lived in a converted boat behind the pub when they were first married.

The Tradesman's Arms closed on 27 January 1969. It stood vacant for a while, and then the whole site – pub, green, former houses and workshops – was sold to a builder from Surlingham. Everything was demolished very quickly when there was rumour of a preservation order being applied for. The road was widened and new houses were built on the site, but the name lived on in the bus stop – a name guaranteed to sort out the locals from the rest! All that remains now are a few tiles and the wrought-iron arm that once held the pub sign – at the antiques shop in the old forge opposite.

The World's End

At the top end of the Common, also on the Norwich Road (B1113), stands the World's End – described by a local as 'the somewhat superior pub' of the two, with a full licence and accommodation for people and (in earlier days) horses. The present building probably dates from the seventeenth century with later additions and, like many old pubs, it is said to be haunted. It has hosted many celebrations in its long history: the *Norfolk Chronicle* of 25 October 1809 describes the golden jubilee of George III at Mulbarton, when

... the King's health was joyfully drunk, to the comfort of all the poor in the parish. The World's End house, where the poor were handsomely regaled, was brilliantly illuminated and decorated with arches, the gentlemen met, and the evening was spent with the utmost harmony and conviviality.

Besides being a fully licensed inn, the World's End was used for auction sales (e.g. of 'Carpenters' and other houses west of the Common in 1873) and for petty sessions during the nineteenth century. It was obviously a thriving country inn: 'Petty sessions are held on the 1st Monday of each month, at the World's End inn, where there is an Oddfellows' Lodge, and a good bowling-green, much resorted to, in summer, by company from Norwich' (*White's Directory*, 1845).

The bowling-green was extended, or incorporated, into a much larger 'Pleasure Ground' during the days of William Todd, in the 1880s and 1890s, which attracted groups from Norwich:

... Every summer along came the Brewer's men, their wives and their children. The horses would be dressed up with plumes and ribbons, and all the people in their Sunday best... As soon as the cavalcade arrived, the horses would be taken to the stables, and the people would all make for the pub. They'd have dinner there, and boy what a dinner! And speechifying of course.

The forecourt of the World's End with five people and a dog. Note the sign and milepost on the left, and the pump in the yard. Date uncertain – this copy has 'R.E. SMITH' (landlord 1915–22) added on to the original plate above the sign on the wall, but the photograph is probably older.
(PHOTO CONTRIBUTED BY BRYAN TUNGATE)

The World's End with an Austin 7 and its proud owners.
(PHOTO CONTRIBUTED BY ENID FOX)

Mulbarton – 'the Beauty Spot of Norfolk'! A business card advertising the facilities of 'Ye Olde World's End' in the days of Mr William Denny, proprietor (c.1925).
(CONTRIBUTED BY VIC GRAY)

A bill from the World's End, October 1888, signed by the landlord, William Todd, and paid by Mr Turner of Paddock Farm for 'botts' of beer and lemonade and 'galls' of ale.   (CONTRIBUTED BY MULBARTON MIDDLE SCHOOL)

Hunt horses outside World's End, in the 1930s (before the bar was extended). (PHOTO CONTRIBUTED BY MRS J. SWIFT)

Bowls game on the World's End bowling-green, c.1910.
(PHOTO CONTRIBUTED BY VIC GRAY)

The World's End with Mr W.H. (Billy) Swift (landlord 1937–57) standing in the doorway. On the right is part of the brick extension which was added by the Brewery to both front and back of the bar in the late 1930s. The sign has been moved to the taller part of the building.
(PHOTO CONTRIBUTED BY MRS J. SWIFT)

Then on to the Common for Sports. My! Didn't I love the barrel-rolling… Those men who were going in for the race would gather at a certain place, then at the word 'Go' they'd roll those barrels at a spanking pace – just using one hand to keep the thing a-rolling… When it began to grow dark, the horses would be harnessed to the drays, and off they'd go at a fine trot, the women holding torches aloft. Many's the time I've followed them most of the way back.'

The World's End had plenty of stabling and store-rooms on what is now the car park, and employed an ostler and groom. Over the years it was extended and modernised – though Stanley Ramsey remembered his father going there every evening at 11p.m. to pump water for use the next day.

Numerous clubs have met or held functions in the World's End, including a bowls club, the Oddfellows, the British Legion (after the First World War), and the

Mulbarton Knuts outside the World's End when W. Denny was the proprietor, probably early 1925. Left to right, back row: *Mr Kedge, W.F. Alborough;, W. Kedge (with kitten), S. Huggins, Russell Dent, William Denny junr, W. Kedge, ?, Mr Cullum;* middle row: *Sid Funnell, A. Kedge, Mr Kedge, R. Kedge, Pat Carver, Leslie Andrews, Peter Thomas senr, Mrs Denny (wife of landlord), Lee Hemnell, Gordon Andrews, Russell Andrews, ?, J. Sizer, Mr Denny;* front row: *Mrs R. Dent, J. Buxton, Mr Wharton (with dog), F. Smith, Mr Smith, Ernie Midlane, William Denny (landlord), ? (sitting behind child), A. Smith, ?, ?, Mrs S. Funnell, ?.* (PHOTO CONTRIBUTED BY BILL ALBOROUGH)

Mulbarton Boxing Club photographed at the back of the World's End. The club was formed by Lenny Dack in the late 1940s, and met in the World's End clubroom. Left to right (standing): *Lenny Dack (organiser), Billy Alborough, Roy Dawson, Alfred Swift, Russell Johnson, 'Skippy';* front (kneeling): *Weaver (originally a London evacuee), Freddie Hall.* (PHOTO CONTRIBUTED BY MRS J. SWIFT)

The line-up for the Boxing Day football match in the snow, 1982, between the men's darts team (disguised as ladies) and the women's darts team (dressed as men), outside the World's End. (PHOTO: BRYAN TUNGATE)

The sign of the World's End in 1975. (PHOTO: JILL WRIGHT)

The World's End darts team has raised money for a number of local charities. Taking part in a 24-hour darts marathon to raise £519 for the Edith Cavell Day Centre in 1988 are, left to right, back row: Steve Walters, Les Riches, Paul Tufts; third row: Mike Revell, Pat Marshall, Steve Cook, Andy Stevens, Keith Dye; second row: George Henderson, John Thurston, Maurice Law, ?, Michael Hunt; front row: Phil Condron, Paul Kirby, John Riches, Mick Chamberlain, Dave Allen.

(PHOTO: BRYAN TUNGATE)

Women Unionists' Association. When the Parish Hall was almost next door, groups such as the Men's Social Club also had close links with the pub. The Swardeston and District Horticultural Society held its Annual Meeting and first Winter Exhibition in December 1933, with classes for vegetables and flowers 'for cottagers only'. A boxing club run by Lenny Dack had its home in the Function Room and gave shows, and the World's End Gun Club became the Norwich and District Wildfowlers Association.

Much more recently, the Humbleyard Rehearsal Orchestra practised in the Function Room.

The Oddfellows

The Mulbarton Benevolence Lodge of the Manchester Unity of Oddfellows was formed on 3 February 1843; its 'Lodge House' was the World's End. The Loyal 'James Turner' Juvenile Lodge, established on 14 September 1888, was named in honour of James Turner of Paddock Farm. Both clubs were well patronised, with members from Mulbarton and a surprisingly wide area around. Presumably many were local people who moved away temporarily but still wanted to keep their membership. From the beginning of the school log-book in 1875, half-day holidays are recorded for the Oddfellows events:

1881: July 29th – A holiday was given on Monday in consequence of the Meeting of the Oddfellows at the World's End (this is a general holiday for the labouring classes and mechanics).

1895: July 29th – No school. Oddfellows F. Society meeting – many of the boys belong to Juvenile branch and requested holiday.

Kelly's Directories indicate a membership in 1904 of 'about 590 members including juveniles; Mr John Thrower of East Carlton, is secretary'. By 1922, there are 'about 500 members, including juveniles; Mr Herbert R. Cunningham is secretary' (he was still secretary in 1933).

An annual dinner for Lodge members was held at the World's End but cost 2s.6d. per person in 1875, so was likely to have attracted only well-off members. However, a clue to the popularity of the Loyal Benevolence Lodge is the 'Pence Book' that has come to light. This ledger lists members and their payments for each half-year from 1861 to 1869 and is called the 'Pence Book' because members paid 1d. (one old penny) a day for a six-day week, which amounted to 1s. a fortnight. This was the equivalent of National Insurance – a contribution towards 'benevolence' when a man could not work or a family needed help with doctor's or nursing fees. The book begins in July 1861 with 288 members (men only), and finishes in December 1869 with 318 members. The oldest member seems to be Henry Brown of Wreningham – aged 63 in January 1865. Very few others are aged 60 or more; most are in their twenties and thirties.

For a sample half-year in 1865, there were 44 names listed as resident in Mulbarton – some have descendants here today. Most had subscriptions owing and three names were crossed out due to 'non-payment'. Following names through the ledger, we find that George Emms (aged 33 in 1865) moved to London in July/December 1869, and in the same year Richard Moore (aged 25 in 1865) moved to Newcastle. James Catchpole's place of residence is

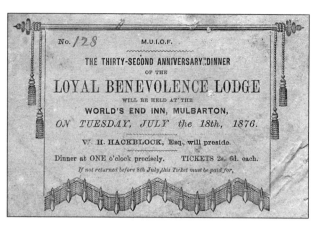

The 32nd Anniversary Dinner was held in the World's End on 18 July 1876. A ticket which reserved a place for 'Brother Samuel Dye' (the wheelwright) has the programme printed on the back: 'The Committee being anxious to make the Anniversary pass off satisfactory to all, the House having to close at Ten p.m., you are requested to attend to the following instructions: 1st To meet at the Lodge House at 10.30. 2nd To Mulbarton Church, for Divine Service, at 11. 3rd To Dinner at 1 p.m. 4th To hear Speeches after the tables are cleared. 5th To parade round the Common after the Speeches.' (Were they really in a fit state to parade after all those toasts?)

(CONTRIBUTED BY DAVID WRIGHT)

given as 'America'. He is excluded for non-payment by the end of 1864 – hardly surprising if he had emigrated, or was he working on a farm of that name now lost under the A47 Southern Bypass?

The Junior branch continued to flourish during the inter-war years, when it met in the Parish Hall on the fourth Monday of the month. A Women's branch was formed by 1920, which met twice a year. A local newspaper report of 20 January 1932 describes the children's annual party:

Juvenile members of the Loyal Benevolence Lodge of Odd Fellows, M.U., were given their annual tea in the Mulbarton Parish Hall, arranged by the Secretary, P.P.G.M. H.R. Cunningham and Mrs Cunningham. A capital tea was provided for the large number of juveniles. The secretary had obtained an acrobatic and conjuring party [from Roydon and Scole] known as Rick, Rack and Ruin. They gave a thrilling performance. The Odd Fellows song was sung by the Deputy G.M.F. Foulger. The remainder of the musical items were given by the juveniles and Mrs Howard... Membership is now 153. Presentations were made to five 'Sisters' of the juvenile branch for assistance in the social work of the branch, and Freddy Rice was presented with an attaché case for having won a scholarship. At the close of the programme refreshments were handed round, and each member was the recipient of an orange and a balloon.

The Oddfellows continued to meet at the World's

Above and below: *Two small items in the front of the Pence Book show why the Oddfellows Benevolence Lodge was so popular: a doctor's certificate of 1874 certifying that Bro. Edward Harmer is 'incapable of following his employment' and a Steward's request to the Treasurer to 'Pay Brother William Smith the sum of one Pound' sick pay for two weeks.*

(CONTRIBUTED BY MULBARTON MIDDLE SCHOOL)

End until 1980, when the committee transferred to the Village Hall for its quarterly meetings. With the decline in numbers, the Mulbarton Lodge amalgamated with New Buckenham.

The Reading Room

There are very early references to a Reading Room in Mulbarton, even before the Wingfield Hall was built. The first mention is in the 1891 census, when Maria Godfrey had the occupation of 'Caretaker of Reading and Coffee Rooms'. Was she the lady these lads pestered some years later?

In our village... we had a reading room; but the only paper I ever see'd was the E.D.P... We boys had fun and games there. One thing I remember was to pull a heel iron from our boots, put it in the fire, and when we heard the gates we'd get it out and throw it in the middle of the floor. Time and time again it would be picked up and dropped with a yell. The caretaker lived next-door and she used to make tea, coffee or cocoa at a penny a cup. Three of us would go regular like and say – 'Cup of tea please' – 'Cup of coffee please' – 'Cup of cocoa please'. She'd get real mad and say 'Can't you boys have the same?' 'No ma'am,' we'd say, 'We wants different'. She'd be that mad her wig would slip up and down – that's true it did, and didn't we boys laugh!

The Parish Hall, or Wingfield Hall

A new Parish Hall, incorporating the old 'Reading Room', was built on land next to the Methodist Chapel. It was usually called the Wingfield Hall and was possibly financed by a bequest from Mrs E. Dorinda Wingfield of Mulbarton Hall (Chapter 9) and built soon after her death in 1906. Mr H. Church is listed as 'Secretary of Reading Room, Wingfield Hall' in a directory of 1908. It was run by trustees 'for the purposes of providing a Reading and Recreation Room for the inhabitants of Mulbarton and for such charitable purposes for the general benefit of the said inhabitants as the Trustees think fit.' After the death of Lady Wingfield problems arose around 1917–18, possibly over a trust fund and/or the tithe rent charge on the land. The first entry in the Parish Hall Trustees' Minutes Book records a meeting at Lodge Farm on 18 March 1919 when the chairman (the Rector) 'referred to the kindness of Mr and Mrs Hill in buying the Rent Charge and handing the Hall to the Parish…'

At an open meeting on 3 November:

Mr Tuddenham gave a brief explanation as to the manner in which the so-called Wingfield Hall was now a Parish Hall invested in Trustees who would carry it on for the beneficial use of the Parish. He stated that through the kindness of the late Mr J.W. Hill the room was secure to the Parish, whereas it was at one time in great danger of being lost for Parish use.

In May 1920 the trustees began a process for obtaining a new 'Scheme' from the Charity Commissioners, 'to safeguard the Trustees'. They also put the charges up – and required the Reading Room to pay the same as other users.

The Hall had one large room and a stage with curtains. By 1920 dances were taking place – though the Trustees 'could not sanction 2 Dance nights in succession' nor on Sundays nor during Lent. The dance on Wednesday, 3 December 1919 ran from 7.30p.m. until midnight and cost 1s.3d. per person (6p), refreshments not included. Mr Funnell (the baker) did the catering – and allowed bicycles to park on his premises (opposite) for 2d. each! Mrs Cracknell (from the shop that is now Butler House, at least 100 yards from the Hall) lent her piano for free. The trustees agreed to have it tuned at their expense, and later to buy one for the Hall. A Piano Committee was set up, which duly reported back, obtained a piano and agreed its letting terms and security. Nesda Gray recalled: 'A wonderful big Hall. I have enjoyed many sixpenny hops, singing and dancing, run by Mr A. Bussey *[church organist]* to help Hospital Funds.'

The minutes indicate that members of the Reading Room (renamed the Men's Club) met most evenings, and organised whist drives, dances and

Looking across the frozen pond to the Wingfield Hall (left of the chapel) *with its prominent chimney. 'The Village Hall, or Reading Room as some called it, was opposite the pond, next to the Chapel and Mr Frost's garage.' (Nesda Gray).* (PHOTO CONTRIBUTED BY TERRY BURCHELL, FROM PHILIP STANDLEY'S COLLECTION)

In 1921 the trustees of the Wingfield Hall discussed 'a suitable plaque in memory of M.J.W. Hill's generosity' in rescuing the Hall for the parish. This brass plaque was suitably inscribed and installed.

In 1975, the closed Wingfield Hall still stood between the garage and the Methodist Chapel. (PHOTO: BERNARD AMBROSE)

A children's Christmas party in the Wingfield Hall in the 1950s. Children around the table include Christine Kent, Christopher Ramsey, Juliet Lofty, Lewis Cooper, Robert McKelvy. The adults include Dick Tungate, Mrs Hemnell, Mrs Andrews, Helen Barrett, Berta Lincoln, Joan Widgery (schoolteacher), Joan Ramsey. (PHOTO CONTRIBUTED BY JULIET AMOS, NÉE LOFTY)

socials. But the Hall often functioned at a loss, and had occasional problems with behaviour, as on 21 May 1920: '… a complaint had been made respecting the Reading Room Social "winding-up", and it was decided that in future, when a like Social is held, the Rules of the Room must be strictly observed.'

Other users of the Hall included the Mothers' Union and Girls' Friendly Society (Mondays). In 1920: 'It was agreed to let the room for Political Meetings (irrespective of party).' Every Wednesday night was reserved for socials and other entertainments such as film shows, concerts and pantomimes. From a news report of 18 April 1933:

A concert was held in Mulbarton Parish Hall on Tuesday… on behalf of local charity… The programme consisted of pianoforte solos, duets and comic songs… by performers from Norwich. A play 'The Bathroom Door' was well performed by Miss Ramsay [and five other ladies] and 'Impossible Perkins'… Selections on handbells were given by Mr F.W. Middleton…

The Red Cross Medical Aid Dept had a cupboard and sessions were held at which medical stores were given out from it. A Sunday School must have met here as 'it appears that [they] use the piano for hymns, Miss Muskett having offered to pay a small sum per annum for this privilege' (minutes, 10 July 1922). We also know from the school log-book that the Hall was used in school hours for a week in the summer for the older girls to have cookery classes.

Improvements were gradually made. In 1924 'Mr Cunningham offered to give a lamp for use in the room and Mr Cracknell offered to give the oil.' In 1927, the trustees had a new cloakroom built at a cost of £30 – and refused to pay more when the builder (Mr Barrett) asked for more. Towards the end of 1931, the Men's Club wrote to the trustees 'with regard to equipping the Room with electric light.' The estimate for installation was '£8.13s.0d., with extras for special billiards lights'. The trustees agreed to pay £4 and the Men's Committee the balance. By December they had agreed to have a locked fuse box and 'four 60 watt bulbs be purchased with a view to economy'.

The main memory of the hall was that 'it was cold!' It had two fire places at opposite ends and bucket toilets. Norma Mickleburgh went to keep fit classes and remembers that 'when we danced past the coal fires, smoke filled the room.' She walked from Swardeston for the weekly film shows – 'we sat on long forms to see them'. Dances were a regular feature, with the 'Bunwell Swingers': 'Lenny Potter, Jimmy Abendroth on the piano accordion, and Duggy Brighton on the drums.'

In 1962 there was a major refurbishment: the interior was redecorated throughout for £70, a new stage was given by Mickleburgh & Rutland and curtains by Mrs Lilian Mickleburgh. At about the same time, Mulbarton began to grow and people remember the hall as the meeting-place for clubs such as the Good Companions (founded 1959), Young Wives, Women's Institute, Youth Club, Keep Fit, bingo, whist drives, occasional jumble and other sales, Parish Council meetings and the monthly baby clinic. The Wingfield Hall closed in 1972, but two years later a 'new' hall opened.

Members of the Reading Room, or Men's Social Club, outside World's End, 1924 or 1925. Left to right, back row: ?, *Mr Wharton, F. Smith, ?, ?, Mr Martin, Mr Kedge, Mr Stubbings, A. Stubbings, ?, Mr Nicholls, Mr Nicholls, F. Ellis, Sam Miller;* middle row: *?, E. Midlane, William Denny junr, Mr Huggins, A. Kedge, S. Huggins, G. Buxton, R. Kedge, Russell Dent, Mr Hooney, P. Thomas, J. Carver, Pat Carver, J. Blazer, Jimmy Baxter, J. Sturman, ?, ?;* front row (seated): *Gordon Andrews, W.F. Alborough, Lee Hemnell, Mr Pearce, W. Kedge, R. Andrews, R. Kemp, William Denny (landlord), A. Smith, Mr Wharton, ?, Mr Briggs, H. Lake (secretary), ?, Mr Kedge.*

(PHOTO CONTRIBUTED BY BILL ALBOROUGH)

The Men's Social Club

The Reading Room was the forerunner of today's Social Club – but for men only. The rules at the front of the Minutes Book, duly amended by the trustees of the Parish Hall on 3 November 1919, include:

Rule 3 – Ordinary Members shall be men and youths of good character living in Mulbarton or its immediate neighbourhood, over 14 years of age.

Rule 10 – The Reading Room shall be used for Reading, Writing, and such lawful and orderly Recreation and Instruction by Lectures and otherwise as the Trustees may approve. But no person in a state of intoxication shall be permitted to enter or remain in the room… all betting and gambling of any kind, all swearing and bad language, all disorderly or improper conduct, and all loud talking to the annoyance of others are strictly forbidden.

Rule 15 – The Committee shall decide what Newspapers shall be taken in, and what Books shall be bought. [With variations over the years, these were the *Daily Mail*; the *Mirror*; *Pictorial*; *Chips*; *John Bull*; *Answers*; *Titbits*; *Eastern Daily Press*, provided by Mr Funnell; *Daily Herald*, provided by Mr Beare.]

The Club was open every weekday except Wednesdays, 7–10p.m., from the first Monday in October until the last Saturday in March. Messrs H. & W. Lake were Joint Secretaries, Treasurer and Librarian from 1919 to 1928. Rules were added, for example, on 3 October 1921: '… no Bicycle lamp be brought into the room attached to a bicycle but that they be taken off and stored in the fireplace or another suitable spot.' The name was changed in October 1925: 'It was decided that in future the Reading Room should be known as the Mulbarton Mens Club' [*sic*]. Subscriptions went up to 1s.6d. [8p] per quarter – yet the club still ran at a loss and 'a big endeavour should be made to get fresh members'.

Over the years, activities included billiards, darts, boxing and table tennis – generating much discussion on how each should be financed. A minute of 1 October 1928: '… delight to place on record the fact that the Club had won the Billiards League shield and medals for the past season.' In 1934 a game of billiards cost 2d. 'paid before the game', or 1d. per game for those under 16. A minute of 3 October 1933: '… felt the game of Draughts had been neglected in the Club and the Treasurer undertook to purchase some Boards etc. to encourage the game'.

Tensions between the Club and other users of the Hall are frequently hinted at in the minutes – especially over fees and repairs. By 1933 two Hall Trustees agreed to meet 'the Chairman and Secretaries of the Men's Club and explain charges and insist on keeping of rules…' They duly met at the Rectory on 16 November for 'a frank meeting about use of electric light… the billiards table… piano. Gambling, betting and bad language prohibited; no boys under 16 to be admitted; and club hours 7–10p.m. only (not Wednesdays).'

In return for new rental arrangements, the trustees paid the electricity bill, took over all the fittings and provided curtains for the windows. From now on the Men's Club was treated like any other user. Mounting debts nearly closed the Club in October 1935, but the deficit was turned to a small profit in 1936 – and there the (unsigned) minutes end. In a Radio Norfolk interview in 1988, Stanley Ramsey revealed that the famous Wingfield Hall dances were started to raise money to replace a clock and repair the fireplace in the Hall, damaged by the Men's Club!

The Labour Club

This filled the gap left by the demise of the Men's Club – and was for ladies, too. Bob Mickleburgh was a leading organiser and, besides meetings and socials, his son recalls that: 'my father organised day trips to various seaside resorts each summer. Destinations included Great Yarmouth, Gorleston, Wells-next-the-Sea, Felixstowe and Clacton.'

Bob Mickleburgh (left) on one of the outings he organised to Wells-next-the-Sea, rowing with Cecil Miller (coach driver) and Ray Abendroth. Brenda Collins recalled: 'There was a boating lake there and when we had left the beach, usually because the tide came in and everyone had to leave off cockling, we were able to hire rowing boats and enjoy ourselves on the lake.'

(PHOTO CONTRIBUTED BY BRENDA COLLINS)

Sunbathing at Lowestoft – an outing for the Mulbarton branch of the Labour Club organised by Bob Mickleburgh in the early 1950s. In the foreground (left to right) are Mrs Gittings, ?, Renee Gardiner with daughter Janice Gardiner and mother Mrs Copeman (in hat), Cissie Robinson with daughter Frances Robinson, and Mrs Tuddenham (in deckchair, extreme right).

(PHOTO CONTRIBUTED BY PETER MICKLEBURGH)

Brenda Collins and others remember:

After the war ended Bob Mickleburgh and Lenny Dack used to organise coach trips to Wells-next-the-Sea and we used to go out on the sandbanks gathering huge bags of cockles. It was one of the few seaside trips we had in those days and they were greatly enjoyed. We used to take a picnic and the coach parked on what was called Abraham's Bosom at the end of Beach Road at Wells.

Bob Mickleburgh's wife, Lilian, recalled that they always called at a pub on the way home, sang songs in the bus and Mrs Kedge was the life and soul of each outing.

The First Mulbarton Players

Formed in 1934, the Mulbarton Players were started by the choir and friends to raise funds for church restoration projects.

Cinderella was their first major production. An undated news cutting of 1935 reports:

At Mulbarton Parish Hall on Wednesday the pantomime 'Cinderella' was presented. The organiser and producer was Miss Ramsay [the Rector's daughter], whose untiring efforts in training the performers were well repaid by hearty cheers from the large audience which quite filled the hall... The pantomime, which was in three acts, was performed throughout in a creditable manner... the two ugly sisters (Mr H. Martin and Mr W. Emms) caused much merriment... A word of praise is due to Miss Lister, who made the ladies' costumes. It is expected the proceeds will amount to £10.

A scene from Pleasure Cruise, *performed by Mulbarton Players in the Wingfield Hall in 1938. The play was written and produced by Cyril Fairman and consisted of five acts. The photo shows 'the moonlight scene on the top deck' – described in the review as 'artistically arranged' with lighting effects controlled by Messrs G. Deller and J. Skae. There was a cast of 15 and the acting was described as 'of a high standard and the chorus girls looked very charming in their numerous novelty costumes.'*

(PHOTO CONTRIBUTED BY JIL WHEELER)

A rhyme about the production has survived, bringing in many local characters and events; here is a taster:

Have you heard all the talk of the Village,
Folks will never forget such a sight:
'Twas a pantomime called Cinderella
We gave here one Wednesday night.

There was quite a big crowd there to see us
With a chorus we opened a show.
With Rhoda and Daphne and Ivy
Nesta, Hilda and Betty you know.

Mr Fairman, a gallant Prince Charming,
Had lots of lovemaking to do.
Mr Warren, I think, was Danieli,
But we didn't know quite who was who.

And then as the two ugly sisters
Now Mr Emms sure was a scream
Mr Martin was fine as the other
And looked like some wonderful dream.

There was Michael and Frank on the curtains,
And they pulled the job through all right.
Mr Sinden collected the tickets
And Jack Skae managed the lights.

Miss Lister worked hard on the dresses;
She must be an expert, I think.
Mrs Stackyard helped with the refreshments
Then gave us all coffee to drink.

Royal Scandal was the 1936 production, presumably inspired by current events surrounding the abdication of Edward VIII:

At Mulbarton Parish Hall on Wednesday a musical play entitled 'Royal Scandal' was performed before a large audience. The actors were members of the church choir and friends. The producer of the comedy was Miss Ramsay of Mulbarton Rectory, and Mrs Howard, the organist, was the accompanist... In the interval Mr F.W. Middleton gave selections on the handbells.

This was not the last Players' production – in 1938 came *Pleasure Cruise*, written and directed by Cyril Fairman 'owing to the absence of Miss Ramsay, their producer.'

The Village Hall

The Wingfield Hall continued to be used for a variety of clubs and events until it closed in 1972. To repair and modernise the hall became too costly, and in 1970 a committee was formed to raise money for a new Village Hall. Members had their eye on the village school when it was finally closed – as there was no suitable site for a new Village Hall. The old school

The former school in the process of being converted into a Village Hall in early 1975. A small porch has been added, but as yet there are no cloakrooms to the south.

(PHOTO: DAVID WRIGHT)

The interior of the old Village Hall (former school, now dental surgery), late 1987. An enrolment of new members into 2nd Mulbarton Guides with (left to right, foreground): Dawn Frost (patrol leader), Lisa Thorpe, Jenny Birch and Hayley Shaw being enrolled by Jill Wright (Guide Guider) and Angela Spiers (Assistant Guider).

(PHOTO: ROSEMARY SHAW)

was built on common land, so people thought it should only be used for the good of the village. From *Parish News*, Christmas 1972:

A very well attended public meeting was held in the Old School on Monday September 25th. By an almost unanimous vote, it was agreed that the committee should make a bid to the Norfolk Education Committee to buy the old school when it becomes available in April–May 1973. It appears that a completely new building is quite out of our reach and the old school can be converted to a suitable hall fairly easily. A grant towards this has been applied for…

A party for children in the Village Hall to celebrate the Queen's silver jubilee in 1978 (note the cake with Union Jacks, bottom left). (PHOTO: CYNTHIA LADBROOKE)

Mulbarton members of Hethersett & District Lions celebrate with residents of 'Robinscroft' in September 1991 on the new patio they built for this small MENCAP home in Mulbarton. Foreground: John Hewitt (left) and Lions President Rodney Davis. Seated (left to right) are Robinscroft residents Michael, Barbara, Teresa, Timothy and Sandra. Standing (left to right) are Lions members David and Doris Hewitt, Harry Walsh and five of the Robinscroft staff and helpers.

(PHOTO: *EVENING NEWS*, REPRODUCED
COURTESY OF ARCHANT PHOTOGRAPHIC NORFOLK)

In fact the school was in use until Summer 1973. The Committee raised over £7,000 in five years, through a series of Village Festivals and other events such as a Wine and Cheese Happening at the World's End; a sponsored walk; a 'knit-in' and a lottery with 6d. tickets. Grants supplemented this huge local effort. Early in 1974 people were being invited to bring donations in kind – cups, plates, tea towels, etc. – to increase the resources of a hall that had already been in use for some months.

After many problems with the Charity Commissioners, the Wingfield Hall was finally sold in 1975. It was demolished and permission was given for a modern house to be built on the site – named Wingfield House. The proceeds from the old Parish Hall were only about 10 per cent of the cost of the replacement Village Hall, but the final payments were made to the County Council in 1975. The lottery ceased in 1980 and was replaced by a regular grant from the Parish Council, but huge efforts went into fund-raising and working parties to cope with maintenance and improvements such as the new changing rooms. Numerous organisations hired the hall, including the baby clinic; playschool; toddler club and Monkey Club; Guides and Brownies; Youth Club; several dance groups; martial arts; two WIs; Good Companions (for the over-60s); and the Hethersett and District Lions, who raised thousands of pounds for local charities.

Women's Institutes

The Mulbarton and District WI was founded in 1944 when the East Carleton and Mulbarton branch was divided. When the two institutes separated, half the balance was given to Mulbarton: £1.12s.3½d! Gifts from the president and committee amounted to a further £5.10s. and a bank account was opened.

The first committee meeting was held on 11 January 1944 at Brooke Villa (the old Post Office) with Mrs Rose Middleton as President. Vice-presidents were Mrs Hooney (of the Long Lane nursery – responsible for birthday posies); Mrs Massingham (of Mulbarton Hall – magazine secretary); and Mrs Quick (on the social committee). Miss Larter was Secretary; Miss Claxton, Treasurer. Other committee members were: Mrs Eccleston (trading stall); Mrs Gladwell (social committee); Mrs Goodman, Mrs Nicholls (refreshments, 'with three members in rotation'); Mrs G. Stackyard; Nurse Sexton; Mrs Blackman (to meet speaker); Mrs Ladbrooke (press correspondent).

Meetings were held on a

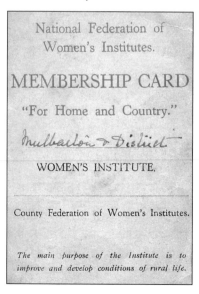

National Federation of Women's Institutes.

MEMBERSHIP CARD

"For Home and Country."

Mulbarton & District

WOMEN'S INSTITUTE.

County Federation of Women's Institutes.

The main purpose of the Institute is to improve and develop conditions of rural life.

Membership card for Mulbarton & District WI, admitting Mrs A. Stackyard on 25 January 1944. Annual membership was 2s.6d (half a crown, now 12p).

(CONTRIBUTED BY EVELYN SMITH,
NÉE STACKYARD)

Tuesday afternoon in the Wingfield Hall. Early meetings opened with reading the 'Alberta Creed' and motto and/or singing 'Jerusalem' and ended with 'God Save the King'. An outdoor meeting was held in August at East Carleton Lodge or Bracon Lodge, and later at The Lodge or Malthouse, Mulbarton. There were summer outings to Sandringham, Hunstanton and Lowestoft along with trips to the theatre, the pantomime and to Old Tyme dances and occasionally to London. Brenda Ford (née Collins) remembers:

My late mother was one of the founder members of the Women's Institute when it was formed in Mulbarton (I still have her badge). She enjoyed it immensely and went to the Royal Albert Hall for their annual meeting where she was a delegate on more than one occasion, along with Mrs Bobbin, another founder member.

The 'Afternoon WI' continued with a similar pattern of meetings and activities for just over 50 years. In 1983 the Mulbarton Evening WI was founded to cater for women who were at work during the day and welcomed former 'Afternoon' members when that WI finally closed. Irene Eagle, elected secretary of the Evening WI at its foundation, continues as secretary of the current Mulbarton WI after more than 21 years of service.

The New Village Hall and Social Club

As the village grew the Village Hall in the old school became too small and was replaced by the present much larger hall and social club with money from grants and the parish rate. A news cutting dated 14 April 1989 reports:

A new era has opened at Mulbarton where a £200,000 village hall has been paid for by the villagers. And together they have helped raise a further £9,500 to build a new Scout and Guide headquarters on the site. The end result is the pride of the village with everyone helping in some way, however small, to turn dreams into reality.

Parish Council Chairman Mrs Val Grogutt says, '... our future plans include a sports hall, bowling-green, floodlit hard courts and a children's play area... Behind the village hall, which is also home for the 525-strong social club, is the new Scout and Guide headquarters...'

Everything achieved in this village is through the care and goodwill of the people who live here. We are proud of what we have achieved, and hope to do more.

Both the Village Hall and the Social Club have been extended since they were first opened. Ronnie and Jane Barrett have raised thousands of pounds at social club raffles and dances for such charities as Children in Need, the Air Ambulance, local play-

In the spirit of service: parish councillors get to work stone-picking on land adjacent to the recently opened Village Hall. Left to right: *Councillors Marina Carter, ?, David Wright, Harry Walsh, Nigel Christian. In the background is an abseiling tower built by Scout leaders for use by Scouts and Guides next to their headquarters.*

(PHOTO: CHRIS CARTER)

'Roll out the barrel'! The first delivery of beer is received by Ronnie Barrett, bar steward (right), from Greene King in preparation for the opening of the Mulbarton Social Club, 1988. (PHOTO: MARINA CARTER)

groups and the Day Care Centre. Some of the clubs that meet in the Hall or Committee Room have their roots in the Wingfield Hall; others were able to start (or restart) because of the extra facilities – among them Short Mat Bowls, the Art Group, Mulbarton Players, the Children's Centre and the Youth Club.

The Present Mulbarton Players

The present Mulbarton Players were founded in 1994 by Chris Scales to raise money for the Hall School for handicapped children in Norwich which had been vandalised and the gym destroyed by fire. He invited local village people to put on a variety show ('Maytime Cavalcade'). The response was overwhelming and the the Players raised £1,500 for the

Mulbarton Players Millennium style: the 'underwater' scene in the panto Dick Wittington, *written and produced by Chris Scales. Miss Octopussy (Richard Pilch,* centre*) is serenaded by singing mermaids* (left to right) *Graham Eagling, Kevin Godfrey, Charlie Yallop and Andrew ('Angus') Curtis. This production raised money for children with muscular dystrophy.* (PHOTO CONTRIBUTED BY GRAHAM EAGLING)

school. The team were so delighted with the response that they asked Chris to carry on directing under the name 'The Mulbarton Players'. Over the years they have performed numerous shows, plays and, most popular of all, pantomimes – 'Oh yes they have!' Richard Pilch and Gordon Spalding took over the reins from Chris Scales for some of the time. The Players have raised £17,500 for various charities, most with a local connection, to which the proceeds of their 2006 pantomime, *Aladdin*, have been added.

Scouting

There has been a Scout presence in Mulbarton from as early as 1910, but little is known of this first group other than that it was run by Miss Cecily Gurney of Keswick Hall. She was very involved in work among youth – especially Scouts and Guides.

From the East Carleton Magazine, May 1914: 'Cooking classes for Scouts arranged by the County Council Education Authority will be held at Mulbarton School on Friday 29th at 6.30 and on June 12th, 19th and 16th, also at 6.30.'

From the school log-book, 1921:

May 24th Empire Day. Timetable suspended and special Empire lessons in Hist. Geog, Nature Study, Drawing, etc. taken instead. Physical Exercise and Signalling display by the Boy Scouts. Half Holiday in the afternoon.

The first Scout group was disbanded and another group started in 1932. This group was known as the 42nd Norwich and the leader was Murray Martin of Silver Fox Farm, East Carleton. Cyril Fairman, then

of Paddock Farm, was treasurer, and a newspaper report on a jumble sale with teas and folk-dancing at the Rectory says that £6.7s.3d. was raised in 1933. Scouts were involved in discussions about celebrations for King George V's silver jubilee in 1935. At one time the troop had 21 boys but unfortunately this group disbanded during or soon after the Second World War.

In 1975 a Cub Pack was formed in the village, attached to the 38th Norwich (Cringleford) Scout Group. Mulbarton's own 1st Mulbarton Scout Group was started in 1982. The Cubs changed their name-tabs and continued to meet in the First School on a Wednesday evening. The Scout Troop was started by Malcolm Court and Derek Edwards with eight boys: two that had been in the Cringleford group and six from the Cub Pack in the village. They met in the Middle School. The group grew steadily over the next few years and a second Cub Pack was started in the Village Hall. The two packs were known as 'Tiger' and 'Jaguar' and enjoyed friendly rivalry and joint meetings. A 'Barn Owl' Venture Unit made its den in the old barn at Lodge Farm for a while. All the sections included a full range of Scouting activities in their programmes – camps, visits, night hikes and other outdoor activities. The biggest problem was – and is – getting volunteer leaders and helpers to run the sections.

In 1989 part of the field purchased for a new Village Hall was leased from the Parish Council and a purpose-built joint HQ with the Guides and Brownies was built with the help of grants and donations and a lot of hard work from parents and leaders. Funds come mainly from subscriptions, the waste paper and bottle banks, an annual jumble sale

The official opening of the new Village Hall, April 1989. Robert Preston (chairman of the Parish Council) is speaking to the assembled crowd, while Valerie Grogutt (former Council chairman) is preparing to help the Ames quads, Ben, Kate, Gemma and Clare, to cut the ribbon to open the hall. (PHOTO: JILL WRIGHT)

The Mulbarton Evening WI float follows the Norwich Union coach which led the opening parade of a rather wet Village Festival in July 1992. Just visible under their umbrellas are (left to right) Janet Bobbin, Pat Frost, Irene Eagle (secretary since the Evening WI was founded in 1983) and Jean Dean. The lorry was lent by David Ireland. (PHOTO: JILL WRIGHT)

Members of all the uniformed organisations gather outside the unfinished HQ building in July 1988 to publicise the need for further support and funds to complete the work. Among the leaders are, far left: *Malcolm Court and Joe Allen, Scout leaders, Alison Howard (Brownie Guider);* far right: *Jill Wright (Guide Guider).* (PHOTO: EVENING NEWS, REPRODUCED COURTESY OF ARCHANT PHOTOGRAPHIC NORFOLK)

Official opening of the Scout and Guide HQ by Dick Condon (right), *general manager of the Theatre Royal, Norwich, in April 1989. More than 400 people gathered, including Norfolk dignitaries of both movements, past and present members of Mulbarton Scout and Guide groups and all who had helped build and decorate the new HQ.* (PHOTO: EVENING NEWS, REPRODUCED COURTESY OF ARCHANT PHOTOGRAPHIC NORFOLK)

Right: *Members of the Humbleyard Branch of the Girls' Friendly Society are joined by other youth organisations for a pageant organised by Miss Cecily Gurney in the grounds of Keswick Hall. Note the contingent of local Girl Guides on the right (Miss Gurney was very involved with Guiding), and the exotic costumes on the left. Occasion and date are uncertain, possibly 1924.*

(PHOTO CONTRIBUTED BY VIC GRAY)

The 2nd Mulbarton Guide company gathers in the old Village Hall (the former school) for the enrolment of Kirsty Read (centre left) and Heather Shaw on 8 November 1988. Surrounding them in a candle-lit circle are (left to right) Jill Wright (Guider), Marie Reeder, Zoe Wheatley, Hannah Kelly, Justine O'Neill (hidden), Jennie Wells, Gill Rochfort, Rachel Punt, Emma Harrison, Emma Court, Claire Tallack, Sarah Bluckert, Michelle Bunting (holding Company flag), Kay Neatham, Hayley Shaw, Katherine Adcock, Kelly Barnard, Charlotte Doyle, Jayne Hewitt, Louise Rochfort, Lisa Thorpe, Jennie Birch (hidden), Terri Farrow, Natalie Packer and Pat Adcock (Assistant Guider). (PHOTO: EVENING NEWS, REPRODUCED COURTESY OF ARCHANT PHOTOGRAPHIC NORFOLK)

Bats in the belfry – 1st Mulbarton Brownies celebrated the 1984 national Brownie Tea-making Fortnight by organising a tea-party in Mulbarton Church belfry, complete with bat masks, bat models and a batty cake. Guests included the Rector, Revd Geoffrey Unwin, his wife Daphne and a Nora Batty look-alike (Kathleen Smith). (PHOTO FROM 1ST MULBARTON BROWNIES' SCRAPBOOK)

and auction and the firework display. The HQ is not only used regularly by all the Scout and Guide groups, but also by a playgroup and occasionally for playschemes and other events.

Guides and Brownies

Guide and Brownie units in Mulbarton were only started in the 1970s, but Mulbarton girls have been part of nearby units for much longer than that. There were units in Flordon and Bracon Ash from the early days of Guiding, and Mrs Finch opened the grounds of 'Woodlands' in Long Lane for camps and outdoor activities. Local girls took part in some of the Keswick Hall pageants and other activities.

The present Guide Company was founded in 1965 as the 1st Flordon by Sue Gilbert and met in a hut in a field beside The Street, Flordon. It then became Flordon and Bracon Ash, meeting at Bracon Ash Village Hall, and finally 1st Mulbarton. A second company was started in 1985 by Jill Wright and ran for 10 years before the two companies were amalgamated. Most members came from the two village Brownie Packs.

The first Brownie pack was registered on 6 January 1971 as the 1st Flordon and Bracon Ash. It met at 'Woodlands' – close enough to Mulbarton for village girls to join. Mrs Finch, who then lived at 'Woodlands', was Brown Owl. Meetings were moved to the First School Hall by 1974, when Margaret Coleman and Liz Valiant were running the

1st Mulbarton Brownies celebrate the Pack's 21st birthday in the Scout and Guide HQ, June 1999. In the back row are (left to right) leaders Lynn Lambert, Gill Smith and Lindsay Watson.
(PHOTO CONTRIBUTED BY LYNN LAMBERT)

pack, followed by Venita Callaby and Lindsay Watson. The pack was re-registered as 1st Mulbarton in June 1978, and flourished under Brown Owls Rosemary Shaw, then Lindsay Watson and Lynn Lambert. Huge demand led to the formation of a 2nd Mulbarton Pack, and while leaders were available there was a Rainbow Group for younger girls. All the uniformed organisations have benefited from long-serving, trained and talented volunteers who have organised varied weekly meetings, exciting challenges, visits, camps, pack holidays and even overseas trips.

❖ CHAPTER 4 ❖

The Village School

Mulbarton's Earliest School?

The earliest reference to a teacher in Mulbarton discovered so far is around 1805, when 'Richard Whiting (Schoolmaster)' was tenant of the house now called 'Carpenters', west of the Common. Did he teach in Mulbarton? If so, where?

In the Church Visitation Return of 1843 questions raised about education are answered by the recently appointed Rector, Revd Richard Lucas:

9. Is there a day school, and how supported?
                    Two dame schools supported by weekly
                              payments of the children
10. What is the average number of scholars? About 50
11. Is it in union with the National Society?   No

White's Directory of Norfolk, 1845, lists Mark Bean Petchell as 'Schoolmaster and Registrar', but where was his school? Did the Visitation Return cause the new Rector to organise education in his parish? Government grants had been available to church schools since 1833.

The records of the Rich Charity (Chapter 1) indicate that a 'substantially built' cottage erected on charity land (now allotment land) beside The Rosery in 1829 was later turned into a school. 'SCHOOL HOUSE' is listed in the 1851 census between households 84 (The Rosery) and 85 (Near Flordon Lane). A map of the charity lands dated 1862 marks a 'cottage now used as a schoolroom', rented by the long-serving Rector, Revd Richard Lucas. *White's Directory* (1883) claims it was pulled down in 1865 (i.e. when the new National School was built) and the land 'is now let as a garden'. Did this school serve all or part of the village – and was it the successor or the alternative to another building that claims to have been a school?

There is evidence that a small building at the south-west corner of Mulbarton Common was also an old school. Certainly hundreds of ink-wells were found when the building was renovated by the present owner! Some claim it was in use as a school as late as 1914, when there were only five pupils. In 1915 it was let to the wheelwright at the Tradesman's Arms opposite. The building was part of the sale of the East Carleton Manor estate in 1920:

LOT 21: The Old Mulbarton School (now used as a Paint Shop), situated at the junction of the roads from Mulbarton and Bracon Ash, and being a weather-board

This small building at the south-west corner of the Common is thought to have once been a school. It is built mainly of clay lump with some brick and tiles – though heavily disguised now. It has one large square room with a chimney for a stove, a tiny entry lobby, and at the side is a manger and hitching rail for a horse. It became the wheelwright's workshop in 1915.   (PHOTO: JILL WRIGHT)

and tiled building with flagged floor. Lean-to Cart Shed attached. The estimated area is 4 poles... Let to Mr F. Swain on a yearly tenancy at £3 p.a.

Mr Swain bought the little building he was using and in 1946 his widow sold it to Cyril Fairman at the Malthouse, who in turn sold it to Billy Goward at the forge in 1957 for use as a store. It is still part of the forge property. In 1976 the County Council proposed to knock it down to widen the road, but the present owner managed to save it.

The Victorian School

In 1865 a new National (i.e. Church) School was opened in Mulbarton on common land obtained from John Steward, lord of the manor, by Revd Richard Lucas, who was chair of the managers. Until 1890 the children paid a small fee, though the managers themselves often paid for the poorest children. Sending children home for the 'school pence' they owed in April and October is often mentioned in the log-book, and those who could not afford it stayed away for a while.

In 1872 the 'New Code of Regulations' required that 'The Principal Teacher must make at least once a week in the Log Book an entry which will specify ordinary progress and other facets concerning the School or its teachers...' The Mulbarton School

The 'National' School opened in 1865: a brick and stone building (now the dental surgery) which originally had one room and, unlike schools in some nearby villages, had no schoolhouse. This photograph may date from 1907, when Sir Edward Wingfield KCB (of Mulbarton Hall) presented the school with a flagpole. On the far right, where the lady is standing, is the wooden butcher's shop (Chapter 8). (PHOTO FROM VILLAGE ARCHIVE)

log-book begins on 8 February 1875, when Elizabeth Smith took charge. The first Diocesan Report explains some background:

REPORT of the Scripture Examination given on 17th June 1875:
The School passed a fair examination, especially when regard is had to hindrances from the illness of the late excellent teacher, the consequent suspense of the School till the appointment in February of the present Mistress, with the prevalence of Scarletina lately among the children. The order and discipline of the School seemed good and the children happy.

Miss Smith must have arrived to considerable chaos. She was unqualified, unsupported and lacked resources for an average of 62 pupils of all ages in one room. Attendance was erratic, depending on the weather, the state of the roads, illness and parents wanting children for fruit-picking, hay-making, gleaning, acorn-collecting and other means of supplementing meagre incomes. The Rector visited several days a week, and at times taught lessons other than scripture. He also provided necessities – some probably from his own pocket: 'March 2nd – received from the Rev. Lucas 2 dozen slates and 2 dozen Bibles.' A little later he gave pen holders and scripture prints.

Other frequent visitors were Mrs Wingfield (of Mulbarton Hall) and Mrs Hackblock (of The Lodge), who were trustees and came to inspect the girls' needlework.

The teacher-in-charge recorded some of the lessons she gave: 'March 25th – Gave a lesson on the Camel' and in April '... on the Rhinoceros'.

To cope with numbers, older pupils were chosen to teach the younger: 'Feb. 25th – Took Maria Brown from 1st Class to teach lower classes.'

Holidays include Easter (anything from Good Friday only to a week); Whitsun (usually a week); harvest (four or five weeks – the start date varying according to when harvest began); Christmas (usually two weeks); a half-day each for Valentine's Day, Ash Wednesday, the Flower Show, the Oddfellows Dinner and other special occasions (e.g. the reopening of the church after refurbishment on 11 November 1875).

Mulbarton does not seem to have been a popular appointment. The school had a succession of mistresses who stayed for a year or less. The teacher for 1876 had a teaching certificate and introduced some innovations.

Jan 24–28 – Allowed the first class to write on paper for the first time.
March 20–24 – Allowed III Standard to use paper for arithmetic.
May 15–19 – Allowed chn, in Infants' Class to go out to play for a short time each day this week.

Her Majesty's Inspector's report of 22 June 1876 was rather alarming:

Some work has been done but the Arithmetic is very weak especially in the second and third classes. The Infants are being taught but little and the Mistress cannot do justice to the School either in Instruction or Discipline without further help. The Accounts should be kept in proper form. The supply of Reading books is insufficient.

The response was immediate – on 17 July an assistant mistress, Miss Jarman, began duties and during the summer the building was enlarged to include a

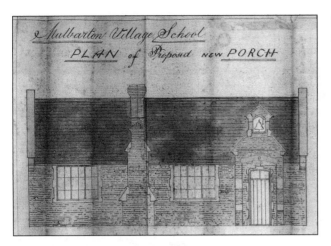

Architect's drawing for the porch and extension to Mulbarton School, 1876.

separate classroom for the infants. The Inspector's Report of July 1877 states:

The school has been improved by the addition of a class-room, and the order has much improved since last year... but... The Infants should have regular daily teaching from the Mistress. The supply of Reading books is still in some parts of the school insufficient...

In 1878 there is a complaint about overcrowding and poor discipline among the boys, 'the conduct of some of whom needs amending.' Perhaps the comment on unruly boys was taken to heart the following year:

On 13 January 1879 – 'Caned two boys who gave their teacher much trouble in the 1st class.'

It paid off – regarding the Scripture Examination (May 1879) it was reported:

That the condition of the children both as regards behaviour speaks well for the care and attention which has been bestowed on them by the mistress. The boys are far more orderly... The Infants did really well especially in Old Testament and Catechism, and the repetition of Scripture was excellent... The great failing noticeably is that the majority of the children leave the questions to be answered by about half a dozen of the quicker ones amongst them. It would be well to endeavour to remedy this. The writing on slates was very good...

The two Monitors deserve praise for their quiet attention and readiness in answering – and also a boy whose name I believe is Rice. He deserves encouragement.

Overcrowding is often commented on: 'Desks should not be five deep. More desk accommodation is needed...' (1879 Inspector's Report). No wonder childhood illnesses spread rapidly and the school had to be closed for epidemics of scarlet fever, diphtheria, whooping cough, measles, mumps and 'flu. It was the teachers' chore to fumigate the premises!

Almost every new teacher comments in the log-book on poor work, but efforts to raise standards met resistance. Eliza E. Bolton took charge on 10 October 1879 and had a hard start:

Have had several times to deviate from Time Table owing to lack of a monitor. Attendance very poor – chn. out gleaning... Order and work of the assistant's class has been very poor... Have had to work Arithmetic with Standard III after school hours on account of their back-wardness in that subject... Devoted some time to the 1st and 2nd stand. The former need thorough teaching; many of them barely knowing their letters. Tried Emma Cooper as a monitor.

Miss Bolton's BIG innovation in the face of poor standards was homework – but, on 17–21 November:

Gave chn. some homework for the first time on Tuesday. Several of the parents burnt the papers containing it: plan seems likely to meet with opposition.

Jan 23 1880 – Several complaints have been made by parents about the school windows being open during school hours; but it is absolutely necessary to ensuring a healthy atmosphere that they should be.

April 12–16 – Have admitted several children. On Friday a girl named Alborough was taken forcibly out of the school by her father in direct opposition to my injunction that she should remain.

In 1880, schooling became compulsory for all children between the ages of five and ten.

In 1883 a master was appointed. David Walter Parsons took charge on 8 January with Mrs Parsons assisting. He immediately lists 'low standards (esp. in Arithmetic); reading books and slates in bad condition; no school song.' Over the next few weeks he received 'several new slates... 3 doz. Royal Readers and other articles... New Historical readers, Geographical readers, new blackboard and easel...', and later, 'Received for school use 2 dozen *Robinson Crusoe*, 4 dozen other reading books, also Grammar, Arithmetic and Poetry books, Recitation cards and Needlework frame.'

Pupils had to learn and recite poetry, including *The Wreck of the Hesperus* (Longfellow) and *Elegy Written in a Country Churchyard* (Gray) in Standards IV and V.

Mr Parsons instilled discipline: 'Caned Arthur Sturman and Isaac Lake for insulting an old lady of the village', and, 'Admitted two new scholars on Monday. William Beaumont the new scholar was severely punished today for impudence and insubordination.' This punishment didn't impress his brother, James, for a fortnight later he was:

... punished severely today for insubordination; during the master's absence in the classroom he deliberately left the school and went home. He returned with his mother in the afternoon and promised to reform.

Form No. XVII. N.
ENGLAND AND WALES.

EDUCATION DEPARTMENT,

WHITEHALL, LONDON, **S.W.**

18 June 1884.

Mulbarton C. of E. School.

Notice is hereby given to you, that an Order on H. M. Paymaster-General for £ *64.12.10* has been despatched to the Correspondent of the above-named School in favour of the person nominated by yourself and two others to receive the Grant due to it for the past year.

Full Instructions have been sent with the Order.

You are requested NOT to write in answer to this notice, unless there are any circumstances which you wish specially to communicate.

Grant notification to Mulbarton School from Education Department, London, for £64.12s.10d, sent on 18 June 1884. The Inspector's report from earlier that year stated: 'The School has improved during the year especially in the lower part of it… The Infants… do not know much of the Object lessons they have received. The Higher Grant is recommended with some hesitation.'

(CONTRIBUTED BY BRYAN TUNGATE)

In the Inspector's Report of June 1883 it was stated that:

The School… has improved considerably in Discipline and Instruction though many of the children are not yet up to the work of their Standards. Needlework has improved considerably. The Infants need more attention.

There are further improvements by October 1883, when we get a glimpse of the syllabus:

1883, Oct. 26 – The Infants have made satisfactory progress this quarter – Miss Flood takes them for Arithmetic twice a week viz. on Tuesday and Thursday; the first division have their reading lessons in the main room under the master's supervision. Mary A. Barrett and Ann Waller have been monitors past qr.

List of Object Lessons to be given for the next half year…
Animals: Cat, Cow, Dog, Horse, Elephant, Duck, Lion, Fish, Bird, Camel, Mouse, Fox.
Objects: Potato, Apple, Bread, Candle, Coal, Sugar, Salt, Orange, Soap, A Letter, Chalk, The Body.

The lists remain much the same in later years, with additions such as 'Donkey, Reindeer, Frog, Window, Boots and Shoes, Wheelbarrow…'

But there are challenges and encouragements:

1884: March 28th. Admitted three new scholars on Monday aged 10, 8, and 5 respectively, not one could write their names or letters.
May 2nd. The school year ended on Wednesday… Fred Loveday and Harry Larter have attended every time the school has been opened; the latter has not lost an attendance for the past three years.

The 1885 HMI report gives grudging praise and notes:

The classroom was very crowded and with a larger room, which is greatly needed, more variety of occupation would be possible. It would be wise to give the little children some recreation in a meeting of three hours. The classroom required proper ventilation. With hesitation I recommend the higher Merit Grant.

A high turnover of staff and children, plus lack of money for any improvement, must have been frustrating for every head teacher. Pupils could leave on their thirteenth birthday, and many families moved from village to village to find work and/or accommodation:

1888, May 4 – During the year 37 children have been admitted and 33 have left, leaving 115 on books. The school pence has increased 10s.
1889 May 31 – J. Turner has presented the school with a pail, jug and six tin cups for the children's use during the Summer months.

In September, D.W. Parsons resigned after nearly seven years of battling to improve the school.

Arthur George Hubbard (aged 23) and his wife, Maria (21), took charge of Mulbarton School on 30 September 1889. They had to find their own accommodation and lodged in a cottage by the pond with the local 'vermin catcher' and his wife. Their first task: 'Have examined children and found Spelling, Writing and Mental Arithmetic weak. Number on books 106.' They set about acquiring items for a school museum: examples of woollen manufacture on 3 October; specimens of 'Mustard and Starch manufacture from J. Coleman Esq.' on 7 November; followed by exhibits of cotton cloth and thread (from Clarks of Paisley); 'Cocoa Manufacture' (from

The schoolmaster from January 1894 to the end of September 1895, John Albert Vandyke (1852–1916), with his family. A note in the log-book reveals that only 56 children turned up on his first day due to bad weather. Left to right, back row: *Doris, Cecil, Gladys Mary;* front row: *Mary Selina Vandyke, Margery* (child), *John Albert Vandyke.*

(PHOTO CONTRIBUTED BY MULBARTON MIDDLE SCHOOL)

Cadbury's); 'Steel Pen Manufacture' (from Gillette's, Birmingham); and 'Lead pencil manufacture' (from Banks of Keswick).

On 20 March 1891 – 'The new case for the school museum was fixed up on Thursday, the funds being the proceeds of a lecture recently given by the Master.'

Another new cabinet was fixed the next month. Perhaps their enthusiasm helped improve attendance – on 1 May 1891: '... end of school year. Rachel and Mary Banham and Richard Kedge have been present every time.'

The Hubbards only stayed four years but, according to the 1893 HMI report they left the school:

... in good order. The children have passed a fairly good examination on the whole in Elementary Subjects... History and Needlework are good. The Infants are in good order and they are satisfactorily taught...

After a series of temporary staff, a new head, John Van Dyke, arrived with his family in January 1894.

The log-book shows the variety of problems he faced:

1894, Jan 19th – The children I find are very unruly. I have had great trouble with discipline.

Feb 9th – I suppose owing to the high winds the school work has been greatly impeded by volumes of smoke down the chimney.

March 9th – Punished Gilbert Randle for shouting in school... I've drawn the attention of the Managers to the floor of the Cloakroom.

April 4th – ... had to punish Harry Towler for disobedience...

April 13th – I find a difficulty in taking Musical Drill – very limited in regard to space.

June 22nd – Sydney Huggins fell from Tree, broken leg [Returned Aug. 2nd].

June 25 – Today asked for new reading Books, most of the apparatus is very old and unsuitable.

Dec. 3rd – History lessons – Upper classes the Afghan wars; lower standards the Roman Walls and roads. When the girls are at Needlework there is not sufficient desk room for the boys to do their drawing. One class therefore has to go into Classroom, viz Standard I.

According to the January 1895 HMI Report:

The Infants are very fairly taught; more Word Building should be given in the first class and teaching of Number should improve. Objects should always be present during an Object Lesson. It would be well to put matchboarding round the room, which might be made to look more cheerful. The room appears to be insufficiently warmed during the cold weather. Note singing is not sufficiently prepared.

Mr Van Dyke left in September 1895. 'Sept. 20th – Lillian Fisher aged 14 has charge of the Infants for the present, Miss Taylor [*from Swardeston*] superintending their work.'

After Mr Van Dyke resigned, two more heads stayed for a few months each, and then 'J.W.J. Simmonds with Mrs Simmonds and Miss M. Duffield (Monitress) took over.' For Mulbarton School a new era had begun.

The Era of Mr Simmonds

Walter Joseph Simmonds, appointed to the school from 1 September 1896 as head teacher, with his wife as assistant, stayed for over 25 years. He followed what must have been a difficult time for the school, with four teachers in four years from 1893 to 1896.

We can learn quite a lot about him from the school log-book, which he kept meticulously, and from directory entries.

When he started, there were 90 pupils – 34 infants and 56 in mixed school. He found the school far below the standards he expected:

Sept. 4th 1896: I have endeavoured during the past week to ascertain the state of the school... Standards I & II appear to be better than others but I have not been able to go thoroughly into their work. Standard III is weak in every subject, especially Reading and Arithmetic. Standard IV cannot yet do simple and compound multiplication; pence table not even known. Stds V, VI & VII cannot do fractions properly.

One lesson in History appears to have been given within four months and in Geography children did not even know the oceans and continents and could not tell the position of Norfolk. The girls have done no knitting at all, and no needlework has been commenced. The Infants are extremely backward, hardly any knowing letters, and quite one third of the whole number ought to be (by age) in First Standard.

Every subject he tested in the next few weeks he judged 'poor', 'very poor' or even 'disgraceful'.

Mr Simmonds was an enlightened educationist who introduced new teaching methods, subjects and

Mulbarton School photo, dated 1902. Standing with the pupils are the head teacher, Walter J. Simmonds, and his wife, who taught the Infants. He was an innovative head: on arrival, he introduced a football club in October 1896 (cost, half-penny per boy), then organised school photos and a lending library as early as 1898. The original photo had the name 'Horace Lofty' pencilled on the back – he was admitted to the school on 20 January 1902 as an infant.

(CONTRIBUTED BY JULIET AMOS, NÉE LOFTY)

The school log-book open at a page (right) *showing the Scheme of Work 'approved by HMI' for 1902.*
(Photograph with permission of Mulbarton Schools)

equipment, and on 19 January 1897 there is the first ever mention of a science lesson, with an experiment 'with glass jar, lighted candle, basin of water, to show necessity of air, also pressure of air upon water – as introductory to lesson on Diving Bell.'

June 28th – By recommendation of the Inspectors, the girls now have sewing in the Classroom with infant girls, while infant boys come into big room for Drawing on squared slates.
Sept. 27th – Repaired Harmonium...
1898: Feb. 3rd – Showed children a snake's skin about 3 yards long, lent by a parent who had received it from Australia; children were delighted.
Feb. 23rd – Monitress prepared and gave object lesson on 'Common Snake' under my guidance. Faulty methods pointed out to her afterwards.
March 18th – Caught a fine specimen of moth which I allowed children to view under microscope.

And there were other natural history lessons using real specimens.

1899: March 8th – Received this morning a new Globe, a Portfolio of Geography Lesson sheets, Map of Norfolk etc, Map of Palestine, Map of the World in Hemispheres, 4 Scripture pictures, a few small pictures of animals etc, new Blackboard and Easel
1900: June 27th – Game of rounders took place in the afternoon as physical exercise – children taught how to play properly by the teacher.
July 13th – Boys taken under a shady tree to sketch the Mill and Telegraph Poles this afternoon. Several away owing to fruit gathering and haytime.

Other entries give intriguing insights into village life:

1897: Feb. 12th – As George Williams (an infant) was coming to school he was knocked down by a horse driven by a butcher and was badly cut about the head and face. He was at once carried home by his brothers

and will be driven to Norwich Hospital for treatment, I understand.
1902: Oct.7th – Alfred Rumsby when coming to school got run over by a wagon and was carried home again.

Unlike earlier head teachers, Mr Simmonds did not favour physical punishment, but he expected high standards; on 19 December 1898: 'Caned 2 boys for egging on infant boys to throw stones' – the second and last mention of caning since he took charge. On 14 June 1899: 'Warned PH and two smaller boys against being cruel to small birds on the Common.'

There were also occasional discipline problems to deal with:

1908: Nov.23rd – Gave the following boys a good reprimanding on account of ill treatment of girls when going home, one girl was brought back on Friday in a fainting condition through being hit with stick by these boys:[6 names listed]
Dec. 8th – K.H. very disobedient and insolent to Master. Told her to apologise or go home. She refused to speak, consequently I sent for Rector who in turn referred me to Sir E. Wingfield. Lady Wingfield visited and got her to apologise before the whole school. Her temper is diabolical.
1915: July 13th – R.A. this afternoon showed open defiance, upsetting the school, kicking the Master, and breaking his watch-chain, simply because he could not have his own way.

Mr Simmonds valued good relations with parents:

1900: April 23rd – Reopened school today... During the [Easter] Vacation the master was summoned before the Magistrates by the Attendance Officer to give evidence against a parent for not sending a child to school. This sort of thing is not at all pleasing and is likely to cause great friction between parents and teachers.

He had his share of parental criticism:

In 1901, on 21 November – 'Started an experimental Class in Cottage Gardening on the suggestion of HMI. Mr Fisher sent a note objecting to his son Osman learning "Gardening".'

Other innovations and improvements followed, and in 1904 on 16 May: 'Started a Savings Bank on the Stamp Slip System. 17 children made deposits this morning.'

He got new stoves installed in 1903, a drinking water-supply (buckets and ladles) in 1906, and joined the school to the RSPB's Bird & Tree Scheme in 1908–09.

In 1910, cookery became a school subject for the older girls in the summer term. On 22 April it was noted that: 'Arrangements have now been completed for Cookery Course from May to July, on Fridays in the Parish Hall.' The boys do drawing instead (but they do have gardening!)

The schoolhouse (left) *near the school was ready for occupation in 1901. A note in the log-book explains that 'The House is in trust (not properly a school house) but a private residence for the Master for such period as this school remains a Church School. In the event of a Board, the house becomes Church Property. The Rector is the sole trustee and can use it in several ways as the deeds direct him.' When sold, the money was invested for 'The Rector's Fund for Church Purposes'. The original postcard was posted to Miss M. Lofty, Mulbarton, Norwich, 3 March 1908.*

(CONTRIBUTED BY JULIET AMOS, NÉE LOFTY)

Pupils were encouraged to observe special events, and on 17 April 1912: 'Solar eclipse visible today – took children out for three observations with prepared glasses.' (Repeated at the 1921 eclipse).

Walter Simmonds and his wife were the first to move into the new house built behind the school:

1901: March 28–29th – Two days holiday for the purposes of allowing Master and Mistress to remove household goods from Swardeston, where they have resided during the past year. They will now inhabit the new house built by the kindness of Mrs Wingfield and family. [Their joint salary was £120p.a. and their rent was £10p.a.]

Mrs Simmonds had to resign through ill-health at the end of 1904 – the log-book states that: 'The Infants were thoroughly well taught and knew their work well when she left.'

For several years Mr Simmonds struggled with an understaffed and overcrowded school. He supplemented his income by teaching music and was Parish Clerk with a small honorarium from 1903–20. He took an active part in village life, apparently founding a drum and fife band, of which he was bandmaster, and was also involved with the cricket club. He resigned in 1922 after running the school for 26 years, without recording any thanks or comments:

1922: Oct. 31st – Small number present today – average 36 only for today. Classroom disinfected by

teacher, ready for scrubbing later. J.W.J. Simmonds ACP give up charge at the end of today as Head Master after 26⅙ years service in this school. A supply teacher will be in charge until Nov.30th. Stockbook completed and signed by Correspondent yesterday.

Four head teachers came and went between Mr Simmonds leaving in 1922 and Mrs Rowbottom arriving in 1931, but the assistant teachers provided stability. The Misses Jessie Maud Larner and Anna Watson (Mrs Anna Nichols from 1928) joined the school as untrained teachers in 1913, gained qualifications and both stayed until after the Second World War. However, by 1928 the school was on the county's 'A' list of 'condemned' buildings. The managers agreed a list of repairs, sought grants and gifts, and a number of improvements were made in the summer of 1929.

Mrs Rowbottom, Head Teacher 1931–46

The next long-serving head is Mrs Marion Rowbottom, still remembered as 'a lovely lady and a real teacher of the "old school".' Rene Carlton (née Hammond), born in 1923, remembers the school through the 1930s:

The teachers were Mrs Nichols (Infants) and Miss Larner (Juniors) who shared one of the council-houses

Mulbarton schoolboys – is it the 1932 football team? The date is written on a football! Sitting at the front on the left is Claude Frost, aged 11. (Contributed by Iris Frost)

Special events are remembered best. In February 1935, the whole school gave a concert in the World's End clubroom in aid of the School Sports Fund. The local newspaper reported:

The infants gave a display and performed a little play, 'The Princess of London'. Juniors and seniors appeared in amusing items, including 'The Travelling Doctor', 'The Friendly Waiter' and 'Darby and Joan'. 'Engaging a servant' was a sketch by the seniors. Well executed dances included 'A Scottish Reel' by the seniors, and a skirt dance by one of the senior girls.'

Later the same year, Mulbarton pupils were among the 1,300 Norfolk children taken to visit London on two special trains. Rene Carlton still remembers the huge excitement:

I will always remember the whole school (probably not the Infants) going on a trip to London by train. Mr Lincoln took us to Swainsthorpe Station in the back of his van and picked us up again when we arrived home. That was very exciting for everyone, going on the steam train.

in Long Lane. Mrs. Rowbottom, the Headmistress, lived in the School House. It wasn't just the '3Rs' – the girls did dressmaking at school, and we used to walk across the Common to the Wingfield Hall for cookery lessons. The boys played football on the common with Mr Rowbottom and the girls played netball and also went onto the Common for games. There was a maypole on the playground, and we did lots of country dancing. There were no school lunches in those days – none of us lived far away so we went home.

Other memories are less happy – the dentist's visit is still vivid to Bill Alborough:

A little white caravan came and stood by the school. Children went in one at a time to see the dentist, and were given a piece of paper specifying the treatment needed. I remember taking home such a piece of paper for my mother to sign saying I needed several extractions – every time she took it from behind the clock I said

Pupils on the Common after school, c.1938. Describing the school dress at this time, Tony Kent wrote: 'Boys wore shorts to school and hobnail boots. Girls wore gymslips and knickers that covered all from navel to top of knee. Thick elastic held them in position. As the legs had elastic to hold them down, girls carried hankies, coins and sweets there. These knickers were known as "Harvest Festivals" – "all is safely gathered in"!' (Contributed by Iris Frost)

'no', but eventually I had to agree. It was a bit 'cissy' to have your mother go in the caravan with you. I did have the teeth out – all together. How I got home afterwards I shall never know…

Mrs Rowbottom and her faithful assistants saw that education was continued throughout the war years, despite the disruption of air raids, evacuees coming and going, and new staff duties such as inspecting gas masks and dishing out food supplements to undernourished children. In 1941 Mr S. Ramsey presented the school with a wireless for current affairs, and children were immunised against diphtheria. The efforts of the staff were rewarded: in 1943 one boy passed the scholarship to City of Norwich School and another moved to the Junior Technical College. In Mrs Rowbottom's final year two girls won scholarships to grammar school – one was Brenda Ford (née Collins), who remembers the school in the 1940s:

During the course of the war I became five years old and started school at Mulbarton. I can remember walking down Long Lane from the Woodlands (about a mile) to school and back each day and sometimes going home to dinner as well. It seemed a long way to a small child, but there were several of us who walked together – the Baker family, who I believe were evacuees from London, and Gerald Collins and later Myrtle Bullen – as we all lived close together on the lane. It was a pleasant walk as there was virtually no traffic. The bread delivery van was one of the most likely motor vehicles to come along and sometimes an Army lorry but we were quite safe.

There were about 72 pupils and a green curtain divided the Juniors from the Seniors… Mrs Nichols was the Infant teacher and I can remember her singing 'All things bright and beautiful' whilst she dusted the classroom first thing in the morning. I can also remember the awful milk placed in front of the fire in the winter: the bottles nearest the fire were 'cooked' whilst those on the other side were still frozen…

Bryan Tungate started at Mulbarton School in 1944:

We had to walk over the common to reach the school. There were no car rides to school like there are today. Also it meant walking home at midday for food as there were no school dinners then. Some bread and jam sandwiches were what we usually had. One winter, 1947, it snowed for weeks and it was a long walk then. Dad and all the neighbours would help out by digging a bit of a pathway for us as we were not allowed to stay at home just because it snowed. Our teachers were locals; they were sure to know who was missing, everyone knew everyone in the village then. If we were away the School Attendance Inspector would be after us. The school was heated by an old iron 'slow but sure' stove and when we dropped a bit of cheese on it there would be a big stink and the teachers would get upset.

Evelyn Smith (née Stackyard) adds:

The larger room had a coke-burning stove with pipes leading from it to heat the two classrooms. It wasn't very efficient, and on very cold winter days we were allowed to keep our coats on. I remember, too, the milk bottles thawing out around the stove. We could all have milk – I think it was 2½d. (just over 1p) a week. The cardboard tops were saved and we made raffia table mats, etc., with them. The 'milk monitor' for the week had to walk across the common to tell Mrs Lincoln at the dairy how much milk to deliver. I remember going there once and being amazed to see chickens wandering all round her kitchen!

The lessons were Reading, Writing, Arithmetic (every morning we had to say one of the tables), Poetry, History, Geography, Needlework, Art and Religious Education.

At playtime we played ball games and hoops. The playground wasn't fenced in, and when you were in the Senior class you could play on the Common opposite. There was an annual Sports Day, with schools in the area competing.

The Junior teacher, Miss Larner, is remembered as being 'very strict… she was a dead shot with a book.'! Everyone seems to remember the green curtain ('You could jab people through it with your compass point!') and the toilets:

There was a trap door at the back where the buckets were taken out by the cleaner (scavenger) and the contents were buried in the School House garden… One day some lads opened the trap door and put stinging nettles inside…!

Miss Larner left in September 1945. A year later Mrs Nichols and Mrs Rowbottom also left at a time when the English education system was facing huge changes.

The County Primary School

The 1944 Education Act promised a new era for schooling in Britain: from 1947 the school-leaving age was raised to 15 and all children were entitled to a suitable free secondary education guided by the 11+ results. It also demanded big improvements in buildings and resources. The managers of Mulbarton School knew they could never meet the new demands and asked for the school's status to change from that of a 'Voluntary School' to a 'Controlled School'. Norfolk was reluctant to take over the school, but in October 1946 the managers informed the County that they did not have the funds to meet expenses, thus forcing the takeover. So from January 1947 the pupils attended 'Mulbarton County Primary School'. That year, the first group of 14+ pupils moved on to secondary schooling in Wymondham.

Mulbarton School: boys of Mr Cobb's class on the Common near the school, probably 1947. Left to right, back row (standing): Basil Moore, Frank Cobb (master), John Canham, Ronald Bobbin, Colin Haverson, Philip Cooper, Peter Bailey, Alan Dawson, Bryan Tungate; front row: Raymond Abendroth, Kenneth Hammond, Peter Mickleburgh, Clifford Robinson, John Williams, David Ladbrooke, Bernard Rayner, Trevor Gardiner.

(PHOTO CONTRIBUTED BY CLIFFORD ROBINSON)

The 1950s began with Mulbarton as a primary school with about 50 pupils aged between five and eleven and two teachers. Those over the age of 11 went to Wymondham Secondary Modern, except for a few who passed the 11+ to go to grammar school. Some of the improvements of the 1950s included the borehole sunk in 1953 for a more reliable water-supply than from the well in the grounds of the school house, and flushing toilets, installed in 1956.

As the 1950s drew to a close, clerical assistants and 'dinner ladies' were appointed in County schools and a tiny kitchen was added. The secretary, Mrs Lofty, worked in a corner of the classroom with no telephone to disturb her work – only the teacher and children in the background! No telephone was installed until 1964.

Jil Wheeler remembers the 1960s, when she taught at the school:

Meals were cooked at Swardeston School and transported to Mulbarton by car. The large classroom served as a dining-room – the meals being served by two stalwart dinner ladies, Mrs (Nanny) Mickleburgh and Mrs Fish. By the time school began in the afternoon the washing-up had been done and Mrs Mick and Mrs Fish were eating their own school dinners in a corner of the classroom. Nothing escaped them – Mrs Mick felt it her duty to loudly inform the staff of any misdemeanours committed by the children.

As more houses were built in the village so pupil numbers went up. In 1965 a mobile classroom was installed and the new addition to the school staff was a welfare assistant.

When the older children were eventually housed in two mobile classrooms, anything between 40 and 50 infants occupied the main building's two classrooms, with one teacher and a welfare assistant… PE was taken outside if the weather was fit. Dancing and movement activities were only possible indoors if the furniture was moved into the tiny cloakroom. On one memorable day, when the older children were away on an outing, a torrential downpour caused the roof to leak and all the infants had to be crammed into one room for safety! Christmas concerts were sometimes performed on a 'platform' of desks and the piano had to be played from the adjoining room to accompany the children singing.

A New School for a Growing Village

In 1970 the first part of what became Mulbarton First School was built. There was a large open area for two classes, children's cloakrooms, a kitchen/washup (now the school office), a staff room (now the head teacher's office) and staff cloakrooms. In February 1970 two infant classes moved into the new building, while the junior children remained in the old school. Mr Derek Chamberlain, who moved from

Mulbarton School photo taken on the Common, early 1950s. Left to right, back row: *Frank Cobb (junior class teacher), Peter Hornsby, Ronald Barrett, David Fish, David Hornsby, P. Howard, Ronald Hammond, F. Bunn, Brian (Eddie) Thrower, William Wharton, Michael Cook, Brian Cross, Mike Millington, Keith Sparkes, P. Walker, Robert (Mack) McKelvy, J.A. Hornsby (headmaster);* third row: *Joan Widgery (infant teacher), Mike Hindle, ?, William Kent, Diane Robertson, Margaret Sparke, Margaret Carver, Faith Tuddenham, Una Barrett, Maureen Norman, Myrtle Bullen, Margaret Tungate, Frances Robinson, Carol Hanworth, Ruth Tuddenham, Janet Abendroth, Louis (Lew) Cooper, Michael (Oscar) Thrower;* second row: *John Cooper, Mervyn Wymer, ?, John Sturman, ?, Phillip Cotton, Larry Hindle, Jennifer Mickleburgh, Christine Kent, Carol Lake, Pauline Cotton, Patricia Collins, Gloria Wilde, Sandra Hawkins, Sylvia Dack, Angela Williams, Hilary Bunn, ?, ?;* front row: *?, Cynthia (Cindy) Thrower, Andrea Barrett, Christopher Hindle, David Webb, Christine Hindle, Rodney Ladbrooke, ?, Stephen Wilde, Paul Muirhead, Susan Barrett, Diane Muirhead, Angela Lincoln, Lynn Collins, Rosamund Farrow, Ruth Barker, Penelope (Penny) Kedge.* (PHOTO FROM VILLAGE ARCHIVE)

Mulbarton School pupils, mid-1950s. Left to right, back row: *Miss Stockwell, ?, ?, Michael Frost, David Webb, Mr Hornsby (head teacher), David Hornsby, Charlie Sturman, ?, ?, Joan Widgery (teacher);* third row: *?, Rodney Ladbrooke, Cynthia Thrower, Andrea Barratt, Donna Muirhead, ?, Susan Barratt, Jennifer Mickleburgh, Carol Lake, Mervyn Wymer, Christopher Hindle;* second row: *?, Christine Kent, Mary Carlton, Julie Swingler, Christine Hindle, Ruth Barker, ?, ?, Lynn Collins, ?, ?, ?;* front row: *?, Stephen Wilde, Alan Hammond, Chas Sturman, John Thurston, ?, ?, Keith Thrower, Christopher Ramsey, Paul Muirhead, Roger Hanworth, Michael Allison.* (CONTRIBUTED BY JULIET AMOS, NÉE LOFTY)

A Christmas Concert in the old school, 1968–69. The cast of The Queen of Hearts *was mainly from Anne Barclay's class (now Mrs Dack).* (PHOTO: *EASTERN DAILY PRESS*, REPRODUCED COURTESY OF ARCHANT PHOTOGRAPHIC NORFOLK)

Swardeston School in the late 1960s, remained head of both parts of the school.

The day of the move was reported in the *Eastern Evening News* of Friday, 13 February 1970:

Removal Day came to Mulbarton Primary School today and swiftly and with a minimum of fuss a 100-strong workforce swept into action armed for the job with prams, sledges, home-made trolleys and even wheelbarrows. And a happier workforce it would be hard to find. For the pupils, spending the day moving equipment down the road to the new infants' school, with maybe a sneaky snowball fight here and there, was infinitely preferable to the complexities of maths and grammar.

Though it is only the infants who are moving into the new building, almost the whole school took part in the removal, their various methods of transport piled high with boxes of maps, instruments and other equipment…

The juniors finally moved into extensions to the new building in September 1973 and, as reported in the *Eastern Daily Press* in July:

Children of Mulbarton School left a lot behind them when they broke up on Friday. Not only will they never return to their old school, which is more than 100 years old, but in future they will not have Mrs Lilian Mickleburgh to help them at lunchtime as she has for the last 27 years.

In 1969 Mulbarton First School begins to rise from its foundations. (PHOTO: JIL WHEELER)

The school hall (now the First School Hall) was included in this phase and this was much appreciated by staff and children. There was also a kitchen, which meant meals were no longer sent from Swardeston School, and a bungalow for a caretaker,

Throwing snowballs in the playground of the newly opened school, 1970. The teacher (back right) *is Anne Barclay (now Mrs Dack). This building was only the first phase. A new block to hold another 80 infants and another to take 320 juniors was built – and further additions were made later as the village grew.*

(Photo: *Eastern Daily Press*, reproduced courtesy of Archant Photographic Norfolk)

which later became Mulbarton Surgery. Meanwhile, after much fund-raising, the old school building was acquired as a Village Hall (Chapter 3).

At Christmas 1973, the head teacher could report that the school was together again:

After three years of having a school in two parts it is very satisfying to be able to say that we are all once again together. Life has been very hectic for us all this term, what with new children from Swardeston and Tacolneston and also new teachers… What a change it all means. A lovely new hall for dining in and for P.E. and dancing – a lovely kitchen with a first class happy staff… A very Happy Christmas from all of us at the school to everyone in the village and elsewhere, with a plea to all builders: Don't build too many houses too quickly at Mulbarton.

In 1977 the one school became two: Mulbarton First School for pupils aged 5–8, under first Mrs Linda Craig (1977–80) and then Elizabeth Pierce from 1980, and Mulbarton Middle School for pupils aged 8–12. Mr Chamberlain continued as Middle School head until he retired in 1982 and was followed by Geoffrey Dixon and Beulah Chatten. At the time of writing,

Miss Pierce is set to become Mulbarton's longest-serving head when she retires in December 2006.

'Moving Day', February 1970. The day of the move from the 'old' school to the new Infants' School was cold and very snowy. The new building had new furniture but books, toys and equipment were transferred from the old school. The children brought prams, carts and sledges and it was 'all hands on deck' to help.

(Photo: *Eastern Daily Press*, reproduced courtesy of Archant Photographic Norfolk)

Aerial view of Mulbarton School in 1975, when the Bluebell Road estate (left foreground) *and Lark Rise estate* (top right) *were being built.*

(PHOTO: DAVID WRIGHT)

Pupils of Mulbarton First School show their paintings to Revd W. Awdry (author of the Thomas the Tank Engine *series of books) in October 1983. Left to right: Steven Wright, Richard Moore, Revd W. Awdry, Toby Wheatley, Richard Smith, Julian Bunting.*

(PHOTO: EASTERN DAILY PRESS, REPRODUCED COURTESY OF ARCHANT PHOTOGRAPHIC NORFOLK)

The first reunion of former pupils of Mulbarton School held in the old school (by then the Village Hall) in March 1989. Among those who came were (left to right): *Jean Smith, Maurice Norman, Peter Mickleburgh, Colin Rumsby, Angela Williams, John Williams, Lily Mickleburgh (school cook for many years), Gerald Collins, Clifford Robinson, Colin Kedge, Vi Barrett, Brenda Collins, Vera Hammond, Norma Kedge, Doreen Abendroth, Olive Allard, Dawn Mickleburgh.*

(PHOTO: BRYAN TUNGATE)

Mulbarton Middle School leavers, summer 1988. Most of the pupils from Mulbarton have been named. Left to right, back row: Colin Mower, Matthew Hammond, Tony Howell, ?, Steven Wright, ?, ?, Richard Roebuck, Andrew ?, Darren Mace, Wayne Ladbrooke, Andrew ?, Paul Farman, Leo Lonergan, David Nash, Stephen Rowe; third row (standing): Richard Beckett, Emma Sercombe, Sophie Daniels, ?, Julie De'Ath, ?, Kerry Bobbin, ?, Lisa Smith, Nadine Thrower, ?, ?, Joanna Hinchley, ?, Helen Waring, Jo-Ann Buckenham, Nassira Powell, Connie Smart; second row (seated on chairs): Lucy Carver, Angela Reilly, ?, ?, ?, Sarah Bluckert, Mr Ball, Mr Bell, Geoffrey Dixon (head teacher), Mrs Finch, Nicola Middleton, ?, ?, Sarah Haisted, ?; front row (on floor): Martin Drury, Mark Faulkes, Stewart Adcock, Julian Bunting, ?, Richard Moore, Richard Smith, ?, Stephano Casaccio, Andrew Rudd, Ben Sparks, Chris ?, Toby Wheatley, Rob Cole, Mark Woodhouse. (PHOTO CONTRIBUTED BY STEVEN WRIGHT)

Not only did Mulbarton continue to grow, but children were bussed from Wreningham, Ashwellthorpe and Tacolneston to the Middle School. When Bracon Ash and Swardeston Schools closed, younger children were bussed to the First School. Increasing numbers meant mobile classrooms and new extensions. But there were better facilities for the village, too, which were used by evening classes and some organisations – especially the various branches of St John Ambulance for different age groups. Now the wheel has come full circle, as Mulbarton's schools change again to become an Infant school (ages 5–7) and a Junior school (ages 7–11).

Mulbarton First School reception class pupils, 1986 – as drawn by themselves for a tea towel.

CHAPTER 5

Church and Chapel

The oldest building in Mulbarton, with its greatest treasures, is still used regularly for the purpose for which it was built: to worship God. There was probably a church here nearly 1,000 years ago, in the reign of Edward the Confessor (1042–66); certainly a church is mentioned in the Domesday Book of 1086. We have no idea how big it was or how old, but the church we have now probably occupies the same spot.

The Church Building

It is hard to know if there is any truth in the story that Thomas de St Omer, lord of the manor of Mulbarton, built or rebuilt some or all of the church as a penance. In 1285 he is supposed to have claimed the ancient 'liberty of infangenthef' to judge for any theft in his domains and hang those guilty. That year he tried, condemned and hanged Walter Godwyne of East Carleton, but apparently poor Walter should not have been hanged, either because he was innocent or because Thomas St Omer had no right to hang him. According to Norfolk historian Francis Blomefield, writing around 1800, 'it was ordered that he should be disseized of such liberty and the gallows pulled down', and he does not mention church-building.

The generous view is that Thomas repented and offered to help build the church to save his soul. The less generous view is that a court (then administered by church authorities) imposed a penance on him, to be paid in cash or kind. Thomas probably appointed the first known Rector, Ralph de St Omer (1329), one of a number of Mulbarton Rectors related to whoever was lord of the manor and patron of the living!

Thomas's daughter, Alice, married Sir William de Hoo (Chapter 1), who is said to have built the church – did he complete work started by his father-in-law? According to Blomefield, they were buried in the church and their portraits were in a stained-glass window in the north wall of the church until 1800, along with pictures of Sir Thomas de St Omer and his wife and the coats of arms of both families. The windows of the nave and tower are in Decorated style (prevalent roughly 1290–1350). The windows and roof of the chancel (at the east end) are in later Perpendicular style (around 1350–1530).

One notable Rector, Sir Richard Torkington (Rector 1511–26; 'Sir Richard' because he was a priest but not a university graduate), set out on a pilgrimage to Jerusalem in March 1517. His pilgrimage took one year, five weeks and three days, and finished when he returned to the shrine of St Thomas à Becket in Canterbury. He wrote the oldest diary of English travel ever published, unfortunately now long lost. It began:

Mulbarton Church viewed from the pond before 1911. Both the large tree and the thatched Church cottages have now gone. (Photo contributed by the Rector)

Font in Mulbarton Church. In the background are panels with the Lord's Prayer and the Creed which were at the front of the church below the east window until the mid-1930s.

Thys ys the begynnyng of the pylgrymage of Syr Rychard Torkyngton person of Mulberton in Norfolke. And how he went towardys Jherusalem all a lone to the tyme he came to Veneyse.

Traces of pre-Reformation practices can still be seen in Mulbarton Church: the 'Stoup' for Holy Water just inside the door on the right, where newly consecrated salty water would be placed each Sunday; a Piscina behind the pulpit, where the cup was washed after Mass on a side altar; and another Piscina on the south side of the present Communion table. The large slab under the main door may possibly be the top of a pre-Reformation stone altar, and a stone on the outside of the porch may be the remains of a 'Mass clock', or sundial, to show the times of services. Certainly the font is medieval, and its base may have come from the original church. Just think how many generations of babies have been baptised there as a sign of belonging to Christ's Church!

Through Reformation, Revolution and Restoration

Henry VIII took the English Church out of the Pope's jurisdiction, but kept his title 'Defender of the Faith'. An inventory carried out in 1552 lists items that, considered superfluous with the Reformation in place, should be handed over to the king, Edward VI:

1 Chales [Chalice] with a patent [Paten] of sylver... A Cope of blew velvet embroidered...' another Cope; six 'olde vestments... a Tunicle of Sylke... a cross clothe... a Canapei cloth...

It is unlikely that Mulbarton handed over these items before the king died in January 1553, so they were still available for Catholic services under Queen Mary!

Drastic religious changes probably only made a gradual impact on rural parishes such as Mulbarton. Alan Percy was Rector from 1526 to 1560, through the reigns of Henry VIII, Edward VI, Mary and Elizabeth, and presumably managed to change from Catholic to Anglican twice during that time! He testified to the good character and orthodoxy of the Rector of Hethel, who was hauled before an ecclesiastical court in the reign of Queen Mary. Clergy of the time had to cope with changing from Latin Mass to English Prayer Book, installing a Bible, moving the Communion table, etc. The next Rector (or his curate) bought the large new silver chalice (Communion cup) and cover inscribed 'YE TOWNE OF MULBERTON, 1567', with silver-marks to show they were made in Norwich.

Mulbarton's Church Registers are amazingly complete from 1547 to the present day. Elizabethan entries give us little glimpses of the people who worshipped in the church and the hardship of their life and death:

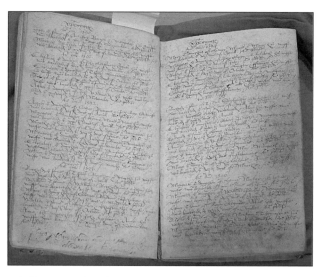

Mulbarton Church Register for the 1590s, now in the Norfolk Records Office.

(PHOTO: JILL WRIGHT, WITH PERMISSION OF NRO)

Mother Begerlle was buried ye xiith daye of December 1550.

Mother Wright, wyddowe, was buried, 1558.

28th April 1558, John Husband and Elizabeth Crowe married.

24th August 1558, John, son of John and Elizabeth Husband baptized.

24th August 1558, John, son of John and Elizabeth Husband buried.

In 1558 there were 19 burials and six early the following year – far higher than average – so there may have been an epidemic .

The Rector from 1571 to 1616 was William Richardson, who 'lived incumbant of the said Towne over fortie yeares.' His son, Thomas Richardson, may be the only man from Mulbarton to be buried in Westminster Abbey. Thomas came here at the age of two and must have sat and listened to his father's sermons. He was sent to Norwich School and his mother died when he was only 13. He became a lawyer, then a judge in Norwich and then London. In 1620 he was elected an MP, and was promptly elected Speaker of the House of Commons, knighted on his first appearance at Whitehall in 1620, and went on to become Lord Chief Justice. Although he made an important ruling that 'the prisoner ought not to be tortured by the rack, for no such punishment is allowed by law', he could also be very harsh: at a trial in Salisbury in 1631, someone aimed a flint at his head – but as he was 'leaning low on his elbow in a lazy reckless manner' it only hit his hat. He quipped, 'You see, if I had been an upright Judge I had been slain', but he ordered that the man's right hand be cut off. In his diary, John Evelyn (whose father was then Sheriff of Surrey and Sussex) wrote, 'My father was afterwards most unjustly and spitefully molested by that jeering judge, Richardson, for reprieving the execution of a

Memorial to Revd Anthony Frere, Rector of Mulbarton 1616–60, in the floor of the chancel. Buried next to him is his wife Elizabeth, who died in 1653, daughter of Henry Hartstonge of the Old Hall.

A memorial in the chancel of Mulbarton Church to former Rector Benjamin Lany, and his wife, who lived to 103.

The memorial to Sarah Scargill, placed in the chancel by her husband, Daniel Scargill, Rector, is in the form of a book. The poem (below), inscribed on copper pages, speaks of his undying love for her.

Over the years, monuments and tombstones were added to the floors and walls of the church. A particularly sad memorial near the vestry door in the chancel dates from 1678 and records the short life of Eliza Carr, 'for sixteen years a maiden, thirteen months a wife and twenty days a mother'. The Latin inscription plays on the words: 'There remains for time immeasurable to measure maidenhood by the year, matronhood by the month and motherhood by the day'. But some people lived to a great age – one monument commemorates Mary, wife of Rector Benjamin Lany, who died aged 103 years, and their daughter, who died aged 95.

The most unusual monument is book-shaped with a copper cover that opens to reveal a poem penned by Daniel Scargill (Rector 1672–1721) in memory of his first wife, Sarah (née Le Neve), who died in 1680 after seven years of marriage. It begins:

Dear Love, one Feather'd minute and I come
To lye down in thy darke Retireing Roome
And mingle Dust with thine, that wee may have,
As when alive one Bed, so dead one Grave.
And may my soul teare through the Vaulted Sky
To be with thine to all Eternitie.

He married another Sarah and the death of his second wife is recorded in the register with the note, *Nulla secunda* (second to none). He seems to have had two excellent wives! However, Scargill's early Christian life was controversial. He was expelled from Cambridge University because 'he gloried to be an Hobbist and an Atheist' (i.e. he agreed with the political philosopher Thomas Hobbes, who published *Leviathan* in 1651). But he had second

woman, but out of this he emerged with as much honour as trouble.'

William Richardson's successor was Anthony Frere (Rector 1616–60), who must have been flexible enough, and popular enough, to survive the changes of Cromwell's time, when Rectors of some neighbouring parishes were 'ejected'. He took an unusual wedding on 18 August 1642, when the three daughters of George Burton were married at the same ceremony: Barbara (aged 29) to John Moore, Sarah (22) to Samuel Beart, and Rose (18) to John Colman. Frere seems to have lived just long enough to see the Church of England restored under Charles II, and either he or his successor must have ordered the larger silver Paten (Communion dish), which was made in Norwich around 1660–61. The Book of Common Prayer, introduced in 1662, was used for all services for over 300 years and is still used at the 8a.m. Communion service.

thoughts, solemnly recanted and was restored to the university and allowed to continue studies for Holy Orders. Daniel Scargill was quietly ordained by the Bishop of Norwich in his private chapel and a few days later made Rector of Mulbarton.

Nineteenth-Century Makeovers

In 1812 Revd Richard Spurgeon arrived in Mulbarton from Martham, where he had been curate-in-charge. He set about repairing and 'beautifying' Mulbarton Church 'at his own expense' in 1815. Quite how he managed to bring a load of 'spare' ancient stained glass from Martham Church is uncertain, but it is now part of our beautiful east window. A window on the south side of the chancel also has some ancient fragments, along with figures from an abbey in Germany, whose glass was sold as a 'job lot' to a Norwich merchant when the abbey closed!

The patchwork of stained glass may have been from Spurgeon's own collection. He was an avid collector – after he died in 1842, the contents of Mulbarton Rectory was sold in 1,025 lots over five days and, according to the 40-page catalogue, included:

Fine and rare old carvings, in wood, marble, ivory and bisque; beautiful enamels and miniatures; picturesque

East Window of Mulbarton Church: here we have fifteenth-century glass showing (left to right, centre) *Adam and Eve leaving Eden; Adam digging with a spade in bare feet; and a figure labelled Potettates (Powers), subduing a demon. Martham Church still has Eve spinning, and the 'Thrones' and 'Principalities' to go with the 'Powers'!*

marbles, casts and medallions; ... very valuable specimens of ancient painted glass; oil painting, prints, etching and drawings; a large collection of splendid Oriental and other China; trinkets and antiquities; capital library of books...

Lot 142 was a 'Roman sepulchral urn... dug up at Caister near Norwich by the late Rev Richard Spurgeon, and Roman lamp.' Lots 187–230 were painted glass – mostly small pieces it seems, some of which may have come back to the church and were incorporated in the windows of the south side of the nave when they were reglazed in the 1980s. A rare piece of seventeenth-century Flemish glass shows St Paul being visited in prison by Timothy and Epaphroditus. Poringland Magna claims that stained glass from an ancient screen was taken to Mulbarton – if so it may be part of the jigsaw in the chancel windows.

Old glass in the south window of the chancel of Mulbarton Church. On the right there is a king or bishop holding a model of a church, and on the left a child is being taught to read. The teacher's head may be a Jewish rabbi, but the body is dressed as a woman – probably Anna, traditionally the mother of the Virgin Mary.

The two kneeling figures of a monk and a nun in the south window of the chancel of Mulbarton Church are from the cloisters of the abbey of Steinfeld in Germany. Some of the glass was sold in Norwich in 1804.

The church from the south in 1822. A lithograph of Mulbarton Church before its Victorian enlargement and 'restoration'. The porch, with its sundial, is noticeably different since the Victorian 'makeover' in the 1870s.

(CONTRIBUTED BY DAVID WRIGHT)

The pews in the chancel are much older than the Victorian pews in the nave and aisle. The beautiful carved ends are intertwined with corn and vines – symbols of the bread and wine of Communion. The small table in the foreground of this picture is covered with a cloth which is one of several embroidered in the Democratic Republic of Congo and given to Mulbarton Church by people of Bukavu Diocese.

We usually think of the Victorian era as a time of full churches. In the Visitation Return for 1843, the recently arrived Rector, Richard Lucas, stated that services were held at 11a.m. and 3 p.m.; there was 'free seating' for 140, that all was in 'good order' and that the churchyard was grazed by 'sheep only'. At the time of the 1851 census, a national 'Census of Accommodation and Attendance at Worship' was also taken. Mulbarton had one church for a total population of 557, and attendance on Sunday, 30 March (Mothering Sunday) was 45 at morning service and 120 in the afternoon – with 30 children at Sunday School on each occasion.

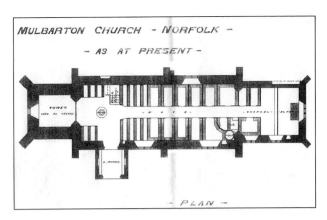

Plan of Mulbarton Church before 1875. Mulbarton Church had one aisle, a west gallery reached by stairs, and box pews.

(FROM THE CHURCH'S COPY OF PLANS NOW HELD BY NRO)

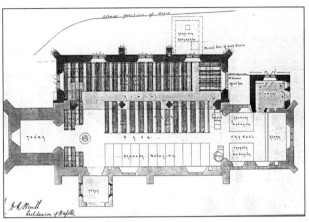

Plan for the enlargement of Mulbarton Church, 1875. A new north aisle and a vestry were added, the gallery was removed, new pews were installed, the floor level was raised above the under-floor heating system and the porch was redesigned.

(FROM THE CHURCH'S COPY OF PLANS NOW HELD BY NRO)

The next big 'makeover' was under Revd Richard Lucas, who set about restoring and enlarging the church in the 1870s. The box pews were replaced and a plaque on the pulpit reads: 'The pulpit and prayer-desk were given by several parishioners at the time the church was benched by the Rector: October 1872.' To build the new north aisle, the north wall was demolished, including the spiral staircase to the former rood (crucifix) loft. The new north wall included a chimney disguised as a buttress. Heating pipes were laid over the floor slabs and the nave floor raised level with the chancel. The west gallery, where a small band of musicians used to play, was removed, and a vestry was added through a doorway in the chancel. The porch was remodelled, demolishing the old priest's room above the entrance. The rendering on the outside of the building was also removed to reveal the flints, giving the church a totally new look, but exposing the flints to the weather. The cost was estimated at £850, and by the time the plans were approved in March 1875, £730 had already been

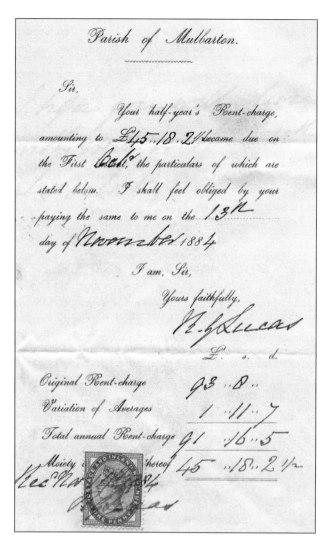

Rent bill for Glebe (church land) from the Rector, Revd R.G. Lucas, to James Turner (farmer and churchwarden). Rent of £45.18s.2½d due on 13 November 1884 – and receipted with a 1d. stamp on that date. Inside is written 'I hope you will dine with me the 13th at 5 o'clock'! The clergy still relied on rents and tithes for their income.

(CONTRIBUTED BY BRYAN TUNGATE)

promised. Work did not take long: the 'Reopening of Church after refurbishment' on 11 November 1875 is recorded in the school log-book. In the following year Mrs Caroline Lucas, the Rector's wife, died and a new stained-glass window was added on the south side of the chancel. In 1887, the small organ at the back of the north aisle was replaced with a splendid pipe organ, installed to commemorate Queen Victoria's golden jubilee.

Into a New Century and a New Millennium

The early years of the twentieth century saw more changes: a stained-glass window at the west end of the north aisle in memory of Mrs Emma Dorinda Wingfield in 1907; war memorials placed in the porch and on the south wall of the church (Chapter 10);

The interior of Mulbarton Church before the First World War memorial was fixed to the south wall or electricity was available. Behind the Communion table at the east end are boards inscribed with the Lord's Prayer, Creed and Ten Commandments, which were removed in the 1930s and put in the tower.

(PHOTO CONTRIBUTED BY TERRY BURCHELL, FROM PHILIP STANDLEY'S COLLECTION)

and the panels with the Lord's Prayer and Ten Commandments moved to the entry to the bell-tower when the chancel was redesigned in 1937. A carved and highly painted panel of Mary Magdalene meeting the risen Christ was placed behind the Communion table in memory of Revd W.E. Eaton by his daughters, but is now covered by a curtain. Electricity was installed in 1934, which later enabled the organ to have an electric blower in 1949 and the heating system to be changed in 1957 from the old boilers that needed stoking to the tubular heaters still used today.

National events were commemorated with special services. The school log-book records:

1936 Jan 28th – The school was closed to-day for King George V's funeral. The children attended a memorial service in the Church at 10 am. This was taken by the Rev. Ramsay.

The following year there was the Coronation:

On Sunday 9th May, special forms of service will be used, issued by the Archbishops… These services take the form of a solemn preparation for The Consecration of Our King on May 12th. On Coronation day there will be a special service at 10 a.m. This service will be over in time for listeners in their own homes to hear the broadcast of the actual service at Westminster Abbey which begins at 11 a.m.

This extract is from the Mulbarton parish magazine, started by Canon Ramsay, who had moved to Mulbarton from East Carleton, where he had published a magazine since the beginning of the First World War. There were special local services too:

Mulbarton Church from the south. This postcard was posted in Rochester to an address in Wymondham on 8 November 1906.
(PHOTO CONTRIBUTED BY MALCOLM AND VALERIE JONES)

The first mass road users' church service this year [1938] was held on Sunday at St Mary Magdalene Church, Mulbarton, and was arranged by the Norwich Viking Motor Cycle Club. Some time before the service hikers, cyclists, motor cyclists and car drivers were arriving in good numbers, all attired according to their mode of transport. Many leather jackets, riding shorts, and driving coats were seen. About 250 attended…

The big event after the Second World War was when the clock in the church tower was dedicated as a village war memorial by the Bishop of Norwich on 8 October 1950.

Revd A. St John Heard, whose ministry began in the war years, ran a clothing club to help parishioners. Brenda Ford (née Collins) remembers: 'His wife was an invalid so we did not know her, but he was one of the few people who had a private car which he used to drive along the common at about 5mph!'

Sandy – Revd Cecil Sanderson, Rector 1960–78 – and his wife Mary are remembered for their hospitality. Many meetings and fund-raising garden parties were held at the Rectory. One participant remembers:

… country dancing in my gingham skirt which I had made for the occasion in dressmaking lessons. Reverend Sanderson's wife always made Rice Crispy cakes covered in chocolate.

Sandy was keen to make newcomers to the village feel welcome, and started monthly family services, for which Mr Bussey compiled a booklet with an order of service and lively hymns. *Parish News* began, and Sandy helped design the village sign and the layout of the new Rectory, in which he and Mary lived for less than two years.

Sandy's successor, Geoffrey Unwin, moved members towards a more evangelical viewpoint. 'Mission Praise' gradually replaced 'Hymns Ancient

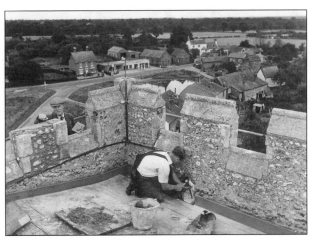

The church tower being repaired in the early 1950s. Beyond are the Post Office, Frost's garage, the Parish (Wingfield) Hall, the Methodist Chapel and the World's End.
(PHOTO CONTRIBUTED BY IRIS FROST)

Certificate recording the baptism of Arthur Stackyard in Mulbarton Church in 1906 and signed by the then Rector, Revd J. Carleton Steward. (CONTRIBUTED BY EVELYN SMITH)

& Modern', new forms of service were introduced, bright banners and kneelers were stitched, guitars were heard for the first time and new links were made with home and overseas missions. Although some people left, the church was more in touch with young families in the village. Today, Mulbarton Church describes itself on its website as 'a lively

Revd Sanderson and his wife Mary at the doorway of the (old) Rectory during a wedding reception held there in August 1973. (PHOTO CONTRIBUTED BY NORMA MICKLEBURGH)

The sack race at a church garden party held on the front lawn of the Rectory, early 1960s.

(PHOTO: DEREK VALIANT)

Fancy-dress parade at a fête in the grounds of the Rectory in June 1965. Left to right: Grant Smith (cowboy), Paul Hindle (chimney-sweep), Debbie Ryan (gypsy), Andrew Mickleburgh (pirate), Jane Mickleburgh (Queen of Hearts).

(PHOTO CONTRIBUTED BY NORMA MICKLEBURGH)

Young Wives Group members in fancy dress with Revd Geoffrey Unwin at the Patronal Festival Garden Party at the new Rectory in July 1984. Left to right, standing: Edna Hewitt as Cleopatra, Audrey Batchelor as a clown, Angela Edgar and Roz Catton as fishermen.

(PHOTO: JOHN HEWITT)

Left: *Typical church fête? Sheltering from the downpour are Debbie Ryan (left) and Andrew Mickleburgh under a hastily covered stall in the grounds of the Rectory in June 1965.*

(PHOTO CONTRIBUTED BY NORMA MICKLEBURGH)

evangelical and charismatic Anglican Church Family.' A visitor from the past would find the building similar, but might be surprised at the informal and enthusiastic worship with music group, flags and a multimedia approach, thanks to modern technology. But the purpose remains the same: to honour God, learn from his word and be equipped to serve.

The Bells

The six ropes hanging in the tower show there are now six bells, but this was not always so. The first known mention of the church tower and a bell is in the will of Thomas Caukhill (1393), who left a sum of 40s. towards a new bell. The 1552 inventory lists three bells, which must have rung out when Queen Elizabeth I passed through Mulbarton on Saturday, 16 August 1578 on her way from Bracon Ash to Norwich. Two more bells were probably added during the massive expansion of change-ringing in the seventeenth century. The Mulbarton ringers travelled far and wide during the eighteenth and nineteenth centuries to ringing competitions, which were popular events in Norfolk and Suffolk over a long period. They won a prize at Bedingham in 1842 and rang 1,200 changes at Forncett in 1844.

The five older bells are inscribed: bell No. 4: - 'anno dni 1616'; the tenor bell (which weighs nearly half a tonne!) – 'JOHN BREND MADE ME 1653'; bell No. 5 – 'THO NEWMAN MADE MEE 1714'; bell

The new treble bell inscribed: 'Given by his parents in memory of Geoffrey Alfred Frederick Middleton, Sapper, Royal Engineers, killed in action at Dunkirk, May 28, 1940. Dedicated 27th Oct. 1946.'

(PHOTO CONTRIBUTED BY EVELYN SMITH)

No. 3 – the old bell was inscribed 'anno dni 1612' but was recast in 1904; the former treble (now bell No. 2) – recast 1808, now inscribed: 'THOMAS MEARS & SON OF LONDON FECIT 1808'.

The crown of bell No. 4 has three shields, one with an intertwined ABW, the monogram of William and Alice Brend, whose company was casting bells in Norwich from 1586. At the time of John Brend (1634–58), the founder of the tenor bell, the foundry was at All Saints' Green, Norwich (near where John Lewis now stands). Thomas Newman (1701–44), founder of bell No. 5, was probably a travelling bell founder. A brass plaque tells us that 'These bells were re-hung at a cost of £100 in commemoration of the Diamond Jubilee of Queen Victoria – 1897.'

In 1904 a new bell-frame was installed, with space for six bells. This was filled in 1947, when a treble bell from Whitechapel Bell Foundry was given in memory of Geoffrey Middleton by his parents, Frederick and Rose Middleton. Frederick Middleton, sub-postmaster, was a bell-ringer and for some years Master of the Company at Mulbarton.

The Mulbarton peal is tuned in the key of A major. Two peals are commemorated in the ringing chamber; the peal on the full set of six bells was rung:

On Monday Oct. 27th 1947, in 2 hrs. 48 mins A peal of Plain Bob Minor consisting of Seven different extents. Miss Nancy Hall Treble; Fred W. Middleton 2; Mrs. F.C. Goodman 3; Herbert Nichols 4; Harry J. Hall 5; F. Charles Goodman Tenor. Conducted by F. Charles Goodman. The first peal of Minor on the bells.

The ring of six was very popular with visiting peal ringers in the 1950s and 1960s, when over 50 peals were rung. The bells still have an important part to play in the life of Mulbarton Church: they are rung for weddings and special occasions with much help from ringers from neighbouring parishes. On Sunday, 23 October 2005 a 'final salute' for the 200th anniversary of the death of Nelson was rung by Petra Parker, Barry Pilgrim, Derek Jones, Chris Samson, Tom Taylor and George Moore (tower captain).

The Choir

Evelyn Smith (née Stackyard) remembers the choir in the 1940s and 1950s:

I was 10 years old when I joined Mulbarton Church choir, where the organist and choirmaster was Arthur Bussey. He was an excellent organist and choirmaster, but he was very strict. Choir practice was every Friday evening, and we attended Church for Morning and Evening services. If we sang at a wedding we were paid 6d. each (2½p).

Every year we joined other choirs from Norfolk to sing in Norwich Cathedral on the Saturday nearest to St George's Day. We rehearsed in the afternoon, and

Mr Bussey took us for tea at Purdy's Restaurant on Tombland. Then we sang in the evening – it used to be a wonderful occasion. In the summer we always had an outing to the seaside, and every Christmas a visit to the pantomime at the Theatre Royal.

Brenda Ford (née Collins) adds:

We always sang special anthems during the Church's year for Easter, Whitsun, and Harvest Festival. The church was always full for special services and well decorated, but not so full for the regular Sunday services. The choir were seated near to the organ and in the earlier days the organ had to be pumped by one of the boys. Once an electric pump was available there was not so much subdued giggling in the choir!

Mr Nicholls, husband of a teacher at school, was a warden at the Vale Hospital in Swainsthorpe which was a sort of workhouse for elderly men. He used to bring them to church at Mulbarton sometimes. He was a very nice man and used to sing Bass in the church choir when he was not on duty. I can always remember him singing the 150th psalm at Harvest Festival in his lovely bass voice – 'Praise God in His Holiness...'

Reg Warner told a Radio Norfolk interviewer that he earned 12s.6d a year for pumping the organ in the 1930s. A later choir member who pumped the organ was the future England footballer, Maurice Norman.

Choir outings were a tradition – the school logbook records that in the years before the harvest holiday dates were fixed, the whole school closed for the occasion, as both staff and pupils were usually involved in the choir:

On 22 July 1881: '... A holiday was given on Monday as Mistress went with the Church Choir to Yarmouth.' It was Yarmouth again in 1883, and Lowestoft in 1898. In later years the school was not allowed to close – but pupils still went on the outing.

On 8 August 1910; 'Choir outing today – 12 choirboys absent on this account.'

Long before Mr Bussey took the choir to the pantomime there were Christmas parties. A local newspaper reported, on 29 January 1932:

The Mulbarton Church choir were on Friday entertained to a supper at the Rectory by the Revd A.R. Vaughan Daubeney and Mrs Daubeney... After supper games, dancing, etc. were enjoyed, and songs were rendered by members of the choir; there was also community singing... Selections and change ringing was given on the handbells, and an enjoyable evening was spent... This is the first Christmas [the Rector and Mrs Daubeney] have spent at Mulbarton...

Church Choir, October 1946. Left to right, back row: *Joy Cooper, Barbara Lightwing (née Hall), June Haverson, Jean Smith (née Baker), Jean Hornsby (née Smith), Lillian Gladwell (née Lincoln), Daphne White (née Bailey), Margaret Cross; Evelyn Smith (née Stackyard), Joan Cushing (née Larter);* middle row: *Maurice (Monty) Norman (footballer), Doreen Tunney, 'Daddy' Green, Mr F. Middleton (postmaster), Herbert Lake (undertaker), Herbert Nicholls, Muriel Taylor (née Kedge), Nancy Hall;* front row (seated): *Mrs Lake, Arthur Bussey (organist), Revd A. St John Heard, Mrs Hall (organist), Nurse Sexton (district nurse), Philip Cooper.*

(PHOTO CONTRIBUTED BY BRYAN TUNGATE)

Mulbarton Church choir 1953. Left to right, back row: *Joy Cooper, Gillian Baker (later Philpott);* middle row: *Hazel Baker (later Stone), Brenda Collins (later Ford), Arthur Bussey (organist); Revd A. St John Heard, Herbert Nicholls, Margaret Canham, Sylvia Cooper;* front row: *Peter Hornsby, Barbara Hall (later Lightwing), Jean Baker (later Smith), Mrs Hall, Jean Smith (later Hornsby), Joan Larter (later Cushing), Nancy Hall, David Hornsby, ?.*

(PHOTO FROM MULBARTON CHURCH)

Church choir with Revd (Sandy) Sanderson after a wedding – possibly 1964. Left to right: *Nigel Smith, ?, Heather Coleman, Juliet Lofty, ?, Val Fox, L. Smith, John Smith (?), Revd 'Sandy' Sanderson, Rose Marie Evans, Kathleen Tooke, Sally Evans.*

(CONTRIBUTED BY JULIET AMOS, NÉE LOFTY)

Mulbarton Church choir outing to Yarmouth, 1948. Left to right, back row (beginning with lady between two boys): *Mrs Sparke, Mrs Lake, Mr Hall, Jean Smith, Muriel Kedge, Joan Larter, Arthur Bussey (organist);* front row: *Margaret Sparke, Michael Goodman, Colin Haverson, Barbara Hall, Brenda Collins, Daphne Bailey, June Haverson, Rosemary Morris, Evelyn Stackyard.* (CONTRIBUTED BY EVELYN SMITH)

Church Choir 1987 – almost the last robed choir of Mulbarton Church. Left to right, back row: *Tara Riddington, Hazel Pledger, Alison Dixon, Revd Geoffrey Unwin (Rector), Gillian Wilson (organist), George Faulks (lay reader), Rachel Wills, Alice Lince (née Mitchell, choirmistress), Andrea Dodgson;* front row: *Fiona Jones, Jo-Ann Buckenham, Karen Riley, Elizabeth Burchell, Katherine Adcock, Christine Hobbs.*

(PHOTO CONTRIBUTED BY ALICE LINCE)

Children of Mulbarton Church Sunday School perform 'The Parable of the Great Feast' for the Anniversary and Prizegiving in November 1986. The bandages are part of the props! (PHOTO: MAVIS BASTIN)

Mulbarton Church Sunday School with Fidele Dirokpa (then Bishop of Bukavu, now Anglican Archbishop of Congo) in 1991. The church supports the Dioceses of Bukavu and Kindu in the Democratic Republic of Congo and has received a number of visits from Congolese clergy. (PHOTO: JILL WRIGHT)

Sunday School

There was a Sunday School with an average of 50 children in 1843, supported by voluntary contributions, according to the Visitation Return. The 1851 church census return gives 30 children in Sunday School at each service – though we don't know how many were the same children! For most of the twentieth century, Sunday School was held in church before the service from 10a.m. (later 9.30a.m.), which made a long morning for those who stayed for the choir. One memory from the 1930s: 'The Sunday School teacher was Mr Blackman. He had travelled the Bible lands as a soldier. What tales he told! He brought the Bible to life…' In the 1940s and 1950s: 'We had a Sunday School run by Miss Larter, a sweet little lady who lived up the corner by the pond.'

Clifford Robinson remembers:

… little books and stickers for attendance, and if you collected enough you could go on the Sunday School treat which was usually to Gorleston. We were taken to the Brunswick Hotel for fish and chips and ice-cream for tea.

Despite the decline in Sunday School nationwide, Mulbarton's flourished through the 1980s, when it was very ecumenical, with its Methodist leader, Mavis Bastin, helped by Daphne Unwin, the Rector's wife. Overseas links were encouraged, through child sponsorship and support for mission partners. Later this was strengthened with visits from Congolese clergy. But immovable pews and hot tubular pipes inhibit interesting activities, and it was largely the need for better Sunday School and crèche facilities that made the Church Council consider a modern extension. To add a room to the side of the church would interfere with graves and the first quote for a matching flint building was a quarter of a million pounds! No one could justify that expense, and other suggestions, such as a mobile classroom, were blocked by the planners. Then the house next-door-but-one came on the market, and within weeks the asking-price had been promised by church members as gifts or loans. It was purchased in 1993 and refurbished for use as a community facility. The Sunday School – renamed CCC (Children's Christian Club) – could now function during the service and enjoy refreshments, games in the garden, and there was a 'loo'! The final loan payment was made in 2005: Mulbarton Church fully owns Harvest House!

The Methodist Chapel

The former Methodist Chapel is next to the World's End, where the road narrows by the village pond. Across the front are the bold words: PRIMITIVE METHODIST CHAPEL 1900. The 'Primitive Methodists' had broken away from the Wesleyan Methodists, who, they thought, had become too 'comfortable' and had lost their original enthusiasm. Thanks to the researches of one Mulbarton Chapel member, Evelyn Vincent, its story has been preserved.

The first mention of Methodists in the area was in 1823, when Mulbarton was among the first group of societies to send quarterly contributions to the Primitive Methodist circuit funds. In 1837 the circuit

Mulbarton Methodist Chapel and 'pond shop', summer 1992.   (PHOTO CONTRIBUTED BY JILL WRIGHT)

looked for a room to rent for regular Sunday services, and in the following year there is a report of meetings being held in the home of David Spurgeon junr. By 1840 the circuit was looking for another base and found a meeting-place to rent. The Mulbarton congregation was 'asked if it would be responsible for the weekly shilling rent, but warned that if they declined then preaching would have to be conducted in the open air'. They declined, and do not seem to have supported open-air meetings instead. In March 1841 a village mission failed to get enough support to restart a Society, although there may have been occasional meetings over the next 30 years. A mission organised by the Queen's Road (Norwich) Primitive Methodist circuit in 1872 resulted in a Society being formed with nine members, who seemed to meet in Bracon Ash, but no building plot for a chapel could be found there.

In 1898 plans were made to build a chapel in Mulbarton. A small corner of the orchard of Mulbarton Mill was obtained and, on 8 August 1899, the foundation stone was laid by Mrs Murrell (wife of Councillor Robert Murrell, a trustee at Queen's Road), Mrs D. Warn and Miss Kate Hollidge (wife and daughter respectively of two other Queen's Road trustees), Mr W. Spurgeon, Mr A. Green and Alfred Calvert (circuit superintendent minister). The *Eastern Daily Press* reported that £40 was laid on the stones for the new chapel. These stones can still be seen in the former chapel building, now two apartments. The chapel was ready for the opening celebrations on 16 November 1899 and in April 1900 regular services began. The chapel, which could seat 150 people, cost £292, of which £140 was still owed when it was opened. Adjoining the chapel was a stable for the visiting preacher's pony, if he was fortunate enough to have one. Otherwise, preachers walked many miles to take services.

The chapel was very active in these early years: there were two services on a Sunday, one in the afternoon and one at 6.30p.m.; there was Sunday School in the morning, with four teachers and 32 children, a Band of Hope with five adult and ten young teetotallers and a Christian Endeavour Society, with 10 members. The Mulbarton school log-book mentions pupils leaving early for 'a Chapel tea Meeting' on 3 July 1900; and on 6 July 1904: 'The Methodist Sunday School Treat this afternoon, consequently nearly one third of school away.' Mr Emms, from East Carleton, was appointed Chapel Steward, and Mrs Cooper, of The Rosery, Mulbarton, was also a founder member. It was said that after Mr Emms got too frail to attend the 6.30p.m. service, his housekeeper could be seen walking alone on the dark winter nights lighting her way with a hurricane lantern, so punctual that people could set their clocks by her.

In 1925 there were 25 chapel members and the Sunday School had one teacher and ten children. By the late 1920s, however, the chapel had almost closed

Mulbarton Methodist Chapel viewed across the pond soon after it was opened – and before the Parish (Wingfield) Hall was built. (PHOTO FROM VILLAGE ARCHIVE)

Mulbarton Methodist Chapel interior after redecoration, with better heating and lighting installed. Mrs Lucas is arranging the flowers. The cross on the front wall was given in memory of Mrs Cooper, a founder member.

(PHOTO CONTRIBUTED BY BILL ALBOROUGH)

down. As in most villages, the congregation fluctuated in numbers according to whether farm workers moved at Michaelmas (in the autumn, when agricultural tenancies were – or were not – renewed). However, in the 1930s some young men from the Queen's Road Methodist Church, Norwich, came to help out with the Sunday School. The annual outing to Yarmouth was very popular with the children.

Also in the 1930s, James Bobbin from Swardeston was invited to become Steward at the chapel. His family worshipped at the Nonconformist chapel in Swardeston (started by Surrey Chapel, Norwich) until it closed down. So began the long association of the Bobbin family with Mulbarton Chapel. At the outbreak of war in 1939 the young men from Queen's Road Chapel were called up into the Armed Forces and Mrs Gertrude Sturman, sister of Mr Bobbin, took on the Sunday School. Several prizes for attendance have survived – inscribed using a 'John Bull' printing set.

Chapel Harvest Festival offerings on display, mid-1980s. The service was followed next day by a supper and sale, which was an important source of income for the chapel and its mission giving. (Photo contributed by Patrick Bobbin)

In 1944 James Bobbin died and his son, Arthur, became Senior Steward – an office he held for 47 years. Alice Cooper, daughter of one of the founders, was organist. Caretaking was carried out by Mrs Alborough, later helped by her sister, Mrs Lucas, who often decorated the chapel with flowers they had grown themselves. During the 1940s and 1950s a trustee, William Trower junr, treasurer of Mulbarton Chapel, sometimes met the assessment out of his own pocket as collections were so low. Accounts for 1945–52 show that collections were around 5s. at each service, totalling between £6 and £7 per quarter.

The chapel was threatened with closure again in the 1950s as there were so few members, but Arthur Bobbin was able to convince the minister, Revd Perry, and the Circuit, that the chapel should remain open. Then several families from Swardeston joined, a new trust was formed, and chapel members took on the management of their own affairs in 1960. Arthur Bobbin and Frank Sadd acted as stewards, Mr Vincent became treasurer, and Mrs Vincent the unofficial organist. A 'Women's Bright Hour' was started, supported by several friends from the Anglican Church. From the end of the 1960s, chapel services were held only in the afternoon, but visitors could be sure of four well-sung hymns and a helpful sermon.

Support from larger churches in the area was much appreciated by Mulbarton members. On special occasions the Chapelfield Road choir, or Hethersett Methodists, or those from Park Lane,

Norwich, would help out at the service, and then afterwards tea and cakes would be served. With no kitchen the kettles had to be plugged into sockets wherever they were available:

One socket was in the pulpit: the preacher would be asked to switch the kettle on just before he announced the last hymn. Depending on the length of the hymn and the final prayer, it has been known for steam to be seen rising, leading to comments that hot air was coming out of the pulpit!

The annual Spring Sale is first mentioned in 1965, when £18 was raised for chapel funds. The last recorded Spring Sale, in 1991, raised £398. This event was held in May in the Village Hall and everyone helped, including friends from the Parish Church. Arthur Bobbin's plant stall was particularly popular. The other 'big' event was Harvest Festival – vividly remembered by Mavis, wife of John Bastin, a local preacher:

My main memories of Mulbarton Chapel go back to the Harvest festival when the pulpit area was adorned with Arthur Bobbin's sacks of home-grown potatoes, boxes of apples, etc. Not for him the daintily arranged baskets of fruit and sophisticated flower arrangements which constitute today's harvests! Chapelfield Road choir came over to sing for us on the Monday evening and offered exorbitant bids as the boxes of apples, etc. were auctioned to swell Chapel funds.

Arthur Bobbin died in 1991, and with him passed one secret – how to manoeuvre coffins into the chapel! His funeral, in January 1992, was the last to be held in the chapel. It was a crowded and decorous occasion, but his son told us that some time afterwards the undertakers admitted that they had had to stand the coffin on end to get it to the back door.

Frank Debenham succeeded him as senior steward and took on the job of opening the chapel each Sunday and switching the heating on, until the trek across the Common became too much for him. Revd Booker persuaded members to hold morning services in the school or Village Hall, a warmer venue where refreshments could be served, so the chapel building closed for worship from 1993. As numbers continued to decline, however, it was decided to offer the remaining members lifts to Chapelfield Road Methodist Church, Norwich.

On 26 November 1995 the last Methodist service was held in Mulbarton Village Hall, followed by a luncheon arranged by Mrs Gail Clifford and family and a willing band of helpers. Revd Gerald Cole was there, as were representatives from the Norwich Circuit and the local Anglican Church. All joined in the tribute to almost 100 years of Methodism in Mulbarton and to several generations of people keeping faith with their Lord.

❖ CHAPTER 6 ❖

Fields, Farms and Farmers

Although Mulbarton has grown so much in recent years, when viewed from the air the village looks surprisingly small and compact, surrounded by large hedged fields and small areas of woodland. That farmland is largely the reason for the existence of the village. Over the years hedges have been removed, farms have been amalgamated and the old field names almost forgotten – but not quite…

Fields

About 1724 James Balls, lord of the manor of Mulbarton, had a map made of his domain showing roads, buildings, fields and landowners. The land was divided into furlongs of various sizes (a term for an area of land as well as a measure), and many of these were further subdivided into long narrow strips. The area of the Common is given as just over 45 acres, and the rest of the land was divided into 22 furlongs with wonderful names, including: Sowdle Field, Brome-Dale, Catmay (later Catmere) Hurne, Catbridge Field, Castelins Wongs, Chapps Hill, Porter Bush, Nether Gate, Drink-Hill, Kenningham Hurne, Yesmer and Burtch Field (later Birch Field).

A century later, every parish was surveyed under the Tithe Act of 1836, which fixed a rent charge for every field and piece of land in lieu of tithes of produce. The Mulbarton 'award' was made in 1841, and the map and accompanying rent-charge book is now in the Norfolk Records Office. The 1724 furlong names appear again, with variations in spelling and with some additional field names: Tee Close (by the road to Swainsthorpe), Dirty Close, Great and Little Brick Kiln Pastures – all words associated with making clay-lump 'bricks'. There were also Hulver Bush (an old name for holly), Ashery, Cherry Tree Close, Swamp Close, Dry Close, East and West Crow Fields, First and Second Cuckoo Fields, Sarah Barley's, west of the Common (probably should be Sarah Burley, a member of a large Mulbarton family, who died in March 1770). Several fields are named according to their size, although Hundred Acres only has an area of 4½ acres! Many of these names have been used as road names in present-day Mulbarton.

Farming

In Victorian times there were five farms in Mulbarton, only two of which still exist today: Paddock Farm, and Kenningham Hall Farm. Both were owned for decades by different branches of the Turner family, whose family line is recorded on two memorials in Mulbarton Church. The land of Old Hall Farm and Malthouse Farm was sold off separately from the farmhouses during the last century, and Lodge Farm was split up more recently.

Mr Turner's Farm

The farmhouse facing Norwich Road – 'the Turnpike' – is marked on the 1724 map of Mulbarton. Detailed records survive from Paddock Farm which tell us a lot about farming in Mulbarton before the days of mechanisation. The earliest accounts are a summary

Mulbarton harvest, building a haystack, early 1900s.
(PHOTO CONTRIBUTED BY JOHN BETTS)

Paddock Farmhouse and part of the cattle sheds, summer 1992, before the front fence was put up.

(PHOTO: JILL WRIGHT)

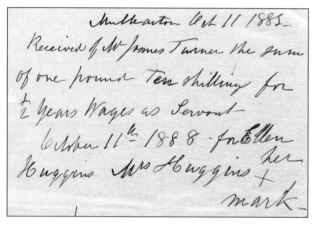

Servant's wages for six months to 11 October 1888. Ellen Huggins earns £1.10s. (£1.50p). Note she is unable to sign her name. (CONTRIBUTED BY MULBARTON MIDDLE SCHOOL)

for the years 1769–79. In 1770, Mary Pitcher was paid £1.14s. (£1.70p) a year, Will Poll £6.6s., Robert Chapman £9 and Mary Nixon £9.9s. (see Introduction for £.s.d). This was in the days of John Turner (1712–96), who married Bridget Johnson in Norwich Cathedral. Their second son, James Turner (1750-1829), married Rebecca Spratt in Mulbarton Church and is presumably in charge in January 1801, when 16s.10d. (84p) was paid out for 'trashing [threshing] oats', £1.8s.3½d for 'trashing barley' and £1.16s.11d. for 'trashing wheat'. Will Chapman (possibly the son of Robert Chapman of 1770) was paid 10s. for six days' work.

James and Rebecca Turner are followed by a son and grandson, also called James: James Turner (1805–50), who married Mary Ann, and their son James (1834–89), who never married but who kept meticulous accounts whilst his father's estate was being settled. In 1850, James Turner junr employed eight men and two boys on a 179-acre farm, taking on extra men and women at seed-time and harvest. Two women worked in the house. Because he owned his own farm he did not have to pay rent, but he did pay tithes to the church, the poor rate and other taxes.

For a typical six-day week, a man earned 8s. and a boy 3s. At harvest, when they are working much longer hours, all the men receive £1 and the boys receive double wages at the start of the harvest. At the end of the harvest they received the balance due to them: on 6 September 1850 this was £2.17s.0d. per man. Women earned only slightly more than boys: 'Woman Albro' received 2s.6d for 3½ days' threshing; Mrs Bailey 3s. for four days' work in the barn; Mrs Kedge only 1s.9d. for three days' work in the barn and 2s. for her harvest wages. On another occasion, the Kedge children were paid 6d. (in total) for 'dropping beans'. Most of these workers lived in 'tied cottages' belonging to Mr Turner, for which they had to pay rent. For example, James Sleight lived with his widowed father and grandmother in a cottage 'near Turnpike' (Norwich Road) for which he paid £4.15s.0d. rent and 1s.6d. tithe a year, out of wages averaging 8s. a week.

The account book lists payments to local tradesmen: £5.5s.10d. to Mr Rice, blacksmith, to settle his account, £5 to John Rice for thatching (including £1 for thatching three haystacks), 2s. to Mr Dye for rubbish collecting and payments to casual labourers for harvest work and to contractors for sowing barley and mowing hay. There is beer for the haymakers (2s. on 6 July) – and later for the harvesters. Farm expenses include seeds, repairs, milling wheat, mending sparrow nets (2s.), 'muck' (10 loads = £2.10s.), a cockerel (2s.) and a collar for a pony (1s.6d.). In October 1850 Mr Turner went to a sale and bought a gig (a light horse-drawn carriage) for £5.15s., a harrow (£3), a water trough (8s.6d.), harness for a horse (£2.4s.0d.) and the horse itself (£21).

A great variety of produce from the farm was sold. The wheat went to Mr Cremer at the mill by the Common for flour (80cwt for £74). Mr Cremer also bought the barley, hay and straw. Oats were sold to Mr Todd at the World's End for the horses. Some animals went to the local butcher, Robert Girling (who rented a cottage by the Common from Mr Turner): six pigs for £14.9s.6d., one fat pig for £2.10s., one sheep for £1.15s.6d., one calf for 10s. and eight beasts (cattle) at £17 each. In July 1851 he sold four shorthorn bullocks at Smithfield Market, London, for £68, and the next week another four for £64. Horse hide went to Mr Cunningham (for 5s.) and cow hide to Mr Turner (5s.6d). Butter and eggs were supplied to Mr Girling and Mrs Todd, with faggots, wood, and parsnips sold to the farm workers for small amounts.

Life on Mr Turner's farm does not seem so very different 30 years on. In 1881 it had been under restrictions for foot-and-mouth disease, but was declared free by March. In November 1884 James Turner dined with the Revd Richard Lucas and paid almost £46 annual rent for Glebe land. During the winter of 1884–85 he was employing eight men, two boys and two women to do such work as washing, carting stones, chopping turnips, trimming hedges and clearing drains (ditches). For a six-day week the men were paid between 10s. and 15s. a week, the women and boys between 4s. and 5s. a week. Mr Turner's corn was ground by Alfred Thompson at the windmill by the common, and he paid 15s. for a 'light carriage' licence to Samuel Gowing at Mulbarton Post Office. Maybe this was the carriage repaired by H.W. Howes Carriage Works, Prince of Wales Road, Norwich, in 1887 for 10s.

Harvest Home

James Turner's farm account book for 1866 gives a detailed diary of the harvest, when everything was done by hand. The ten men and boys who cut, stacked and threshed the wheat and barley are either the men who were working for him in 1851 or their sons, helped by four wives. This account, with original spellings, has details added from information elsewhere in the same book about field sizes and crops:

Thursday 9th August – Began Harvest today in Dry Close [8½ acres], the wages to be the same as other [years] per head, 6£.

Friday 10th – Began to cut Bush Pytle [4 acres]. Finished by 3 o'clock, went into Sarah Barleys, din about 2½.

Saturday 11th – Cutting Wheat in Sarah Barleys [12 acres].

Monday 13th – Began to cut Barley in Wheelwright Pytle [6½ acres]. Finish Sarah Barleys by 12 o'clock. Began to cut the Ten Acres [actually 9½ acres].

Tuesday 14th – Cutting Wheat in Ten Acres.

Wednesday 15th – Finished cutting Wheat in Ten Acres. Finished cutting Barley in Wheelwrights.

Thursday 16th – Thunder. Finish cutting Peters Close [6½ acres]. Went into Six Acres and finished it [7½ acres].

Friday 17th – 10 till 3. Men began to work on bottom

for stack in Ten Acres to put the Sarah Barleys about 10 acres of it on. [Using turnips, etc., from the previous winter as a base for the sheaves.]

Saturday 18th – Finished the stack off first thing. Began another stack with the rest of Sarah Barleys. Began to thrash wheat from Ten Acres at 12 o'clock. Left off for dinner and finished at 5 o'clock and sent in to Cremers [Miller] 55 comb. Top the stack up from Ten Acres, 1 load from Bush Pytle.

Monday 20th – Did not begin to Cart till 10 am. Began Bush Pytle unto stack in Ten Acres. Finished it from the Dry Close. The rest into barn – about 5 o'clock.

Tuesday 21st – Began to cut Swamp Barley [8½ acres]. Began to Cart Barley from Six Acres to stack in Ten Acres.

Wednesday 22nd – Damp. Cut the Catmer Hurn [5½ acres]. Went on with Swamp.

Thursday 23rd – Dry. Finish cutting Swamp. Turned the Wheel[wrights] Pytle and part of Peters Close. Began to cart Wheelwrights Pytle. Finish it off.

Friday 24th – Dry. Trimming Wheat. Stack Turning. Barley in Peters Close begun. Jn Larter not well – left at 3 o'clock.

Saturday 25th – Turning in Swamp and [Catmere] Hurn. Cart Barley from Stack in the Field.

A list of wages follows: £6.10s. to Mr Dawson; £4 to C. Waller; £5.10s. to Mr Sleight; £6 each to John Larter, Mr Kedge, H. Larter and James Barrett; £2 each to W. Banham and E. Rice; £4.14s. to Cole; 15s. to W. Kedge (boy); £1 to Mrs Kedge; 6s. each to Mrs Sleight, Mrs Kedge and Mrs Larter; 5s.3d. to Mrs Dawson.

Monday 27th – Finished carting Swamp – 5 loads into the second stack and finished with Barley from the Catmer Hurn. Carted part of the Wheat rakings into barn. Thatching Barley stack in Ten Acres. Heaping Barley from 8 o'clock until 5 o'clock all day.

Tuesday 28th – Finished getting the Wheat and Barley. Raking up Wheat into barn, Barley into Bullockshed. Thatching Barley stack in Swamp.

Harvest at Mulbarton with horse-drawn cart, early 1900s. It is believed that the people include Mr Potter, Mr and Mrs Tooke and Mr and Mrs Albert Rice.

(PHOTO CONTRIBUTED BY EVELYN SMITH)

Harvest in Mulbarton, possibly during the First World War. The horse is pulling a hay-rake.

(CONTRIBUTED BY TERRY BURCHELL, FROM PHILIP STANDLEY'S COLLECTION)

A double line in the account book shows the harvest is over. It was thirsty work: Mr Turner pays Mr Dye (of the Tradesman's Arms) just over 7s. for beer! But there is still plenty to do – mowing vetches in Burnt House Close, turning vetches, driving muck, barn jobs and thrashing. Mr Dawson has gone off to Norwich; the other regular workers are back to regular wages: between 4s.6d. and 6s. to the men; 1s.6d. to the boy.

Paddock Farm to the Present Day

After James Turner died in 1889, the farm was rented out to tenants. A 'James Brown, farmer', is listed as living at 'The Paddocks' in 1896, and Robert William Daplyn is resident on the 1901 census and listed in directories from 1904 to 1916. Arthur W. Fairman farmed both Malthouse Farm and Paddock Farms in the early 1920s, then his brother, Herbert James Fairman, moved from East Carleton Manor Home Farm to Paddock Farm until his brother died in 1942.

The next tenant was Fred Jackson, who always had a walking stick and usually wore a brown smock. The bend by Catbridge Lane was nick-named 'Jackson's Corner'. He exercised his common rights and people remember his cows wandering along the main road to and from the farm. Chris Mickleburgh remembers regularly taking a small churn to the farm

Paddock Farm House on Norwich Road, c.1910. The pond is much smaller now. (PHOTO CONTRIBUTED BY DAVID WRIGHT)

The Paddock Farm name-plate when the tenant was Herbert James Fairman, brother of Arthur Fairman of Malthouse Farm.

(PLATE OWNED BY INGRID FAIRMAN – PHOTOGRAPHED WITH PERMISSION)

Aerial view of Paddock Farm and its barns in June 1986 – before the barns were converted into housing.

(PHOTO: DAVID AND JILL WRIGHT)

Putting straw on the strawberries at Paddock Farm, probably May 1989. Left to right: Graham Barton (driving tractor), John Shaw, Jonathan Shaw. The buildings of Paddock Farm are on the horizon. (PHOTO: NIGEL FROST)

and watching the milk being ladled in. After Mr Jackson moved to Carleton Rode around 1957, Paddock Farm came back to a member of the Turner family. Colin Preston, whose mother was a Turner, was given the family farm as a wedding present by an uncle in the mid-1950s.

Like many of his ancestors, Colin Preston served as a churchwarden for many years. He ran Paddock Farm as a mixed farm, growing sugar beet and cereals, with cattle fattened for market. Then he turned to fruit crops, especially strawberries, which were supplied to the Norfolk Show each year. Local women and teenagers picked the soft fruit, but as labour became scarce (or too expensive) an increasing amount was opened for 'Pick Your Own'. People still come to pick soft fruit, apples and onions.

Management of the farm passed to Colin's son, Robert, who expanded the business to include a farm shop and then a butcher's. Colin Preston introduced some exotic species to the farm – llamas, pot-bellied pigs and some exotic goats that were popular with the children of customers. More recently, the great barn and bullock sheds have been converted into housing, and several local businesses have used the studio above the shop.

Steam on the Farm
(More memories of Tony Kent)

To a true Norfolkman, the traction engine drivers were 'Thas th'owd boyze wut druv tha troshin tarkle'. What drivers! The steering wheel had a large knob on the rim which the driver gripped. The steering rods were chains, and when the driver wound the wheel one side tightened and the other slackened. Towed behind the engine was the drum, and behind that the pitcher (elevator). Imagine going along the average country lane and taking that lot through a 12-foot gate in one swing. They did it day after day. If the entrance was too muddy, the tackle would be unhitched, the engine taken in, and everything was winched in, and those boys could put the tackle to an inch. Now came the rough part. In the winter the tackle left huge ruts, and a boy with a horse-drawn 3-wheeled water cart had to negotiate those to keep the engine supplied. Much would be spilt. Frequently, the cart would overturn and lose its load, and the boy was called anything but a boy!

Each set of tackle had a crew of two – some had three. These were driver and drum feeder, who cut the strings on the 'shoofs' (sheaves) and fed the corn into the drum. Strings had to be kept out. Some had a 'chaff and coulder' man who bagged up the chaff and cleared the coulder (weed seeds, husk, barley havers) from under the drum. His was a twilight world of dust. It was often the 'not so bright' who 'done' this job.

The threshed corn was weighed off the drum as 'combs' – 12 stone oats – 16 stone barley – 18 stone wheat – 20 stone clover. Two men lifted it into a wagon which was shoulder-height and it was then taken home to the barn. It was carried off 'one man – one bag' and stacked upright, two sacks high and one flat on top. Chaff from oats and wheat was bagged up at the drum and taken to the fodder barn to be used as animal feed. These same engines were used to drive chaff cutters, which cut up an entire stack of straw in a day, and to drive balers, that tied the bales with wire.

Notable local drivers were Bob Loveday who smoked a 'snout-warmer' (a short pipe), often upside-down. He lived in Mulbarton and rode a 'sit-up-and-beg' bicycle with his back ramrod straight. When loaded with alcohol he caused many a bet on a dark night as his bike rear light zig-zagged along the road, sometimes disappearing into the hedge accompanied by much rich Anglo-Saxon. Sid Sheldrake was an owner-driver from

Traction engine working on a farm at Bracon Ash – the Contractor is G.J. Desborough of Wattlefield, near Wymondham (who is listed in a 1916 directory). The Wallis Patent engine has the registration AP527 and is powering a reaper. Some of the workers are in uniform – soldiers were sent to help with the harvest during the First World War but this was very unpopular as it kept wages depressed.　(PHOTO CONTRIBUTED BY JOHN BETTS)

Traction engine powering equipment to thresh the corn and build a straw stack on a farm at Swardeston. Quite a crowd turned out for the photo! Contractors would visit several farms in an area, so the same team are likely to have worked in Mulbarton.

(PHOTO CONTRIBUTED BY JOHN BETTS)

Swainsthorpe... Harry Smith from Hapton had about the first of the tractor-drawn tackles. Harry drove a Marshall Diesel with a single horizontal cylinder which bounced when on tick-over. When the going was hard it threw out raw fuel. The tractor did not have the weight of the traction engines, so more winch work was needed – but NO water carting!

From Horse to Horsepower

Until late-Victorian times, the only workers on the farm were people and horses. Gradually more and more machinery was invented for horses to pull, but plenty of farm workers were needed to control them.

The first sign of mechanisation was the steam traction engine. Then came the diesel engine and tractors. The shortage of workers in the First World War – both men and horses – gave a boost to mechanisation and tractors were brought in from America, although horses remained important until well after the Second World War. Chris Mickleburgh worked for Dr Burfield at Kenningham Farm from the age of 11 until he was 14:

During the war, children were allowed off school for 11 half-days in term-time for farm work, and all the *holidays. Dr Burfield kept horses as long as he could – he had eight horses and one tractor, and used horses for ploughing. After the war he'd take his horses to the Norfolk Show at Keswick, all trimmed up with braids and brasses.*

In the late 1940s Clifford Robinson worked for Brigadier Harris when he first left school, and horses were still important on Old Hall Farm. He would water the two Suffolk Punches and the shire horse at the pond by the Old Hall, and take them to Newton Flotman to be shod by Bob Thrower, the farrier. 'The brigadier's racehorses were stabled behind the Old Hall. Thrashing was done down the loke (the track), where the corn was cut and put straight onto the cart.' He remembers the horse that shied, scattering sheaves everywhere. It galloped back to the barn, where the stable door was open – but the cart got wedged!

The 'Ag. Labs' and their Union

The small number of farmers employed a large number of agricultural labourers. In the 1851 census for Mulbarton, 526 inhabitants were living in 124 dwellings. Of the 219 who record an occupation, 97 men are 'Ag. Labs' – agricultural labourers – and a further 11 are general labourers, making up half the workforce. It was the same in 1871 – exactly half the Mulbarton workforce were 'Ag. Labs' As the twentieth century dawns, the proportion begins to dwindle: 78 'Ag. Labs' and four general labourers out of 212 workers in the 1901 census. As Dorothy Tungate recalls, until the 1940s:

... the menfolk mostly worked on the land, sugar beet being mainly a crop after the corn harvest was finished, pulled by hand by rows of men with hessian bags tied round their legs in wet weather, and earlier on when young plants were 'singled' by hand – a back-breaking job I fear in all weathers.

Men and boys with their pitchforks for the hay harvest, about 1936. Left to right: *Mr Beaumont, Mr Kedge, William Stackyard, Roger Brewington – others not known.* (PHOTO CONTRIBUTED BY EVELYN SMITH, NÉE STACKYARD)

Then mechanisation began to take over from the labourers, and today the remaining farms are worked by their owners with, literally, one or two highly skilled workers.

Agricultural labourers always had to cope with long hours of hard work for low wages. If they complained, they risked losing their jobs and tied cottages. During the First World War farm workers were in a strong position to negotiate for better wages and conditions: both labour and farm horses were in short supply due to the war, and there had been a series of poor harvests. A strike threat in 1915 led to an historic meeting between representatives of the Union of Agricultural Labourers and farmers, promising a wage rise and union recognition. In August 1917 the Corn Production Act led to guaranteed minimum prices for six years, a minimum wage for farm workers of 25s. a week and an Agricultural Wages Board with representatives of both employers and workers.

George Edwards, from Fakenham, was President of the National Union of Agricultural Labourers until

Agricultural Labourers' Union meeting at Mulbarton on 15 July 1917. The procession from the World's End area passes the chapel, Parish Hall, Post Office and pond, with band and banners, on its way to the Common.
(PHOTO CONTRIBUTED BY IRIS FROST)

Agricultural Labourers' Union meeting on Mulbarton Common on 15 July 1917. VIPs (probably including George Edwards) sit on a hay-wain. Were the soldiers there to keep the peace? In the distance (right) is the school. (PHOTO CONTRIBUTED BY IRIS FROST)

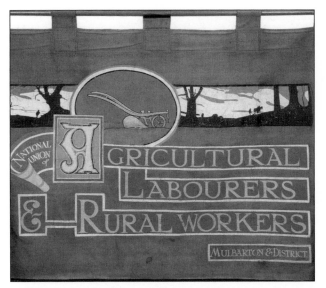

Banner of the Mulbarton Branch of the National Union of Agricultural Labourers and Rural Workers, which is now stored in the Gressenhall Museum of Norfolk Life.

(PHOTO CONTRIBUTED BY JOHN BETTS)

1928. He had been a farm worker himself and, campaigning tirelessly during the First World War, was nicknamed 'the farm worker's friend'. He frequently toured South Norfolk speaking at workers' rallies, and Mulbarton Common was a favourite venue. People came from far and wide: Roy Riches of Starston, near Harleston, writes:

I well remember going to his [George Edwards's] meetings on a Sunday on Mulbarton Common and Burston Green as well as other places. This poor under-sized man was very religious; he was a Primitive Methodist and always opened and closed his meetings with a prayer and a hymn with a local Silver Band providing the music and in this area it was mostly the New Buckenham Silver Band. Many of the men and women who followed George Edwards were also Methodists.

Cynthia Goward, wife of the Mulbarton blacksmith, spoke on Radio Norfolk about a 'Labour Conference' [sic] that was held every year on the Common for farm labourers on a Sunday afternoon and evening: 'I remember George Edwards spoke there once.' Nesda Gray remembered:

The first Sunday in July every year was a big day called Demonstration Sunday. The New Buckenham Band would play and march from the Swardeston Dog [the pub] to Mulbarton Common for a big meeting. Mr Emms and his three sons all played in the band – they lived in Birchfield Lane. At 8 o'clock most of the crowd would drift to the World's End or Tradesman's Arms.

These rallies continued into the 1960s: the Mulbarton branch had its own banner.

The Fairmans of Malthouse Farm

The Malthouse is opposite the south-west corner of Mulbarton Common. During its history it has been a house plus malt house; a separate house and a farmhouse; and one house – as today (Chapters 7 and 9). From the 1860s to the 1880s Samuel Fiddymont lived and farmed there. He owned 110 acres and, according to the 1871 census, employed three men and three boys. The Fiddymonts and the Fairmans were large families from East Carleton and Intwood, and two Fairman brothers married two Fiddymont sisters.

James Fairman (born 1821) married Mary-Anne Fiddymont (born 1824) and took over the Malthouse. Their fifth child, Anna Fairman (1857–1956), remembered newspaper accounts of the American Civil War and the assassination of Abraham Lincoln, which she read to her father when she was young and his eyesight was failing. After working in Wales as companion to Mrs Douglas Pennant of Penrhyn Castle, she returned when her mother died and her father's health failed in order to carry on the family farm. In the 1901 census she and her elder sister, Jane, gave their occupation as 'Agriculturalistic'! Anna Fairman sold Malthouse Farm to her nephew, Arthur William Fairman (1879–1942), son of her brother Samuel, who was farming there by 1908, and is later described as 'cattle-dealer and butcher'. He ran a very successful business, selecting cattle in Scotland and Ireland as well as locally and supplying meat to some top London hotels. A shed that still stands in the grounds was the slaughterhouse. For some years he also farmed Curzon Hall Farm, East Carleton (187 acres), and the land of Paddock Farm, which was taken over by his brother, Herbert James Fairman (1884–1943).

Arthur Fairman died in 1942 and in a newspaper obituary it states that he farmed Malthouse Farm for 35 years and worked until three weeks before his death at the age of 62. His brother, Herbert, gave up

Malthouse Farmhouse around 1901, when it was owned and run by Anna Fairman and her sister Jane.

(PHOTO CONTRIBUTED BY ELIZABETH CLIFFE)

The wedding of Arthur Fairman (of Malthouse Farm, Mulbarton) to Gladys Scales of City Road, Norwich (his second wife) on 3 March 1925 at East Carleton Church, was followed by a reception at his brother's home, Paddock Farm. Left to right, back row: ?, ?, Herbert Scales, Arthur William Fairman (bridegroom), Gladys Scales (bride), Herbert James Fairman (brother of bridegroom, father of Cyril), Alice Fairman (wife of Herbert), ?; front row: Margaret Scales, Elsie Scales, ?, Olive Joyce Fairman (daughter of Herbert, sister of Cyril), 'Aunt May', Laura Scales (mother of Gladys), ?.

Left: Anna Fairman on her 90th birthday in July 1947. She died shortly before her 100th birthday.

(PHOTOS CONTRIBUTED BY INGRID FAIRMAN)

Paddock Farm and moved to Malthouse Farm but died in 1943. The farm and wholesale business, with its abattoir and butchery, then passed to Cyril Fairman (1916–99), son of Herbert and Alice (née Fairman – Herbert married his cousin). After the war, his great-aunt Anna returned to live at the Malthouse, too. Cyril is remembered in the village for his work with Scouts, with the Players and with other organisations (Chapter 3), and for his alsatians, Stella and Solo. He added battery chicken houses to the business. John Rumball remembers:

I think there were two sheds in 1946 – must have been half a hundred hens; I remember the butcher hanging up, say, 40 hens (when they no longer produced) by their feet on the fence and slitting their throats… When the butcher killed the bullocks I was not allowed to watch. Jack Landamore made butter from two Jersey cows he milked. The cream was separated by an Alfa-Laval separator and I remember it was hard work turning the machine. The cream was then put into a wooden churn which was then turned by hand supported on a cradle. A small glass window enabled it to be watched as it thickened. Butter pats were then used with salt to form the blocks. Washing up these

separator fins and barrel took an hour… My grand-mother, Lily Rumball, was his housekeeper in the mid-'70s. I remember Cyril used to throw dinner parties about every six weeks and the house ate the fat of the land, as you can imagine from the resources to hand!

Cyril gave up the farm in the 1970s and moved from Mulbarton to run the Cliff Hotel, Gorleston, and the Brunswick Hotel, Great Yarmouth, and Jack Landamore went to be chef.

Lodge Farm

Lodge Farm (now Willow Grange) is in Rectory Lane next to The Lodge, and has been associated with that house for centuries (Chapter 9). On the 1841 Tithe Map the narrow house is aligned north–south, which can still be seen today as the older part of the building. It was probably soon afterwards that a large and much grander extension was added and a new and more splendid entry was made in this south-facing side.

The farmhouse and farm probably remained in the ownership of The Lodge, but were leased out separately. Randall King was the tenant farmer from

Seen here in January 2005, the imposing south-facing front of Lodge Farm was probably a late-Georgian addition to an older farmhouse. It has been renamed 'Willow Grange'. In the distance (far left) is part of 'The Lodge'.

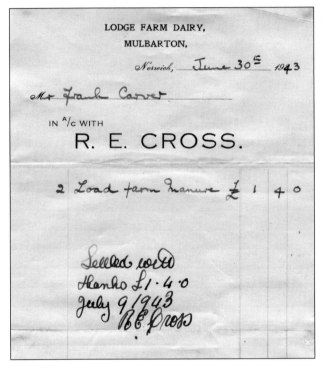

Lodge Farm Dairy: a bill from R.E. Cross for two loads of farm manure for £1.4s.0d. sent to Frank Carver, market gardener of Norwich Road. (CONTRIBUTED BY VIC GRAY)

at least 1864 to 1890. In the 1871 census he is described as 'Farmer of 260 acres employing 10 men, 3 boys, 1 woman.' Then came James William Hill, remembered in the village for buying the 'Rent Charge' of the Parish (Wingfield) Hall and handing the Hall to the Parish (Chapter 3). His wife, Mary, continued to run the farm after his death in 1918. Then came Ralph Ernest Cross, who moved from the Old Hall. He was a churchwarden, and Evelyn Smith remembers that he and his wife came to church in a pony and trap.

During Mr Cross's time, there was a foot-and-mouth outbreak on Lodge Farm, around 1933–34. Rene Carlton (née Hammond) remembers:

My parents lived in Rectory Lane and my father was cowman for Mr Cross. There was a foot-and-mouth outbreak there when I was about 10 or 11. There was a disinfectant dip at the entry and a policeman on duty at the gate. Once the men were on the farm they couldn't leave till the end of the day. I'd go up to the gate to run errands for them – I'd go down to the Tradesman's for beer and cigarettes. The cows had to be slaughtered and they dug a huge pit to bury them. There's a small wood on it now.

The Lodge and Lodge Farm were sold by auction in 1948, when the farm was described as 'the Deep Soil Well-Farmed Residential Agricultural Occupation.' The farmland stretched to south of The Rosary and east of Shotesham Lane. It seems that Mr R. Cross continued to live in the farmhouse and farm the land. In 1958 Brigadier Harris of Swardeston House bought Lodge Farm from Ralph Cross's widow, adding the land to what he already owned from Swardeston House, plus the land that was once attached to Hall Farm and Malthouse Farm, Mulbarton. Brigadier and Mrs Harris died within 48 hours of each other in 1979, and the following year his estate was put up for sale by Irelands, auctioneers – their family firm. Some of the land is now owned by meat wholesaler Barry Brooks of 'The Woodlands', Long Lane, who has established a number of Stewardship paths under an environment-friendly government (DEFRA) scheme.

Following the sale, Lodge Farm and its land were reunited with The Lodge next door, and Mr A. Trafford lived in the house until 2004. Many Mulbarton children have walked along Rectory Lane to see the donkeys in the paddock! In July 2004 Lodge Farm house was up for sale again, but without the farmland. It was described as 'A magnificent 18th Century farmhouse… set in 2 acres.' The asking price was £795,000 – and the new owners renamed it 'Willow Grange'.

Farming at Lodge Farm, 1960–80

Peter Lockhart lived at Lodge Farm as manager of the 511 acres (207 hectares). He is remembered in the village as a former Parish Council chairman, who was very involved in the regeneration of Mulbarton Common and other projects. In his time, much of the land was used for the usual arable crops – barley, wheat and sugar beet:

At first, the sugar beet was still 'singled' and 'topped' by hand – a back-breaking job in all weathers. A considerable acreage of peas and dwarf beans were grown for Birds Eye – up to 100 acres at one time, but this was reduced to 50–60 acres. The peas were harvested mechanically, and a group of farms in the area co-operated to share the necessary machinery. The crop had to be harvested exactly when Birds Eye directed, and to get it to the factory farm-fresh the harvesters worked day and night. The beans were picked by hand – a gang of about 20 ladies from the village were 'on call' to harvest the crop. These ladies also harvested the broad beans that were sold off the farm, and the blackcurrants grown in two fields on either side of Rectory Lane. These were sold to Norfolk Fruit Growers at Wroxham.'

About 150 cattle were kept in sheds at the east end of Rectory Lane (where the farm machinery stores now stand) and were fattened for market. Through the winter, 400–500 sheep were brought in for winter fattening and lambing – though lambing was stopped when the work became too much. There were three house cows by Lodge farmhouse, and Mrs Lockhart remembers making butter along with her other work of supervising the women workers and paying their wages.

Old Hall Farm

Mulbarton Old Hall is behind the huge tithe barn that faces the Common. Although owned by successive lords of the manor, it was let out to tenants. There are references to a farm here in Elizabethan times: the 'Last Will and Testament of John Husbande, one time farmer of The Hall', dated 1574, is in the Norfolk Records Office. In the seventeenth century, Henry Hartstong, gent., was 'sometime farmer at Mulbarton Hall' until he died in 1631. His daughter, Elizabeth, married Revd Anthony Frere, Rector of Mulbarton (Chapter 5).

John Lain was there in 1851, employing ten labourers on 230 acres. He seems to have been followed by William Riches (known to be there 1864–76) and then the Draper family from at least 1883. There may well be a family connection

The Draper family standing by the porch of Old Hall farm-house, around 1900.

(PHOTO CONTRIBUTED BY MARY MELLOR)

The long barn south of the church was built for the manor, or Old Hall Farm. Shown here in 1975, before it was converted first into a kitchen and bathroom showroom and later into a car restoration business (Chapter 7).

(PHOTO: DAVID WRIGHT)

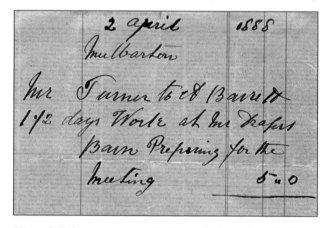

Wage bill for preparing Mr Draper's barn (i.e. the Long Barn) in 1888. On 2 April, Mr Turner paid A. Barrett 5s. for one-and-a-half days work preparing for 'the meeting'. If only we knew what meeting!

(CONTRIBUTED BY MULBARTON MIDDLE SCHOOL)

between William Riches and John Riches Draper. Mr Draper was a governor of Mulbarton School and his death, in April 1906, is recorded in the school log-book. Mrs Ann Mary Draper continued the tenancy, which was due up at Michaelmas 1921.

Old Hall Farm was one of five farms for the sale in 1920 as part of the East Carleton estate:

A Very Valuable Corn Growing Farm... bounded on the west by the Common, on the East with frontage to the road to Swainsthorpe Station and intersected by its own farm road. It extends to an area of about 229 acres.

Besides the house and its outbuildings there were:

Exceptionally Well-built Farm Buildings: Ancient Tithe Barn (about 140 ft long) divided into hay barn, chaff cutting shed, corn barn, stable for four. Also another stable with loft above, cart shed, cart horse stables (for eleven horses), cow houses and sheds, thatched bullock shed and yard, another bullock shed, cattle yard, turnip sheds, cart shed, implement shed.

Also listed are 18 arable fields, three pastures and two orchards.

The purchaser was the Cross family of Cross & Co. (Seed, Oil Cake, Manure and Coal Merchants of 35 Cattle Market Street, Norwich). Ralph Cross was at Hall Farm in 1922, when he employed a farm bailiff, William Buttle. He had what is now Harvest House built for Mr Cushion, his farm foreman. Ralph Cross moved to Lodge Farm, from where he continued to farm the land, and Herbert E. Cross(e) moved into the Old Hall house.

Smallholders

Most country families grew their own fruit and vegetables and kept a few chickens. People with grazing rights on the Common might keep cows. Selling the surplus produce brought in welcome extra cash. When the Church Glebe and large estates were sold after the First World War, more people had the chance to become landowners. The East Carleton estate sale in 1920 included

…numerous small-holdings of attractive and convenient sizes, with Houses and Buildings, Valuable Accommodation lands, Mixed Woodlands, Productive Market Gardens

The estate sale brought a large amount of land in Mulbarton onto the market, and many existing tenants took the chance to buy the freehold to their property.

Some land to the west and south of the Common became a freehold dairy farm, which was sold again in December 1932 after its owner's death. The auction poster tells us that 'a retail milk business, averaging 80–100 gallons weekly, has for some years past been carried on at these', and that the premises are 'eminently suitable for a Butcher, Dairyman or for residential purposes.' It was bought by W. Lincoln, dairy farmer, who sold milk, butter and cream cheese around the village. His was the egg depot, too, grandly called National Farm Packers. After he died his widow, Olive (née Kedge), carried on the business with the help of her children (Chapter 8). Their cob barn is considered a rare enough building to warrant being listed, and both this and the dairy farmhouse have been renovated recently 'for residential purposes'.

Other smallholders included Jack Stackyard, who lived in The Rosery and kept his cows on the Common. 'He'd bike round the village with a can of milk on the handlebars and serve it out with a ladle. His hands and arms always looked so clean.' Ambrose Broom lived in an old railway carriage off Long Lane – 'he kept animals more for a hobby and sold eggs.'

Fruit and Flowers

Mulbarton is only five miles from Norwich and has probably supplied produce to the city for centuries. An inventory of the belongings of Richard Pitcher, 'Husbandman' of Mulbarton, who died in 1591, lists

Above: *Dairy Farmhouse before renovation, with the cob barn beyond, about 1987.* (Photo: Robin Clayton)

Left: *Poster advertising the auction of Dairy Farm, Mulbarton, in December 1932 with details of four lots. The house was west of the Common (now 'Dairy Farmhouse') and some of the land was beside Birchfield Lane.*

(Poster in collection of the Gressenhall Museum of Norfolk Life, photographed with librarian's permission)

93

A field of flowers at Mr Carver's market garden, near what is now the vet's surgery, c.1965.

(PHOTO CONTRIBUTED BY VIC GRAY)

Working in the greenhouse at Mr Carver's market garden.

(PHOTO CONTRIBUTED BY VIC GRAY)

Nesda Gray and her son, Vic Gray, packing flowers for markets in London and the Midlands, c.1965.

(PHOTO CONTRIBUTED BY VIC GRAY)

apples and other fruit among his crops. John Neale, who died in 1716, left:

In the seller... 18 barrells [sic] of cider... 7 layer beds, 2 dozen bottles; In the stamping house: 3 cyder presses... 8 tubs... stamping bottles... 1 spade and 2 combs of apples... 7 bills, 7 bad debts...

This suggests quite a cider-making enterprise, probably using local fruit and selling to Norwich as well as locally.

Market gardening became an important business in the area when good train services from Swainsthorpe and Hethersett Stations opened up the markets in London, the Midlands and Manchester. Flowers picked in the morning were put on an early afternoon train to be at the wholesale markets for the 4a.m. auction and with retailers soon afterwards. Mike Lambert remembers helping Mr Bobbin take boxes of flowers for the Midlands

and Manchester to Hethersett to be loaded onto a freight train from Norwich. If the train was late the station staff would shout to them to hurry so as not to delay the following passenger train, as there was no passing loop.

A number of smallholders in the parish were market gardeners before and just after the Second World War. Allens, 'Rose Growers and Nurserymen', ran Rosery Nursery, east of Long Lane (now the Bluebell Road estate). Their head office was in Bowthorpe, Norwich, and they had an extensive catalogue of roses. They won a gold medal for their roses at the Chelsea Flower Show in 1924. 'Rosery Nursery' is clearly marked on older Ordnance Survey maps. Mr Hooney had greenhouses at the corner of Rectory Lane and Long Lane and described himself as 'Florist and Rose Expert' in his advert in the Mulbarton parish magazine. 'A nice nursery for tomatoes and cucumbers,' say local people, who remember the 'Stephenson's Rocket type engine' used to steam-sterilise the greenhouses during the winter. Mrs Hooney made the birthday posies in the early days of the Women's Insititute. Later, the holding was bought by Pordage & Co., Wholesale Greengrocers. The greenhouses were there until around 1974, when the land was sold for housing.

William (Billy) Emms's market garden in Birchfield Lane had large greenhouses for flowers, fruit and vegetables. Brenda Ford (née Collins) remembers:

My mother used to buy tomatoes from Mrs Emms. She had a nursery business along Birchfield Lane and there were several glasshouses where she grew amongst other things tomatoes. She had a pet monkey in her front garden which always fascinated me as a child, but I was not allowed to touch it as it was of uncertain temperament.

The Great Fire of Mulbarton: Mr and Mrs Frank Carver look at the remains of their thatched cottage on Norwich Road, Mulbarton. Their daughter Nesda Gray (née Carver) wrote in 1988: 'My mother was born in Orchard House in 1887 and I was born there in 1914 and my sister in 1921. In 1926, a thrashing engine [traction engine] coaling up to climb the hill set the thatched roof on fire with sparks. It was rebuilt with a tiled roof...'

(PHOTO CONTRIBUTED BY VIC GRAY)

This photo is labelled 'Family at Hill House, 13 March 1917'. The Muskett family lived at Hill House, the thatched cottage on Norwich Road. Frederick and Alice Muskett ran a market garden and were tenants of the East Carleton estate until they were able to buy the property in 1920. (CONTRIBUTED BY TERRY BURCHELL,

FROM PHILIP STANDLEY'S COLLECTION)

The thatched roof of Hill House caught fire in 2005 – bringing to mind the fire at the next-door house, the Carver family's home, in 1926 (see left). (PHOTO: DAVID WICK)

Eleanor and Frank Carver in the ruins of their home in Norwich Road after it was burnt down. Although the exterior walls were of brick, the interior walls were made of timber infilled with clay lump.

(PHOTO CONTRIBUTED BY VIC GRAY)

The well by the Emms's cottage, next to the road, did not provide enough water for the greenhouses, so a deep bore was put down and a windpump filled the tank, installed on a tower to give a head of water. After Mr Emms died, his property and its entire contents were auctioned in July 1969, in 255 lots – including his wonderful collection of woodworking tools. The cottage was pulled down and new bungalows built (Chapter 11). George Whitmore took on the nursery as a sideline to his normal work and Mr Woolnough still sells his surplus produce from the same bungalow near the Post Office. Nearby, Mr Ladbrook senr bought a small piece of land south of the Common, where he had a large greenhouse to grow flowers for drying, which were sent to London by train. Gradually, the land was divided into plots for bungalows.

North of the old village, along the road to Norwich, were several market gardens. The people here were tenants of the Stewards of East Carleton

Manor until the 1920 estate sale, when they were able to buy the freehold of their property. Frank Carver's cottage, 'The Thatched House', and land near what is now the vet's surgery were Lot 16 of the 1920 estate sale. The house had to be rebuilt after a disastrous fire caused by sparks from a traction engine. Nesda Gray (née Carver) wrote: '... It was rebuilt and my father carried on as Market Gardener and 'flowerist'. He also had 7 acres of fruit trees, so he was well-known in the "Early Market".' Their grandson, Vic Gray, still has greenhouses and runs a small nursery on the opposite side of the road.

North of Mr Carver's land was Hill House Nursery, run by William Church in the late 1800s. He was followed by Frederick and Alice Muskett, who lived in the quaint thatched cottage. Sadly, their son, Cecil, was killed in 1917 during the First World War (Chapter 10). Their nursery was Lot 15 of the 1920 sale, for which they paid £200 in cash and borrowed the remaining £600 from the Steward estate at 5 per cent interest. Their daughter, Celia, married Tom Bobbin, who took over the land. Subsequently the cottage was sold independently from the land, and history repeated itself when the thatch of Hill House caught fire in a disastrous blaze in autumn 2005.

Fur Farming

Coypu are infamous creatures in East Anglia, but few people know that one of Britain's largest coypu farms was in the valley where the parishes of Mulbarton, Swardeston and East Carleton meet. *Myocastor coypus* is a large South American rodent (up to a metre long from nose to tail) with small eyes, large orange front teeth, a long tail and webbed feet. The reddish- or yellowish-brown hairs of its long, coarse

Charles Schofield feeding coypus in their pen, 1939–40.
(PHOTO CONTRIBUTED BY CLIFFORD ROBINSON)

Charles Schofield feeding his 'pet' coypu.
(PHOTO CONTRIBUTED BY CLIFFORD ROBINSON)

Charles Edgar George Schofield feeding coypus beside the stream at the East Carleton/Swardeston/Mulbarton boundary, 1939–40. Coypus are vegetarian, eating all kinds of water plants.

(PHOTO CONTRIBUTED BY CLIFFORD ROBINSON)

outer coat hide the soft velvety slate-grey under-fur, known as nutria (Spanish for 'otter') in the fur trade. This is the reason why the coypu was introduced into Britain in 1929, when fur farms were set up in Norfolk and elsewhere.

Philip Tindal-Carill-Worsley (1881–1946) had bought East Carleton Manor and saw an opportunity to make a profit from otherwise unproductive land. The river and an area in the valley north of Catbridge Lane were fenced off and pens built to house the creatures. By 1938 he had around 300 animals, looked after by his gamekeeper, Charles Schofield. Despite taking every precaution because of their value, it was inevitable that some coypus managed to escape. John Betts remembers meeting what seemed to him a huge animal with ferocious teeth in Bracon Ash at dusk on his way home from school. He turned tail and ran the long way home! Escaped coypus adapted easily in the wild, where they bred rapidly and caused havoc on Norfolk's waterways by burrowing into river banks. Attractive ransoms were offered for any that were shot or caged, and by the end of 1989 MAFF (now DEFRA) believed coypus were successfully eradicated from East Anglia.

The Hunt and the Shoot

From the school log-book:

1881: Dec. 2nd – Attendance would have been much higher if children had not stayed away in consequence of stag-hunting yesterday afternoon.

1884: Feb. 8th – There was a stag hunt on Tuesday which caused three boys to lose their attendance marks...

When fully mature the coypus were killed, skinned and the pelts carefully graded before being sent to the London market as nutria fur. Here Charles Schofield, gamekeeper, is sorting coypu pelts from the East Carleton Manor fur farm in 1939–40. (PHOTO CONTRIBUTED BY CLIFFORD ROBINSON)

This may well have been the last time deer were hunted in the parish, but fox-hunting continued to be a popular pastime for many riders. The local hunt would meet at the World's End. Hunt hounds were kept at Kenningham Hall farm for a time and Mrs

The bag from the shoot – in the Mulbarton/Bracon Ash area, 1912. The photograph includes: A. Watling (Bracon Ash Post Office), Mr Thompson (Mulbarton Mill), F. Swain (wheelwright and landlord of the Tradesman's Arms), D. Middleton, George ('Waxer') Cooper (mole-catcher of The Rosery), J. Hammond, F. Stubbings (Bracon Ash shopkeeper), A. Feltham, P. Stackyard, W. Devereaux and his two sons. (PHOTO CONTRIBUTED BY JOHN BETTS)

Shooting party in the late 1940s on East Carleton Estate. Left to right: *'Pop' (Fred) Jackson (Paddock Farm, Mulbarton), Reginald Bobbin (Swardeston), Commander Crossley, John Berney, Bill Jackson (Paddock Farm), Richard Berney (Bracon Hall), Fred Jackson, Charles Schofield (gamekeeper, East Carleton Manor), Bob Jackson (Paddock Farm), Charlie Frost (Mulbarton garage), Charles Smith, Alfred Archibald Walker, Peter Tindal-Carill-Worsley (East Carleton Manor).*

(PHOTO CONTRIBUTED BY CLIFFORD ROBINSON)

Eileen Gowing spoke of arranging with staff at Swainsthorpe Station to have horses loaded into horseboxes, which were then attached to a train to travel to a more distant hunt.

Mr Turner's accounts and bills from the 1880s show that he bought his shot and gunpowder and had his guns repaired by a gunmaker in Rampant Horse Street, Norwich. The estates and most of the larger farms had wooded areas where pheasants were bred for shooting. Villagers joined in a shoot with their guns or as beaters.

Vermin needed catching, too. One Mulbarton character in the photo of the 1912 shoot is George ('Waxy') Cooper, molecatcher and warrener, who lived in a cottage in The Rosery. Those who remember him say he used his hands to explain where the moles could be found – one hand always contained his mole-digging 'spud', which swung with alarming speed as he said, 'And there's some more over thar'! At harvest, children went to the harvest field to chase and catch rabbits. In the winter, ferrets and snares were used to catch rabbits – rabbit pie was very popular. Rag and bone men visited the village to buy rabbit and moleskins. During the First

World War, Rat Weeks and Sparrow Clubs were organised to rid the land of pests. In 1920 the Parish Council reported to the War Agricultural Committee that 2,000 rats had been killed in one week.

THE MULBARTON & DISTRICT SPARROW CLUB held its Annual General Meeting on Nov. 19th. In the report it was stated that the Club was responsible for the destruction of 13,765 sparrows in the past year, an increase of over a thousand on last year's record. In the four years of its existence, 49,950 sparrows have been destroyed. This figure gives some idea of the usefulness of the Club and the amount of corn saved for national consumption. Mr Hill, in an interesting speech, pointed out that the rareness of hawks made a Club like this necessary, but that there was no fear of exterminating sparrows, who, though they made great depredations in corn, yet were useful in devouring the seeds of the Common Wire Weed, and so helped farmers.

(East Carleton Magazine, December 1915)

CHAPTER 7

Trades and Tradesmen

A trawl through trade directories, old newspapers and census returns, as well as memories and house deeds, builds up a fascinating picture of a largely self-contained village with skilled craftsmen and their trades in Mulbarton. But all these men have their successors today, as this chapter shows…

The Millers

Mulbarton once had two working windmills – and not many people can spot the remains of either today. One was at the north-west corner of the Common; the other was on the boundary of Mulbarton and Swardeston.

On the 1724 map of Mulbarton, the only drawing of a mill is beside a track that is now The Rosery, but no other trace has been found. The next mention of a mill is a declaration under oath by Thomas Mitchell of Moulton, who 'purchased a windmill then standing in the Parish of Dickleburgh' in 1754 from Amos Potter of Tibenham for £50 and moved it to Mulbarton, where he 'Lodged and Boarded with Several Persons' from Michaelmas to Candlemas (1754–55). He then moved with his family, first to a house 'from William Larter of Mulbarton, Gardiner, at a yearly Rent of Two Pounds and Four Shillings' and then to a house rented from 'Kett of Wymondham' for four guineas, which he was occupying in 1756. Was this the beginning of the mill by the Common?

The Smockmill

The mill of Mill House by the Common is marked on Faden's map of 1797. William Toll appears as 'miller' at Mulbarton in the Poll Books for 1796, 1799 and 1802. Some time after that, Andrew Spratt worked the mill in conjunction with Saxlingham water-mill. He died in February 1824, and both mills were put up for sale by auction in 1825; the Mulbarton mill is described in the *Norfolk Chronicle* of 9 April 1825 as:

Lot 2. All that much admired well built Wind Mill, with patent sails, brick and tiled dwelling house, baking office, granaries, outbuildings, garden and productive orchard adjoining, delightfully situate in the pleasant village of Mulbarton by the side of the valuable Common in that parish and over which it has a right of depasturing and is now in the occupation of Mr. Thomas Spratt.

The Mill is certainly not surpassed by any other Windmill in the county of Norfolk, it stands exceedingly well for Trade and is in the best possible state of repair, drives three pair of stones, has two flour mills, horse mill etc. etc. The orchard contains nearly 2 acres and there are about 100 fruit trees of the best quality planted therein.

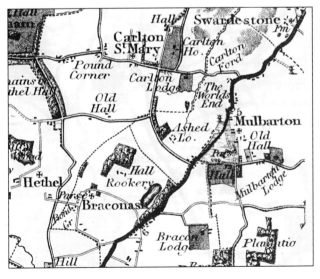

Part of A. Bryant's map of Norfolk as surveyed 1824–26, which clearly shows that Mulbarton had two windmills by the 1820s.

The windmill by the Common was a smock mill. It had a tall, white, 10-sided wooden tower on a two-storey brick base with vertical walls. It was topped with a conical cap and a six-bladed fan which moved round so that the sails faced the wind. Inside there were six floors where grain was ground into flour. This postcard dates from around 1907 – one copy was posted in June 1909.

(PHOTO FROM VILLAGE ARCHIVE)

Mill with chimney and Mill House, c.1907. A steam engine was apparently added in 1883 to keep the mill working when there was no wind. The two men on the windmill are thought to be Mr Thompson and Mr Middleton. The children playing in road are probably the Middleton children from the nearby Post Office.

(Photo contributed by Juliet Amos)

The 'horse mill' presumably refers to a horse walking round and round to turn mill wheels when there was no wind and before steam power was available.

William and Thomas Spratt continued the business, as Thomas signed a notice in the *Norfolk Chronicle* on 24 December 1825 undertaking to use the 'New Imperial Bushell *[sic]*' of 2,218cu.ins from the beginning of 1826. However, they dissolved their partnership in 1828 'by mutual consent', and the following year the mill was for sale again.

At the time of the 1841 Tithe Award, it was owned by Miss Elizabeth Spratt and occupied by Charles Cremer, who is mentioned in a report in the *Norwich Mercury* in August 1843 when the sails were ripped off in a gale:

MULBARTON (re. Storm of 9th August 1843)
Mr Cremer's mill had its sails torn off and then falling on the warehouse adjoining injured it considerably. Mr Cremer's loss is estimated at £300.

From his will, Charles Cremer was evidently related by marriage to the Spratt family.

He stayed at the mill until 1858, and probably retired to be 'a farmer of Bracon Ash' – although he took over the other Mulbarton mill in 1863, and continued to own and rent out both mills. David Blomfield (in 1859), William Howes (from 1863) and Horace Candler worked the mill by the Common until it was offered for sale or to let in the *Norfolk Chronicle* on 22 May 1875:

MULBARTON
To be SOLD or LET, a first class situation as a WIND-

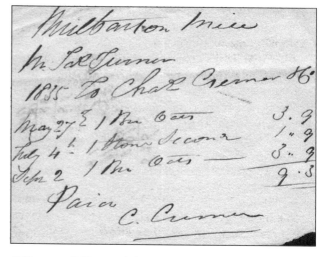

Bill sent to J. Turner (of Paddock Farm) signed by Charles Cremer of the mill by the Common in 1835.

(Contributed by Mulbarton Middle School)

MILL with patent sails, 4 pairs of stones, 1 Flour Mill, with Warehouse attached with 2 Flour Mills, Meal, Corn and Pollard Bins and stowage for a large quantity of goods. A comfortable Dwelling House, Bake office, Granary, 2 Stables and Outbuildings, 2 Gardens, productive Orchard and right of common. The Mill is doing a good business. Possession can be had by next Michaelmas. Apply to C. Cremer, Bracon Ash.

With four pairs of millstones it must have been a busy mill!

In the Poor Rate Assessment book for 1875–76 the owner is Miss Emma Spratt, niece of Charles Cremer's wife. George William Thompson, farmer, appears as the new tenant. By 1884, Alfred Thompson was running the mill – a bill for Mr James Turner for 1884 shows the bill-head changed by hand from G.W. Thompson to A. Thompson. One of two employees in 1893 was William Lant Duffield, who later moved to Mattishall and then to Saxlingham Mill, where Duffield's milling business still exists.

After Emma Spratt died the mill was up for sale again. In the *Norfolk Chronicle*, 1 September 1894:

MULBARTON
The Valuable Property known as Mulbarton Mill, with neat Residence, Gardens, Orchard and Farm Buildings, standing in a good position, with long frontage to the High Road and the Common, with Common Rights of Pasturage.

Messrs. SPELMAN have received instructions from the Executors of the late Miss Emma Spratt to Sell by Auction on Saturday 15 at 3 o'clock at the Royal Hotel, Norwich, the above Estate, now in the occupation of Mr. A. Thompson. The Mill stands well for wind, and with the other buildings is in thorough substantial repair and the total content is about two acres.

Alfred Thompson seems to have bought the property as the sitting tenant. In 1910, according to the *Dereham & Fakenham Times* of 9 July, his mill was struck by lightning:

On Thursday 30th ult. a severe storm passed over Mulbarton and district. The mill at Mulbarton had one of the sails struck and the vanes were shattered, pieces of wood being thrown to a considerable distance. The owner, Mr A. Thompson and his employee, Mr A. Middleton, were working in the mill at the time and were thrown to the ground when the lightning struck the chain which is used inside the mill to pull up the sacks. This is said to be the third time this mill has been struck.

The Mr A. Middleton mentioned is probably related to Mr F. Middleton, postmaster, who moved to

View of the mill from the pond. By 1931 the sails and mill machinery had been dismantled, and a conical roof fitted to seal the mill. (PHOTO FROM VILLAGE ARCHIVE)

The derelict tower of Mulbarton Mill, looking north from the Common in 1934.

(PHOTO CONTRIBUTED BY JUDITH FAIRCLOUGH)

Remains of the base of the chimney of the steam mill adjacent to the windmill, in the Mill House garden.

(BY KIND PERMISSION OF DR AND MRS FAIRCLOUGH)

Mulbarton in 1899 and had a substantial house built next to Mill House as his home and the village Post Office (Chapter 8).

In the early days of the Second World War, when there was some paranoia about a possible enemy invasion, the mill tower and church tower were considered ideal landmarks to guide aircraft to land on Mulbarton Common, so the wooden tower of the mill was demolished, but the chimney remained.

Only the Mill House remains today, along with the base of the chimney. In a very dry year, the outline of the foundation of the windmill reappears in the parched lawn, and one of the French millstones is on the patio. The back part of the house was a simple cottage to which the elegant front was added, probably early in the nineteenth century. The old bake-house, whose chimney can be seen on some old photos, survives as an additional room, but the ovens were removed in the late 1970s. A small building on the southern boundary is a former forge, still with its fireplace and chimney.

The Tower Mill

Mulbarton's other mill is east of the Norwich Road on the border with Swardeston parish. It is first shown on Bryant's Map of Norfolk, surveyed in 1824–26, and the title deeds to the Mill House indicate that the land was once part of the estate of 'John Steward of the City of Norwich Esq.' In August 1822 one strip amounting to 3 roods 19 perches was transferred to 'Mr John Tann of that said City, Bricklayer... upon which he is erecting a Corn Wind Mill', which was probably built in 1823. John Tann must have been a good bricklayer if he built it himself – the tower stands firm today! An advert in the Norfolk Chronicle, 22 September 1827 for an auction sale gives details of the windmill recently built:

Desirable Situation for a Miller, Baker and Confectioner By Mr JOHN CULLEY At the Bell Inn, Orford Hill on

The 'tower mill' at the Mulbarton/Swardeston boundary, was 27 feet high with only three floors. It had two doors on the ground floor – a safety precaution as the sails came to within a few feet of the ground. When it was working, this flourmill had four double-shuttered sails that had to be set by hand, a boat-shaped cap, a six-bladed fan and two pairs of stones. (PHOTO CONTRIBUTED BY MICHAEL LAMBERT)

Saturday October 6, 1827 at 5 o'clock.
Lot 1. A Capital Brick TOWER WINDMILL lately erected, with two pair of stones, flour mill and going geers [sic] complete in excellent repair, also a substantial Dwelling house and 3 roods and 19 perches of Land. All the above premises are situate in Mulbarton in Norfolk, are Freehold, land tax redeemed and are now in the occupation of Mr Samuel Burrell...

The occupant's name is misspelt – it was Samuel Barrell, described as 'Mulbarton Miller' on a later title deed. He seems to have bought the 'cottage with the barn, granary, stables and outbuildings' and also that 'Wind Corn Mill with the apparatus thereto belonging and the parcel of freehold land' from John Tann in April 1833, and paid further money to Edward Steward for the freehold. At the same time, John Tann also sold two cottages in Mulbarton with 'one acre of land (more or less)... now occupied by Robert Daines and William Barrell.' In the 1841 Tithe Award, Samuel Barrell is listed as owner and occupier. He worked the mill until about 1846 and remained the owner until he died in 1862/63. William Barrell was miller from 1853 to 1859 or later.

In May 1863 the documents for the house suggest that everything was sold to the owner of the smock mill by the Common, 'Charles Cremer of Bracon Ash, farmer':

... cottage, barn, granaries... Wind Corn Mill with the sails, cloths, wheels, stones, running and going gears, scales, weights, goods and chattels, appendages and appurtenants thereto belong. And the piece or parcel of freehold land formerly of John Cann [should be Tann] and then late of the said Samuel Barrell deceased in Mulbarton... 3 roods and 19 perches.

William Crane, miller 1863–64, advertised for 'a Single Man to take charge of a TOWER MILL' in the *Norfolk News*. A few months later he advertised the mill 'with comfortable Dwelling House, Granaries and Outbuildings now in Full Trade' to let. The mill was taken on by Robert Ellis (1865–68), followed by William Smith (1872–83), who seems to have introduced steam power.

The owner, Charles Cremer, died at Bracon Ash on 21 January 1886, and his will was proved two months later. His niece, Sarah Cremer, inherited the mill and had 'exclusive enjoyment of the rents and profits thereof since the death of Charles Cremer.' How much income she enjoyed is uncertain, for George Kent took on this mill from 1888 until he was declared bankrupt in 1890.

Huggins and Hart are listed as millers in 1892 (with William George Huggins listed as a corn merchant as well from 1896 to 1900) and Henry Hart on his own from 1904 to at least 1911. He is named as the occupant in January 1904, when Sarah Cremer and Frederick Charles Myhill jointly sold the 'house,

The brick tower mill can be seen in the distance, to the left of Mr Bobbin and his horse, c.1920.

(PHOTO CONTRIBUTED BY MICHAEL LAMBERT)

Remains of the tower mill (near Swardeston boundary) at the end of the garden of the Mill House.

(BY KIND PERMISSION OF MICHAEL LAMBERT)

Interior of the tower mill today showing one of the old floor levels and remains of timbers.

(BY KIND PERMISSION OF MICHAEL LAMBERT)

barn, stable, outbuildings, Windmill, machinery, fixtures and gears' to William Spurgeon of No. 9 Mill Close, Lakenham, Norwich for £225.

In November 1911 William Spurgeon sold the property – still occupied by Henry Hart – to Alfred Thompson, owner of the other Mulbarton windmill by the Common. Alfred Thompson seems to have worked both mills for a time. In October 1922 he sold it to Mrs H. Carver, but by then the mill was out of use. It was derelict by 1926 and was hardly mentioned when it was sold 'by Mr H.H. CARVER, who is giving up housekeeping.'

The sale to H.E. Philpot was completed in June 1926, when the mill still had its fantail and four sails without shutters. It was sold again in June 1934 to J.V.A. Long; in May 1936 to Mrs M.A.D.H.L. Fisher-Rowe; in December 1944 to W.M. Jewson; and on his death the house and land were bought from his executors by the present owners in May 1952.

The Maltster

The Malthouse is opposite the south-west corner of Mulbarton Common. The tall part of the house was the Malthouse itself, which probably dates from the early-nineteenth century. When a malthouse, the tall building had floors approximately 5ft apart, on which barley was spread out, either on tiles with air-holes or on slats to ferment. The tall chimney belongs to the furnace, remnants of which are in the current cellar. A few distinctive perforated clay tiles were found when the house was renovated by Cyril Fairman and were identified as malting tiles by the Norfolk Museums Service.

Trade directories list several 'maltsters' in Mulbarton. In 1847 an item in the *Norfolk Chronicle* on

A view of the south-west corner of the Common with the (tall) Malthouse and Malthouse Farm. To the left is the terrace that incorporated the Tradesman's Arms and the building on the edge of the Common that was once a school building (far left). This postcard was posted on 2 September 1926, and on the back was written: 'c/o Mrs Lansdell, Thorpe House, Mulbarton… Auntie's house is the tall one behind the signpost.' This was then a separate house from the (lower) Malthouse Farmhouse.

(PHOTO CONTRIBUTED BY JO DAYNES)

16 October announced that Mr Charles Cremer of the mill by the Common had taken over the maltster's business at the southern end of the Common.

C. Cremer, Miller and Maltster, Mulbarton
Having engaged the old established Malting Business at Mulbarton (many years in the occupation of Mr Robert Mantes) begs to solicit the favour of a continuance of such Customers who have hitherto dealt there and of the public in general, who will oblige him with their Orders, assuring them that they may rely upon having Malt and Hops of the first rate quality.

Robert Mann (misprinted 'Robert Mantes') is listed as 'Maltster' in 1836 and in the Tithe Apportionment survey. He owned not only the Malthouse but the farm and most other property in that south-east corner of Mulbarton. Mr Cremer presumably had either competition or help from 'James Windett, Maltster and Farmer', who is listed in 1845. Mr Cremer retired in 1858, and it is probably soon afterwards that there were plans to rebuild the maltings into a Georgian-style residence, which were later adapted to convert the building itself into the three-storey house which still stands (Chapter 6).

The Carpenter

In the 1851 census, 11 men give their occupations as 'carpenter'; in 1871 ten men and in 1901 six men. Many of these will have worked for other people – the trade directories from 1845 only list one 'Carpenter' for Mulbarton.

The house on the west side of the Common was appropriately renamed 'Carpenters' – it has a long association with people of that trade. The first recorded tenant is Shelton Cullingford (carpenter) of Bungay and Amy, his wife, who took on the copyhold tenancy in April 1794. They were followed by a schoolmaster, whose widow Elizabeth married William Ollett (carpenter) of Mulbarton, who took on the tenancy in 1814. On 4 June 1821 he asked the

Cottages west of the Common with the carpenter's house and workshop on the right, date unknown. Mr Herbert Lake had his carpentry business there, including coffin-making, and was the local undertaker.

(Contributed by Terry Burchell, from Philip Standley's collection)

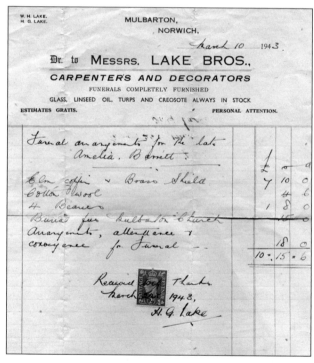

Receipt from Lake Brothers, carpenters and undertakers, for funeral arrangements, 1943. Note the range of items they sell! (Contributed by Bryan Tungate)

Manor Court if he could enclose a parcel of land (possibly common land) about 7 yards by 15 yards on the south side of his dwelling house, dig a sawpit and erect a shed over it. He was allowed to do this – at an annual rent of 2s.6d. Elizabeth Ollett died in 1828, her husband William in 1851 and none of their three children took on the tenancy.

The next known tradesman to live at 'Carpenters' was Alfred Banham (plumber and glazier), who is listed in the 1869 *Post Office Directory*, along with Joshua Banham, carpenter, who lived nearby. He was resident in 1873 when 'Carpenters' and other

Aerial view of 'Carpenters', with other houses to the west of the Common behind, June 1986.

(Photo: David and Jill Wright)

houses were auctioned and he bought his house for £160 and also bought his brother's house, amalgamating some of the land and sheds. Alfred Banham sold the freehold to Henry Lake in April 1910. Henry Lake is listed as 'carpenter' in the 1922 *Kelly's Directory*. He is often mentioned in the school log-book for mending the stove, gutters, downpipes and leaks in the roof, as well as assorted carpentry jobs. His sons, William and Herbert, continued the business. William (Billy) Lake lived at 'Carpenters' and his brother Herbert lived nearby at 'The Nook'. They ran a carpentry business jointly, did painting and decorating and were also the village undertakers:

Along the side of the Common lived the Lake brothers, carpenters and undertakers. When delivering a coffin, they would rush it through the village on a two-wheeled barrow. Country people were 'laid' in the parlour in their own homes and were either carried by bearers or made their last journey on a horse-drawn cart. When a funeral took place, curtains along the route were drawn tight and those who saw the cortège stood facing, men bare-headed.

Tony Kent

In later years there was a woodyard in the village. Jordan's sawmill was on old nursery land east of Long Lane and gave its name to Woodyard Close. The owners also had a sawmill at Cringleford, which later became the Jewson's site. Peter Lincoln remembers a neighbour, Mr Rix, who lived in a cottage near the dairy farm (now demolished), who walked to and from Cringleford every day, six days a week, to work at the woodyard there.

The Blacksmith

There was probably more than one forge in Mulbarton – the windmill near the Common certainly had its own forge. But the building remembered as the blacksmith's shop is an elegant brick building, almost opposite the turning to East Carleton, which probably dates from around 1830. It had stabling for waiting horses in one wing, an enclosed yard, two forges and workshops. Next door is Forge Cottage, a fine thatched house which is technically in Bracon Ash parish. Older residents have vivid memories of Billy Goward at the forge: 'A colourful place – the sparks and the language...' 'I spent hours there in the winter, watching the bellows and the two big fires...'

William ('Billy') Goward worked with and then took over from his father, George. Until he moved to Forge Cottage he lived in one of a pair of cottages next to the World's End that is now one house, Toad Hall. In 1940 he married Cynthia Turner, a mental health nurse who was born and brought up in Swardeston and had served with the Red Cross in Greece and Turkey in the First World War. The main work at the forge was shoeing cart horses and

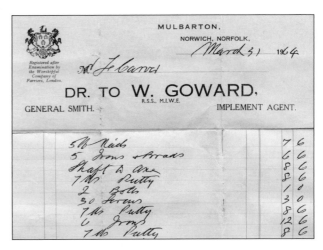

Bill from W. (Billy) Goward, blacksmith, dated 1964, shortly before the business closed for ever.

(CONTRIBUTED BY VIC GRAY)

William ('Billy') Goward, the blacksmith (centre), *relaxing with Charlie Frost* (left) *and Mr Wasey in the latter's garden near the World's End, now the cottage known as 'Toad Hall' (date unknown).* (CONTRIBUTED BY ENID FOX)

The former forge, opposite East Carleton Road. The last blacksmith was Billy Goward, whose widow sold much of the land (including the orchard) for building Forge Orchards and three houses facing the Common.

(PHOTO: JILL WRIGHT)

105

Certificates from the old forge, awarded to the blacksmith. Left are two certificates of the Mustad Horse Nail Co. Right are certificates from the 'Royal Norfolk Summer Show', top right 1925 at King's Lynn, bottom right, 1928 at Norwich.

putting metal tyres on wooden wheels. During the Second World War Mrs Goward helped her husband at the forge, as there was a shortage of labour. On a Radio Norfolk programme in 1982 she described the wheels being brought across the road from the wheelwright's opposite to be tyred:

They were laid on a special platform in the yard; the tyres were made to fit; then heated until red-hot and levered onto the wheels... My husband was the first man to introduce acetylene welding in the Eastern Counties and won gold medals for horse-shoeing.

He was elected Chairman of the Master Farriers' Association in the Eastern Counties, attended annual conferences and meetings around the country, and was presented to King George VI at the Norfolk Show at Keswick.

The forge closed in the mid-1960s; Billy Goward died on 30 December 1968. The land was sold for housing and Mrs Goward had a bungalow built for herself on the corner of Forge Orchards facing the Common. The forge itself is open on Sundays as an antiques centre.

Billy's father, George Goward, was blacksmith from around 1912. Some of the certificates he won at the Norfolk Show are still in the smithy. George Goward was a tenant of the Steward family of East Carleton Manor until the estate was put up for sale in 1920. He took the opportunity to buy the freehold of the property described in the auction handbook as:

LOT 20: The Picturesque Cottage and Smithy with Pasture and Arable Land attached... Situated on Mulbarton Common with frontage to the main road and in the Parishes of Mulbarton and Bracon Ash. The Cottage is picturesquely built of brick with a thatched roof... The brick and tiled Blacksmith's shop consists of Forge House with two forges, Coal House... Shed... two-stall Stable, Hay House, Trap House... Hay Shed,

etc. Meadow and Arable land at rear... Total 4.361 acres. Let to Mr G. Goward on a Yearly Tenancy at the rent of £25 p.a.

Everett Eke is one of the earlier blacksmiths listed in census data and directories (1901 and 1904). Before him was Robert Rice (in directories from 1869 to 1896), who was born in Mulbarton about 1840 and married first Mary Dye (1841–64), who died in childbirth, and then Hannah Dye, both younger sisters of the wheelwright opposite. Robert was the son of James Rice, blacksmith (born in Mulbarton about 1799), who is listed in *White's Directory*, 1845, and whose wife Elizabeth (born Shipdham about 1799) continued the business after his death – she is listed as 'blacksmith' in 1865.

The Wheelwright

Following a tradition going back many years, the wheelwrights of Mulbarton also ran the Tradesman's Arms next door (Chapter 3). Here we meet the Rice and Dye families again. In *White's Directory*, 1845, and in the 1851 census, Robert Rice (born in Bracon Ash about 1808) is listed as wheelwright and beerhouse keeper. He is a single man with a housekeeper, Elizabeth Dye, a 35-year-old widow born in Wreningham. She is probably related by marriage to Samuel Meadow Dye (1806–66), carpenter and wheelwright, and Mary (née Dady, 1808–83), most of whose 12 children were born in Tasburgh. Their fourth child, Samuel (1836–77), also a wheelwright by trade, moved to Mulbarton (where he is listed as wheelwright in 1869 and 1875) and also ran the Tradesman's Arms beer house. In 1871 he was employing two men and a boy. He married Charlotte Sarah West (1845–94, born in Kessingland), who took on running both businesses after his death in October 1877. They had five children, and their eldest son, Edward (born 1868), followed his father's trade and took full charge of the business after his mother's death. As an example of how close Mulbarton families were then to the poverty line, Edward's younger sister, Ellen (1870–99), married Edwin George Hunting and died when their third child was born. In 1901 we find the widower and his three young children living in the Henstead Union Workhouse at Swainsthorpe (now The Vale).

Edward Dye married Emily Swain, 'lady's maid' at Mergate Hall and daughter of the licensee of the Carpenter's Arms in Corsham, Wiltshire. Their eldest son, born in 1898, was named Edward Swain Dye. The next wheelwright and licensee of the Tradesman's Arms was Frank Swain, who married Blanche Carver, daughter of the licensee of the World's End. In 1915 he rented the 'Old School' (a small building opposite the Tradesman's Arms, between the blacksmith's and the Common) as a cart-finishing workshop, and bought it in 1920 in the sale of the Steward estate. When sold by Blanche Swain in 1946 it was described as 'cartshed formerly used as a paint shop'.

The wheelwright was an important person in the days of horse-drawn carts and carriages, but with the coming of cars, lorries and tractors his trade was taken over by the local garage…

Frost's Garage

The Mulberry Nursery now occupies the site of the garage. Charlie Frost and his sons, Claude and Desmond, built up a good reputation, and when they had the Ford franchise people came from a wide area to have their cars serviced.

C.J. Frost advertised regularly on the back page of the *East Carleton Magazine*. From 1915:

C.J. Frost, Cycle & Motor Agent, Mulbarton, Norfolk. Sole agent for BSA, New Hudson, Premier, Sparkbrook, and other Cycles. Cycles built to Customer's own specification from £3.3s.0d; second-hand cycles from £1.

He offered 'car tyres – any make; gas and oil lamps from 3s. and 1s. respectively; inner tubes from 1s.6d. fitted; pram tyring a speciality.' And he was selling Pratt's and Shell petrol. A footnote in the magazine of January 1917 read: 'We call attention to our ad. Mr Frost is serving with the RNAS and we must not let his business suffer in his absence for want of custom.' The Frost adverts in 1917–18 offered 'Car and Motor Cycle Requisites' and stated that 'Mr C.J. Frost is serving in HM Forces but Mrs Frost is carrying on the business with the exception of the execution of repairs.'

With the beginning of a transport boom in the 1920s, the business expanded on what was once the old mill orchard. In 1928 Mr Frost opened a business in Tacolneston, too. He advertised 'Hercules Cycle at

£3.19s.6d… Wireless Batteries in Stock. Charging done. Cars for hire, open or closed. Also Ten-seater Bus.' And there is mention of the hardware department with 'lamp glasses, stoves, brushes, wicks, pails, enamel ware, kettles, tea-pots, etc.'

Mr Frost took on apprentices – Harry Cannell's family still have his apprenticeship papers. Many people have fond memories of the garage under Charlie Frost and his sons. John Rumball remembers taking accumulators from Cyril Fairman's radios to

Harry Cannell, apprentice mechanic and father of Norma Mickleburgh, serving petrol from an early Bowser petrol pump to a car with a Norfolk number plate (AH) at Frost's garage, early 1920s. To the left is a corner of the Methodist Chapel; to the right, across the road, is Mr Funnell's baker's shop. (PHOTO CONTRIBUTED BY IRIS FROST)

Frost's garage seen across the pond in the 1920s, with the main workshop and various sheds, plus large 'BP' sign on Union Jack. To the left is the Post Office; to the right of the garage is the Wingfield Hall, the Methodist Chapel, the World's End and the baker's shop. There was no pavement by the pond. (PHOTO CONTRIBUTED BY IRIS FROST)

Frost's garage still going strong as a Ford agent in 1975. The old Post Office was by now a private house; the Wingfield Hall was unused, but the Methodist Chapel, the World's End and the 'pond shop' were still in use. Today, only the pub remains in business… (PHOTO: BERNARD AMBROSE)

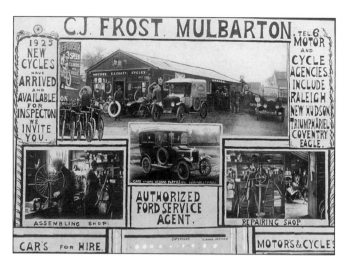

Advertisement for C.J. Frost, 1925 – for 'New Cycles arrived and available', and as an authorised Ford service agent.

(PHOTO CONTRIBUTED BY IRIS FROST)

Charlie Frost holding an old bicycle outside his workshop. The bicycle was renovated and given new tyres, but kept the original horse-hair seat, and is still owned by his daughter-in-law, Iris Frost. The pump has wartime petrol markings. (PHOTO CONTRIBUTED BY IRIS FROST)

Frost's garage in its early days as a garage and 'motor agent', with Charlie Frost standing between the two old pumps. (PHOTO CONTRIBUTED BY IRIS FROST)

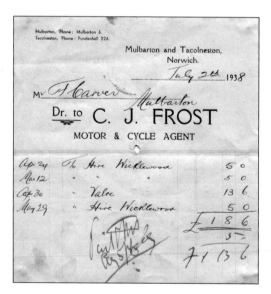

C.J. Frost, Motor & Cycle Agent. Bill issued 2 July 1938 for a total of £1.13s.6d. including tax.

(CONTRIBUTED BY VIC GRAY)

Charlie Frost (left) inspects a 1924–25 Douglas 350cc motorbike owned by a member of a vintage motorcycle club. A pavement now exists by the pond railings.

(PHOTO CONTRIBUTED BY IRIS FROST)

Falcon Acoustics at Tabor House: Rosaline ('Topsy') Lambert (now Mrs Greenwood) winding induction coils, c.1979. CONTRIBUTED BY MALCOLM JONES)

Mr Frost for recharging once a week, and so did Tony Kent: 'C.J. Frost sold bicycles and repaired most things mechanical. He also charged accumulators for "steam" radios. His right-hand man was Mr Cadman from Flordon.'

Dorothy Tungate remembers:

Charles Frost did everything – he sold Valor stoves, bicycles, etc. He used to bring me my 5 gallon drum of Kerosene if I left the empty one at the shop. I bought a Raleigh cycle from him for £9.10s. (now £9.50), and later a child's seat for the back for £6.10s. A lot of money to me, but they were good items, well made in those days.

Brenda Ford (née Collins) had quite a cycle ride from near 'Woodlands', Long Lane, to catch a bus: 'Charlie Frost had the garage for petrol and sold cycles and cycle repair items – most important to us – and he also ran a taxi service.'

On the Frost brothers' retirement, the business was sold to the Thomas family, who owned Swardeston garage. Big plans for expansion are shown by the modern buildings that replaced the old

garage and workshops, but there were problems getting planning permission for paint spraying and other specialist work. The buildings were put to various uses, including a cold store, a tack shop and now a children's day nursery. Car repairs in Mulbarton did not cease, however: Paul Ford of Bracon Ash moved his car repair business to the industrial area (behind the fish and chip shop), where it still thrives.

Mulbarton's International Trade

Modern communications have put national and international markets within reach of Mulbarton's craftsmen and traders. An international business with a link with Mr Frost of the garage is Falcon Acoustics. This modern, high-tech business with world-wide links was run from Tabor House on Norwich Road – the house originally built by Charlie Frost! One of its most popular products was the 'Tabor' hi-fi system – commercially built or in kit form – thousands of which have been sent all over the world since Malcolm and Valerie Jones moved Falcon Acoustics to Mulbarton in 1976. Local people were trained to wind inductors for crossover networks, which were made in workshops behind the house and used in many of Europe's best-known speaker systems. In 2003 Falcon moved to Acle and Malcolm and Valerie Jones semi-retired and moved to Bracon Ash.

Omicron have put Mulbarton on the map internationally with their spares and restoration business for classic cars – especially Lancias of all types. The very title 'Omicron' comes from the name of one of Lancia's many historic commercial vehicles. 'Omicron has the world's largest collection of Lancia spares,' declares *Classic Cars* magazine – all stored in the historic Long Barn facing the Common. The specialist workshops are in the newer barns behind. Andrew and Elizabeth Cliffe explain that the Mulbarton business is becoming even more international:

More and more parts are being specially made either by or for us, in various factories spread right across the world. Sales are also on a world-wide basis with customers in 60 countries, and about 50 per cent of our sales are exported.

Today, the trades may have changed, but Mulbarton still has its skilled workers and small businesses – just look at the adverts in *Parish News* or on the noticeboard in the shop!

Herbert Funnell's bread van (registration AH 7332) parked at Frost's garage, almost opposite the bakery, in the early 1920s.

(PHOTO CONTRIBUTED BY IRIS FROST)

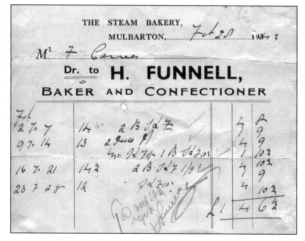

H. Funnell, Baker & Confectioner, The Steam Bakery, Mulbarton – bill for items purchased in February 1943 totalling £1.4s.6½d. (CONTRIBUTED BY VIC GRAY)

Dorothy Tungate with her aunt, Lily Melton (who emigrated to Australia), by the pond in 1950. Behind them is Mr Funnell's baker's shop, with the outbuildings of the World's End visible to the left.

(PHOTO CONTRIBUTED BY BRYAN TUNGATE)

A postcard with 'Hearty Greetings from Mulbarton' sold at Alfred Cracknell's shop. Views (clockwise from top left): frozen pond looking to the church; the garden of 'Woodlands'; 'Woodlands', Long Lane; Mulbarton Hall; the Post Office and the capped remains of the windmill.

(PHOTO CONTRIBUTED BY BRYAN TUNGATE)

✦ CHAPTER 8 ✦

Shops and Services

Today, Mulbarton's population of over 3,000 has a small supermarket with Post Office, a chemist's shop, a farm shop at Paddock Farm, a small store and video shop at a nursery on the border with Swardeston and – from 2007 – a shop in Cuckoofield Lane. But in the past, around 600 villagers were well served with far more shops than today.

The Baker's

The Funnell family – first Herbert and then his son, Sidney – ran the bakery business 'founded 1889'. Peter Mickleburgh recalls: 'Freshly baked bread delivered by Herbert Funnell and his son Sid every other day, excepting Sundays. Their bakery served the village of Mulbarton. The surrounding villages all had their own bakeries.'

Dorothy Tungate reckons she can still smell that bread after all these years:

We had Herbert Funnell, the baker – what lovely bread it was! He made huge 4lb loaves called 'Quarters', all done by hand – no machine stuff then... Mr Funnell delivered loaves with a horse-drawn cart, which was taken into the bakery yard through the big double-gates on Norwich Road, just behind his corner shop. His wife looked after the shop and sold all kinds of groceries and sweets as well as bread and cakes.

The cart was later replaced with a van, serviced at Frost's garage opposite. Sid took over the bakery from his father: '... he had a wealth of jokes which he used to pass on to my father and that generation!' Gerald Collins worked as a baker's boy for two years, starting at 6.30a.m. to knead the dough and grease the pans. Then he would go on the round with Sid Funnell or Mr Skipper and was finished by 4.30p.m.

After Mr Funnell retired, the former baker's shop became a general store and for a time it was part of the 'Mace' group. Its owners included Tom Eynon, Roger Moore and, most recently, Margaret Pitcher. When she was 'bought out' by the 'One-Stop' store in Birchfield Lane, the 'pond shop' ceased to be a shop. In 2005 the house was rebuilt to give better visibility and a wider pavement along the Norwich Road.

The General Store

Nesda Gray wrote, 'My mother from a small child lived with her aunt at the shop opposite the World's End. Her name was E. Gowen, the shopkeeper.' Her parents met through the shop, which supplied goods to Mr Carver, landlord of the World's End opposite.

Between the wars this was Alfred Cracknell's shop.

He sold everything you could think of, even clothes and boots… Everything was in sacks or boxes and had to be weighed up whilst customers waited. Tins of biscuits stood on the floor, open for customers to view. Chairs were provided for customers to 'ease their owd rewmatiks.'

Brenda Ford (née Collins) remembers the war years:

Cracknells' shop sold everything I can think of. My mother used to send her grocery order in there and it would be delivered to our house in a small card-board box – the extent of what our rations allowed in those days!

He also acted as parcel agent and Bryan Tungate remembers that just after the Second World War:

There was a Grocers in Norwich, 'Mr Pimm', where you could go in and order and they would send the parcel of stuff by bus and we would collect from Cracknell's shop in the village who were our local bus company agents. One week our parcel was taken to another village by mistake and we only got it some days later. Unfortunately there was soap powder in the parcel and the aroma from that got into the sponge mix, so Mum's sponge didn't taste too good when she used the mix.

After Mrs Cracknell left: 'This shop was later taken over by a Mr Smith, and finally Len Butler.' Hence the present name, 'Butler House'.

The Shoemaker

Some villagers remember: 'On the Norwich side of Cracknell's was the snob shop (shoe repairer). He was Bert Harbour from Flordon. But a lot of men repaired their own boots' – and many wooden lasts were dug up when the foundations of the garage of Butler House were laid. Mr Harbour moved to prem-ises next to the Tradesman's Arms. 'He cut out little roundels and sold them in packs of three for football boot studs.' But his old shop was probably the Post Office before Mr Middleton took over as postmaster in 1899. Samuel Gowing is listed as 'shoemaker and

Cottages next to the Tradesman's Arms, on the corner of road to East Carleton in the early 1930s. 'There was a small shop (right end) *where Mr Harbor did boot and shoe repairs, and at the other end* (left end) *lived Barney Randall – a bit of a barber... He'd cut our hair on a Sunday morning as we sat outside on a kitchen chair!'*

(PHOTO CONTRIBUTED BY BRYAN TUNGATE)

Village shoemaker – probably Samuel Gowing, who was also village postmaster in the 1890s. (PHOTO FROM VILLAGE ARCHIVE)

sub-postmaster' in directories of 1883 and 1896, and bills signed by S. Gowing were sent to Mr Turner for shoe repairs and also for carriage licences.

Mrs Frost's Haberdashery and Hardware

'Further along the road towards Norwich, Mrs Frost ran a linen shop which sold fancy goods and haberdashery.' First this was in a building beside the Frost family's cottage, but in the 1930s Mr and Mrs Frost built what is now Tabor House and the shop was part of the house. Later it became a hairdresser's salon, and then Falcon Acoustics (Chapter 7).

Mrs Frost had a small hardware and linen shop on the corner of her house on the Norwich Road. She sold all sorts of things from pots and pans to knicker elastic! It was a nice little shop and smelt of a paraffin heater in the colder days – quite a comforting smell as I remember.

Mrs Robinson's Shop, St Omer Close

There was yet another shop on Norwich Road – first in an old cottage facing the road and then, from 1936, in the first house built in St Omer Close:

The Turnpike (Norwich Road) looking north towards Norwich, early 1900s. Through the open gate was Mrs Frost's old shop in a wooden building beside the cottage. Further north along the road is a terrace of three brick houses that are still standing. Mrs Robinson had her shop in the front room of one of the clay-lump cottages in the distance, which were demolished in the 1930s to build St Omer Close. (PHOTO CONTRIBUTED BY IRIS FROST)

Mrs Frost's shop next to her cottage in about 1930. There she stocked hardware, paints, china and haberdashery.

(PHOTO CONTRIBUTED BY IRIS FROST)

Maggie Robinson ran a shop in the front room of her home in St Omer Close. She was Mrs Lilian Mickleburgh's mother, and had owned the orchard that was cleared for St Omer Close to be built.

She sold groceries, linen and newspapers. The doorway and ground floor layout of the house she used to live in are still slightly different from all the others in the Close.

The Butcher's Shop

Several old photographs show a wooden building on the edge of the Common, just south of the school. This was Blake's butcher's shop. The Blake family was linked with the butcher's business for over a century. Robert Blake is listed as butcher in directories from 1839 to 1869. He presumably shared the business with John Blake, who is listed as butcher in 1845 and 1864. The Misses E.A. and A. Blake are an unusual entry as butchers in 1883, followed by Samuel Blake, listed as butcher in the 1890s, then Mrs

The old butcher's shop is on the extreme left of this photograph. Behind the butcher's shop was the slaughterhouse, and several cottages and storage barns occupied the area between the shop and the terrace of houses ('Blake's Terrace') that still exists in the south-east corner of the Common. (PHOTO CONTRIBUTED BY IRIS FROST)

Oliver ('Crom') Blackburn with Samuel Blake's butcher's van outside his mother's old thatched cottages by Mulbarton Church. The telephone number is simply '4'! (PHOTO CONTRIBUTED BY DAVID WRIGHT)

Hannah Blake 'butcher and farmer' and Mrs Mary Blake, 'farmer' in 1904. Samuel Blake (presumably the son of the earlier butcher of the same name) is listed as butcher from 1908 to 1937. It was more than a shop – behind it was an abattoir:

The Butcher was Sam Blake whose employees were Oliver Blackburn, Arthur Stackyard, Horace Lofty, and also Miss Ives, a very lovely housekeeper who made a wonderful Pork Cheese… Animals for slaughter were bought from local farms. Pigs (weighing 300 pounds) were transported in the butcher's delivery van which was later 'slopped out' with hot water and washing soda. Behind the shop was the hanging room, and behind that the slaughterhouse. A huge copper stood in the slaughterhouse: this provided water to scald the pigs which loosened the bristles before they were shaved. The floor was scalded after use and the carcasses were taken to the hanging room where they stayed for 3 to 5 days before going into the shop for cutting and selling. This room also acted as a curing room and hams, bacon, brisket, etc. were pickled in saltpetre. Sausages were made here as well. This room had been built to keep cold – and it was!
Tony Kent

Bill Alborough remembers that while he was at Mulbarton School in the 1930s pupils could sometimes hear pigs squealing as they were slaughtered behind the nearby butcher's shop.

Jane Burrell, sister-in-law of Horace Lofty, remembers the butcher's business after the Second World War:

In 1946 my sister [Phyllis] married Horace Lofty, who was born at Hethersett in 1898, the younger son of William Lofty, listed in the 1901 census as 'Butcher Journeyman'. Horace served an apprenticeship in Norwich and also became a Butcher Journeyman, and eventually became Manager of the Mulbarton Butcher's shop, owned by Mr Samuel Blake… In spite of many villages having a butcher's shop at that time, meat was delivered to surrounding parishes in a van, and it was seldom that Mr Lofty returned home on a Friday night until 9.30p.m. – with frozen fingers. Vans had no heaters then!

The shop was in a substantial wooden building on the common between the terrace of cottages and the [old] school, near the pump that served the cottages. Behind the shop was a cottage and a number of outbuildings – barns, pig sheds, etc. The business was sold to Mr King (of Wood End, Mulbarton) around 1950–51. Mr Lofty had to retire for health reasons and Mr Greenacre took over the management. A new shop was built in 1968 after Mr Bensley had taken on the business. The shop premises were later divided and groceries and greengrocery shared the space.

Mr Horace Lofty died in October 1969, aged 71 years.

Peter Bensley of Hethersett took on the shop at the

age of 31. With £50 to buy some sows and a farrowing house, he began a successful 'farm-to-shop' business, then decided to have his own retail outlets. He bought shops in Norwich and in 1967 took over Mr King's butcher's shops in Mulbarton and Swardeston. His partner in the business was 22-year-old Barry Brooks – who went on to found his own successful wholesale meat business. They demolished the wooden shop and replaced it. 'New Butcher's in £200,000 Farm-to-Shop Venture' was the headline of an advertising feature in the *Eastern Daily Press* of 5 September 1968, which described the growth of the business:

An example of the firm's expansion is that where six chickens a week were once sold, they now sell 35,000 fresh chickens a year. Seven vans [including a Ford Transit, serviced by C.J.Frost, according to his ad on same page!] are in constant use around the shops and two vans full of meat travel from Mulbarton to the city twice a day to serve restaurants, canteens and catering establishments…

Later, the six shops amalgamated to form a limited company, Bensley Kings Butchers Ltd. They once delivered a sirloin joint to the Queen – cut from the supreme champion of the Royal Smithfield Show.

In the 1970 and '80s, Norman Bond managed the butchery until illness forced his retirement and the business finally closed. An estate agent took over the premises for a few years and then it stood empty – the church using it for a 'Christmas Cracker' charity shop in 1993 and 1994. In 1995 it was bought by the surgery, renovated and opened as the Humbleyard Centre for Complementary Therapies in January 1996. In 2006 a butcher returned to Mulbarton – to an annexe of the Paddock Farm Shop.

Cuckoofield Lane Stores

Council-house building at the south end of the village in the 1930s provided an opportunity for a shop to serve the growing population in Long Lane, Cuckoofield Lane and The Rosery. George Larter put a wooden shop at the side of his house, 22 Cuckoofield Lane. 'He sold anything from ½lb of tea to a gallon of paraffin (no EU Regulations then!).' But the Parish Council received a protest in March 1933 saying that 'it was unjust to the other shopkeepers in the village, who were compelled to pay much higher rent values.' The minutes of the next meeting, on 20 April 1933, reported 'higher rent to be paid by the shopkeeper in the Council House'.

The shop continued into the 1950s:

George Larter had a wooden shop in his garden in Cuckoofield Lane. He sold sweets, Corona fizzy drinks and fruit, among other things. I remember when the first bananas appeared after the war – the queue

extended the length of his long front garden path as no-one had seen bananas since the war began!'

When the 'new' council-houses were built on the south side of Cuckoofield Lane around 1960, a shop was included at No. 127. Doris Brighton moved across the road to run it as a general store for many years, ably helped by Mrs Mackerell. In 1972 the Hammonds moved in and used it as a hairdresser's salon for many years

The Paper Round that Became the Only Shop…

The earliest paper round people remember was run by Ernest Beare of St Omer Close, 'Newsagent for Mulbarton and district'. His round was taken over by Mr and Mrs Goodman in Birchfield Lane. The business then passed to Mr and Mrs Bunting, who also bred St Bernard dogs. Mr Harrod senr bought their bungalow in 1957 and continued the newspaper delivery business. Papers were stored and sorted in a wooden hut in front of the house.

Tony Harrod, the postmaster, took over the newspaper round from his father when he came out of the RAF and moved to Mulbarton from Norwich. The newspaper business involved working from 5a.m. to 11.30a.m. and cycling around five villages. When news came of the expansion of the village, Tony Harrod decided to build a shop on the site of the newspaper shed in Birchfield Lane in 1967. He built a store that was larger than needed at the time, but within 10 years it was too small. He took over the Post Office when the one near the pond closed in 1969. His shop became part of the Spar franchise to offer competitive prices in the village, and in later

Ernest Beare, newsagent for Mulbarton and District, with his three-wheeled cycle cart. He would cycle to Norwich early in the morning to collect the newspapers for distribution. The cycle cart was probably made (or adapted) by Charlie Frost. (PHOTO CONTRIBUTED BY IRIS FROST)

Site of the Birchfield Lane shop, 1958. On the far left is 'The Dell', the bungalow of Mr Harrod senr, and the wooden shed where he stored and sorted newspapers for delivery. This is now the site of the Post Office and shop. The caravan and shed were the home of Mr and Mrs Stevens while they built their Cedar Bungalow (Chapter 11). (PHOTO CONTRIBUTED BY MR AND MRS A. STEVENS)

Tony Harrod's 'Spar' shop and Post Office, Birchfield Lane, in 1975, before it was extended. Beyond it is the Harrods's house, replacing the original bungalow called 'The Dell'. (PHOTO: BERNARD AMBROSE)

years he used other franchises. When other villages were losing their shops, this one was expanding. It was enlarged several times in the 1970s: the interior was redesigned and a butcher's department added. In 1983 it was extended frontwards, almost doubling the shop area. Since then offices and a warehouse have been built above the shop (later a second-hand furniture shop). One of Tony's enthusiasms is computers: long before most village shopkeepers had computers he was using one in the shop for the newspaper round and accountancy work.

Although at the time of writing the shop itself is leased to One-Stop, Mr Harrod continues to run the Post Office. With the closure of the 'pond shop', it became the only shop in the village, apart from the Paddock Farm shop.

The old Mulbarton Post Office near the windmill and opposite the pond. Just to the left of the Post Office is the chimney of the bake-house which was part of the mill. This card was posted in 1908.
(PHOTO CONTRIBUTED BY TERRY BURCHELL FROM PHILIP STANDLEY'S COLLECTION)

Vic Gray expanded his video library and nursery to include a general store to serve Swardeston after the closure of the shop and Post Office in that village.

The Old Post Office

Only four families have run Mulbarton's postal services since the penny post began in 1840. In *White's Directory* of 1845, John Todd is listed as being at the 'Post Office' followed by Mary Todd (1854), with Mrs Harriett Todd, 'postmistress and shopkeeper' in the 1869 *Post Office Directory*. Samuel Gowing is listed as shoemaker, parish clerk and sub-postmaster in 1883 and 1896. His successor was Mr Middleton, whose daughter handed over to Tony Harrod, the current postmaster.

Frederick William and Rose Ellen Middleton moved from Brooke in 1899. Two years later they moved the Post Office into their new home opposite the pond, built on land belonging to the windmill. There Mr Middleton completed 50 years' service. Sid Mason remembers walking with his great-grandma, Mrs Pitcher, from the 'factory houses' to the Post Office every Friday night to get a 10s. note as her pension – all she had to live on for a week. When Mr Middleton died in 1949 his obituary read:

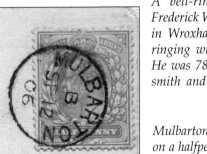

A bell-ringer since he was 14, Mr Frederick W. Middleton of Mulbarton died in Wroxham Church where he had been ringing with others on the church bells. He was 78... He was by trade a shoeing smith and received the certificate of the

Mulbarton postmark of 12 September 1906 on a halfpenny stamp (postcard rate).
(CONTRIBUTED BY MALCOLM AND VALERIE JONES)

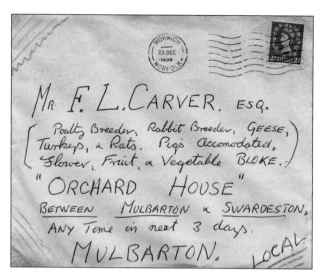

This envelope found its way to Frank Carver at Christmas 1958. No doubt Mulbarton Post Office had some chuckles at the description on the envelope! (CONTRIBUTED BY VIC GRAY)

Mulbarton Post Office, August 1991, when a petition to the Prime Minister against the construction of a chemist shop was being handed in. Left to right: Evelyn Smith (behind counter), Brenda Yallop, Vera White, Pam Howard. (PHOTO CONTRIBUTED BY BRENDA YALLOP)

Worshipful Company of Farriers in 1897. His long service as sub-postmaster was recognised by the award of the British Empire Medal. He had previously received the Imperial Service Medal in 1930...

Mr Middleton's daughter, Vera, took over the reins and continued with the work, helped by her sister-in-law, Mrs Audrey Middleton. When Vera ('Babs') Middleton retired in 1969 she told a reporter that she had first helped her father in the Post Office when she was just 12 years old. 'Because I was so young I needed special permission from the Post Office,' she said. She remembered the mail being delivered to the Post Office by horse and cart from Norwich and later by bicycle. A 13-mile walk in the snow to deliver mail at Mulbarton and neighbouring villages was one of her memories:

We used to stock stationery goods and one old lady bought some sealing wax and without doing anything to it tried to rub it on a parcel. One of the postmen told her: 'It would be a good idea to put a match to it.'

She also remembered the fresh salmon from Scotland which had evidently been held up in the post for some time: 'The roof nearly raised!' A hut by the Post Office housed the doctor's surgery for a short while and became a tea-shop for a time, much enjoyed by the more active ladies from Mulbarton Hall when it was an old people's home.

Mulbarton had other long-serving staff:

... one postman stands out: Bill Haverson DCM, ex-Sergeant-Major, Royal Norfolk Regiment. Bill liked a chat and on Christmas mornings he was ambushed all round the village – a tot here, a tot there...

When Mr Haverson retired, David Hewitt took his place. Les Swingler was a postman for 35 years, and Evelyn Smith assisted Tony Harrod from 1969, when he moved the Post Office counter to his Birchfield Lane store, until she retired in 2001.

The Telephone Exchange

Mulbarton's first telephone subscribers were served by line 201 from the Eaton exchange, Norwich. By 1920 a rural party line had been set up which allowed subscribers to share one line or pair of wires, which zig-zagged across the countryside connecting up all the properties. The Mulbarton line had 14 subscribers. Rental was low and local calls were free, but others could listen in. Whenever a call was put

Mrs R.E. Middleton (left); 'Babs' Middleton and Audrey Middleton at the switchboard of the manual exchange in the Post Office, which closed down on 6 February 1951 after 26 years of operation, 24 hours a day. A new automatic exchange was built in Rectory Lane, which was later superseded by the present Norwich Road exchange.

(PHOTO: EASTERN EVENING NEWS, REPRODUCED WITH PERMISSION)

through, half the telephone bells on the line rang at once, and subscribers had to count the number of times the bell rang in order to work out if the call was for them. Each subscriber had a magneto – a small generator with handles to turn in order to call the operator. The GPO would only open a new exchange for an area if there was a minimum of eight guaranteed subscribers.

At the 1920 annual parish meeting:

The Chairman proposed and the Vice Chairman seconded, that as several people have expressed a desire to use the telephone, the Clerk be instructed hereby to apply to the postmaster at Norwich for a Public Telephone at the Post Office or some other suitable place. Carried nem con.

A new telephone exchange was set up at the Post Office, probably in 1922:

The switchboard was beyond the counter and was a fascinating thing – all those little flaps that jumped when a number was called and plugs that were stuck into the holes under the flaps. In those days there were no dialling codes; one lifted the receiver, waited for the operator to speak, then asked for the village and number.

This was a central battery signalling switchboard – subscribers no longer needed a magneto, but they had to have a battery to give a 'speaking current'. By 1924 the Mulbarton exchange had its own rural party lines serving Bracon Ash, Hethel, and Stoke Holy Cross. By 1928, there were more than 40 subscribers and lines to Flordon and Wreningham.

The Middleton family kept the telephone service available at all hours, with Mrs Rose Middleton still taking her turn at age 78. When the old exchange

Mulbarton Numbers from the 1924 Telephone Directory:
Agnew, Mrs Frank, Mulbarton Lodge – 14
Allen, A.J. and C., Rose & Fruit Growers,
   The Rosery – 13
Betts, Thomas W., Manor Cottage – 17
Blake, S., Butcher – 4
Church, Albert J., Florist, Tomato Grower,
   Roadside Nurseries – 11
Cross, R.E., Farmer, Old Hall – 23
Denny, W., Motor Hire Catering, 'World's End' – 5
Fairman, A.W., Butcher, Farmer – 8
Frost, Charles Jas., Cycle, Motor Agent, Garage – 6
Hill, Mary C. – 27y1 [the old party-line number]
Middleton, F.W., Cycle Agent, Sub-Postmaster – 1
Mulbarton Call Office – 1

Some of these numbers remained the same – for instance the World's End was Mulbarton 5 then became 205, then 50205 and is now 570205.

was replaced by an automatic exchange in 1951, 'Babs' Middleton was sure that 'her' subscribers '… are so used to lifting the telephone and asking for names of persons or businesses that it will be strange for them to have to look up the number.' She nevertheless admitted that pressure of work had increased, with 300 calls a day replacing the original 27 subscribers.

The automatic exchange was housed in a small building in Rectory Lane until January 1994, when Mulbarton got a new computerised exchange on the Norwich Road. This meant all change for phone users: Mulbarton's five-figure numbers were prefixed with the figure 5 and customers in the (then) 0508 area had access to new services. Almost exactly 21 years later, in December 2004, after a well-orchestrated campaign, Mulbarton gained access to broadband.

'The Milk Lady'

Deliveries by local shops were – and still are – supplemented by visiting roundsmen and women. Best remembered is Mrs Olive ('Ollie') Lincoln, 'the

Front view of Dairy Farmhouse after the trees and undergrowth had been cleared, c.1987. The south end (left) was the house and the north end (right) the dairy and store.
(PHOTO: ROBIN CLAYTON)

The listed cob barn west of Mulbarton Common, about 1987. Formerly part of Mrs Lincoln's dairy farm, it has now been renovated into a home by being 'clad' with blocks and re-roofed.
(PHOTO: ROBIN CLAYTON)

Milk Lady'. Born in 1900, she moved to Mulbarton with her husband, Geoff, in 1932 to take on the dairy farm west of the Common (Chapter 6). At first they sold milk from their own cows, going round the villages in their old van with a dip can and ½-pint and 1-pint measures. When dairy regulations came in they decided it was too expensive to install special equipment, so they bought the milk from a farmer in Bracon Ash and bottled it themselves. The whole family helped clean the bottles one at a time by scalding them in boiling water heated in a copper. When filled with milk, cardboard caps were pressed into the tops of the bottles. That was when milk was 2½d. a pint. When the school milk scheme started in 1938, the milk monitor walked across the Common each Monday to give the milk numbers, and Ollie had to fill the third-pint bottles and deliver the required number to the school each day (Chapter 4).

After Geoff Lincoln died in 1939, the children helped even more. Every morning a neighbour, Herbert Lake, went to Mergate Hall Farm, Bracon Ash, with his motorbike and sidecar to pick up churns of milk. Then new regulations came in and Mrs Lincoln had to collect it from the Milk Marketing Board at Harford Bridge (now the Tesco site). Peter Lincoln remembers delivering milk before he went to school, cycling to Hethel with racks of milk bottles fitted to his handlebars. Often this made him late for school, but he was never told off – the teacher must have known the circumstances and been sympathetic. The Lincoln family supplemented the milk business with eggs – their own and those they collected from others. They were washed, packed and delivered to clients in Norwich under the august name of 'National Farm Packers'! Blackberries and elderberries gathered locally were also sent to Norwich. The elderberries were used for dye and wine.

For more than 30 years Ollie Lincoln delivered milk to Mulbarton residents in her little blue van. Other drivers readily believed it when she said:

I've never taken a driving test… and if I did I don't suppose I'd pass… First find out where the gears are, and after that just use your common sense, that's the way I learned!

Up at the crack of dawn, out in all weathers, she always tried to help her customers out – delivering newspapers and shopping, collecting various items for them (including tablets from the doctor), taking people's scraps for her chickens and downing lots of cups of tea. In later years she collected wool to use herself or for her friend Rita Bridgman, who knitted little dolls to sell for charity. She loved her work and said in a radio interview that she'd carry on as long as she could walk. She was finally forced to retire at the end of 1982, after slipping on the ice.

More Deliveries

'The butcher, the baker, the ice-cream man, the coalman, the milkman and the postman,' plus paper deliveries, the fish man and the mobile fish and chip shop used to visit Mulbarton, and many still do. Shops in neighbouring villages also delivered orders.

Jimmy Drake, the coalman, would deliver coal each week. He had a horse called Dolly and a cart. Mother would count the bags in so as to ensure she got what she ordered. He lived in Swainsthorpe but delivered coal in Mulbarton. Whilst loading was in progress [at Swainsthorpe Station], Dolly laid down and slept in the shafts, oblivious of trains passing a few yards away. When loaded, Dolly was given a kick, Jimmy climbed onto the cart and off they went. They worked their way to Mulbarton. Having done several deliveries, the Tradesman's Arms hove into sight, Dolly would trot into the car park, Jimmy trotted into the pub: one slept and one supped. Halfway through the opening period normal service was resumed as far as the World's End, where they both practised their hobbies again… Dolly was switched to auto-pilot and duly arrived home where willing hands took care of both. Tony Kent

Stebbings of Bracon Ash delivered goods in Mulbarton. The delivery cart is loaded and ready to go from The Street, Bracon Ash. (PHOTO CONTRIBUTED BY JOHN BETTS)

The Watling family ran the Post Office stores in Bracon Ash and delivered in Mulbarton.

(PHOTO CONTRIBUTED BY JOHN BETTS)

Coal cart outside the Tradesman's Arms, seen from Mulbarton Bridge. (PHOTO CONTRIBUTED BY TERRY BURCHELL, FROM PHILIP STANDLEY'S COLLECTION)

The fish and chip van parked at St Omer Close with the usual queue, 1976. (PHOTO: GRAHAM EAGLING)

Buying fish from Mr Morley's horse-drawn cart outside Church Cottages in the 1950s – after the war memorial clock had been installed in the church tower.

(PHOTO CONTRIBUTED BY LAURENCE BAILEY)

After the Swainsthorpe depot closed coal was delivered from Flordon by Moys:

Some people had him call round monthly as they had more space to keep the coal than we did. He had a lorry and would hump the sacks round to our shed on his back.

Antonio the Italian ice-cream seller was very popular and he spent most of Sunday afternoon in the village. He used a horse-drawn cart at first, then a motorcycle and sidecar and in later years a real ice-cream van. Peter Mickleburgh remembers, 'One or two of us children would meet "Tony" at the stream about half a mile from where we lived and would get a ride on his pillion back home.'

A 'character' known as 'Old Morley' brought fish and shell-fish on Sunday mornings by horse and dray and had to put up with the pranks of Bryan Tungate and friends: 'One day when he was dozing on the cart on his way home one of us shot the horse with an acorn gun. This was the quickest Morley and his horse ever moved.' This jogged another memory:

Our local policeman, PC Balls, was based at nearby Swainsthorpe and covered a number of local villages. He had a bicycle and if he caught us he would give us a 'clip of the ear'. We didn't want him visiting at all if we could help it.

Many are the Mulbarton families who queued at Russell's fish and chip van – it could be located easily enough from the smell and the smoke. Mr Eagling senr travelled from Banham on a Thursday and Saturday from 1965, and later his sons took over. Before the days of main sewerage, 'the "Honey Cart" drivers always managed to be in St Omer Close when the chippie arrived and would take off their big gloves to eat supper in the lorry cab.' Just before Christmas 1983 the Eagling family opened the fish and chip shop on the industrial estate.

There have always been the occasional callers. The 1841 census recorded a 'tinker' and his son living in 'a cart' by the World's End. A century later:

Mrs Oakley, who lived in a caravan beside the Common, made wooden clothes pegs and called 'sometimes'. When she was knocked down by a van and died her family had a big wreath in the shape of a caravan which they took to the Churchyard.

Other callers included the scissor sharpener, who also sharpened garden shears, and '... had a bike with a trailer on it... his grinding wheel was powered by the cycle pedals.' Then there was 'Mr Parish, who would call with his suitcase selling haberdashery such as darning wool, reels of cotton, anything to do with mending clothes; he would let people buy clothing on account.' The chimney-sweep called every year. And finally:

For us kids the most important visitor was Father Christmas. A few apples and pears with a pair of home-made socks or a pullover to go to school in was about it. One year Dad made us both a wooden aeroplane and my sister got a proper doll. Had we won the Pools?'

Bryan Tungate

Doctors and Nurses

Mulbarton has the Wingfields of Mulbarton Hall to thank for an affordable local medical service. By 1880 Mrs Wingfield had given just over £600 (a large sum in those days) to the Rector and church-wardens to invest to provide nursing care in the parish. The committee of 'The Mulbarton Nurse Fund' appointed Mrs Marratta Clarke (aged 50 and Italian) at a salary of £13 a year, plus £2.10s. towards rent. By 1900 Swardeston, East Carleton and Bracon Ash were also covered, and the committee affiliated to the Norfolk County Nursing Association. Mrs Jessie Ash is listed as the parish nurse in 1904. By 1914:

The Mulbarton & District Nursing Association has been obliged to make a new rule which became operative on October 1st 1914. It was hoped that the voluntary offerings of patients would bring in such a sum that would make up the deficiency in the

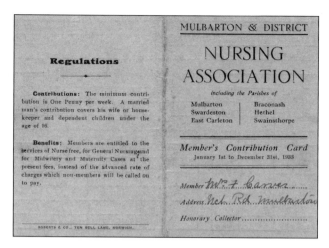

Mulbarton & District Nursing Association Member's Contribution Card, 1933, for Mrs F. Carver of Norwich Road, Mulbarton. The back of the card lists the contributions (min. 1d. per week) and the benefits (free nursing, reduced price maternity). (CONTRIBUTED BY VIC GRAY)

subscriptions, but this has not been the case. Rule 5 therefore reads 'In cases of general sickness the charges for the Nurse's visits will be as under: Class I 2d., Class II 4d., Class III 6d.'

(From *East Carleton Magazine*, November 1914)

A scheme continued into the 1930s whereby people could contribute 1d. a week for cheaper nursing care. Charges in 1934 were: general nursing – 3d. a visit (free to subscribers); midwifery – £1.2s.6d. (15s. to subscribers); maternity – 12s.6d. (7s.6d. to subscribers).

Nurse Sexton arrived as district nurse in June 1920, replacing Nurse Thompson, who left to get married. Her salary was £90 a year:
The Association's other main expenditure was on:

uniform	£1.8s.11d.
bicycle	18s.3d.
insurances	£1.13s.3d.
cottage furniture	£18.0s.6d.
drugs	£3.13s.4d.
fees and sundries	£1.16s.2d.

Income in 1919–20 came from:

voluntary subscriptions and donations	£34.2s.1d.
charges for midwifery cases	£19.7s.0d.
fees for nurse's services	£2.17s.4d.
health visiting grant	£1.1s.3d.
school nursing	1s.7d.

Plus payments from:

the Board of Guardians	£2.2s.0d.
the Local Government Board	£7.12s.0d.
the County Council Grant	£20.0s.0d.
and interest from stock held by the Nursing Association	£21.4s.0d.

Nurse Sexton, district nurse and midwife for Mulbarton, c.1939.

(PHOTO CONTRIBUTED BY EVELYN SMITH)

Official opening of the Humbleyard Centre for Complementary Therapies by Rt Hon. John MacGregor, MP for South Norfolk. Looking on (far right) *is Dr Christine Buckton, prime mover in organising the Centre, which is in the former butcher's shop beside Mulbarton Common.* (PHOTO: MARINA CARTER)

In 1933/34, Nurse Sexton reported 20 midwifery and maternity cases, 59 general cases, two operations, and two cases of TB. In 1937, the Mulbarton parish magazine reported:

The Annual Meeting of The Mulbarton and District Nursing Association was held at The World's End clubroom on April 19th... The annual report stated that Nurse Sexton made 2508 visits to 106 cases which entailed bicycle journeys amounting to 2844 miles... 168 attendances were made to the baby weighing meetings...

These 'clinics' were held in the old Wingfield Hall ('very draughty').

Nesda Gray (née Carver) remembers the midwife: 'Nurse Sexton came to Mulbarton in 1920, and my sister Rhoda was her first baby. My son Victor was the last baby she attended before retiring in 1946.' For Brenda Ford (née Collins), 'Nurse Sexton... was of the real District Nurse breed. She delivered my brother just before the war. She was greatly loved and *[from the 1930s]* lived in one of the council-houses in Long Lane.' Another memory: 'Nurse Sexton had a "sit up and beg" *[bicycle]* and later a Ford Eight.'

Mulbarton did not have its own separate medical practice until the Humbleyard Practice opened in 1980. Dr Deacon, the first doctor to have a telephone

number in Mulbarton (Eaton 201x4 in 1920) had a surgery in Hethersett (phone Eaton 1). By 1928 Dr R.F. Connell had a surgery here (tel. 12) but lived in Swardeston. He was probably followed by Dr Rogerson and then Dr Maingay, the doctors people remember: 'There was no permanent surgery – the doctor held consultations on certain days of the week in the front room of one of the cottages near the pond (now Huntingfield Cottage),' remembers Dorothy Tungate. 'There was no appointment system, we just used to sit and wait, and no prescriptions – he would mix up a bottle of evil-tasting medicine himself. It always cured us!' People remember paying 2s.6d. to visit the doctor and 3s.6d. if he visited them, until the NHS abolished charges in 1948.

With more people working outside the village, the Parish Council stated in July 1952: 'Mulbarton needs an evening surgery and better method for collecting medicines. Parish Council to contact Dr Maingay.' An evening surgery began in January 1953. By the late 1950s the village needed better medical facilities and a small surgery (now the vet's) was built on the Norwich Road to serve Mulbarton and Swardeston. Dr James practised here, followed in 1974 by Dr Leaman, who was instrumental in seeing that the growing village had its own medical practice and modern surgery. Eventually, the new bungalow built to house a school caretaker was acquired from the

The part-built new chemist's shop next to former Village Hall, now a dental surgery, July 1996. Work stopped due to protests over building new commercial premises on common land. (PHOTO: BRENDA YALLOP)

Mulbarton Pharmacy when it first opened – in the former school loos. There was limited stock – and no room for a queue. (PHOTO: BRYAN TUNGATE)

County Council and adapted. It has since been enlarged, and now the village has both a surgery and a complementary therapy centre.

The Dentist and the Chemist's Shop

'Mulbarton Common: Former Village School in nearly ½ acre. Outline Planning Permission for conversion to One Residential Dwelling. Offers invited in the region of £89,000'. This advertisement appeared in 1989 and the former school and Village Hall was sold for commercial development. There was no argument about it becoming a dental surgery (though some lament the changes to the north-facing window) with the office of a financial advisor in the former cloakroom annexe. But plans to build a new chemist's shop on the site of temporary sheds in the old playground was a different matter… There was huge opposition, both to a chemist's shop (replacing the dispensary at the doctors' surgery for all Mulbarton villagers) and to a commercial building on common land.

The first battle was over permission for an independent pharmacy to replace the dispensary in the surgery. Despite local opposition, supported by our MP, permission for a pharmacy was given and work went ahead to build a shop next to what had become the dental surgery. The owner was forced to stop work in May 1993, however, after protests from a newly formed Mulbarton Common Protection Group, who discovered that the shop was being built on common land. The April 1994 annual parish meeting brought discussion and opposition to a head:

Mr Martin explained that the land will always be regis-tered as Common. The old school premises were excluded. But the former school playground is included in the District Council's Management Scheme, and as managers it must oppose any development on the area it manages. For this reason it is proposing to remove a small peripheral area from the Scheme so that the Secretary of State for the Environment can consider an appeal that the chemist's proposed shop can be built there. Mr Martin called on villagers to defend the peripheries of the Common, or further development might be allowed. Some villagers were drawing up a petition, and a vote at the meeting supported the motion that the former school playground should not be with-drawn from the SNDC Scheme of Management.

(News Report, April 1994)

The developers claimed that the land had been fenced off from the Common and had been surfaced as a playground in the 1950s. Villagers fought back by pointing out this 'enclosure' was for community use and safety. The developers lost their case and the owner was ordered to pull the building down by 3 May 1996. Further legal wrangling meant that the half-built shop became a dangerous playground, so it was boarded up by the District Council. The demoli-tion squad arrived in October 1996.

This was not the end of the chemist's shop saga. Permission for a pharmacy still stood – and a tiny dispensing chemist was opened in what had once been the school toilets! Eventually, the financial adviser moved, and the premises became the chemist's shop – with space for parking on what continues to be classified as common land!

CHAPTER 9

Houses Great and Small (and some Residents)

A fascinating hand-written builder's bill for work on a Mulbarton house in 1667 is in the Norfolk Records Office. Rebuilding side walls and partitions cost more than £25; work on doors and windows, including stable doors, cost £2; colour washing 'from gable to gable' and 'from top to bottom' cost over £35. Materials alone cost nearly £116 and labour £60. Unfortunately the house is not identified – if it still exists it is probably the Old Hall near Mulbarton Church. This is the oldest of the 'great houses' of Mulbarton – but the cottages where most people lived are just as important.

Mulbarton Old Hall

Hidden away behind the great barn is Mulbarton Old Hall or manor house – though whether a lord of the

The front of the Old Hall, or manor house viewed from the track that runs eastwards from the Long Barn. Date and the identity of the man at the gate uncertain.

(PHOTO FROM VILLAGE ARCHIVE)

The back of the Old Hall as depicted in a watercolour by Emily Draper, painted in the late 1890s. The building on the right was a dairy. (CONTRIBUTED BY MARY MELLOR)

manor ever lived here is uncertain. It is built beside a moat where an earlier house probably stood. Dr Wells (owner 1940–78) found some cornerposts of a building within the semicircular moat, which is described as 'Scite of Mannor' on some early maps.

The house was owned by successive lords of the manor until sold by the widow of John Steward in 1920 as part of the East Carleton Estate. For all or most of its history it was leased to tenants (Chapter 6). In the auction documents for the 1920 sale, the Old Hall farmhouse is described as:

... an Ancient Edifice of red brick with tiled roof and picturesque haunched gable... surrounded by a high

The front of the Old Hall (north facing) in 1946. This view shows clearly the seven windows on the first floor which are aligned off-centre, suggesting that the right-hand end has been extended. (CONTRIBUTED BY MARY MELLOR)

The back of Mulbarton Old Hall showing the Dutch gable end with new ground-floor windows and a single-storey brick extension added by Dr Wells as a surgery and study. Dated 'Easter 1966'. The extension was enlarged and adapted by the Mellors to be more in keeping with the rest of the house. (CONTRIBUTED BY MARY MELLOR)

brick wall with well-kept Lawn in front and has at the rear An Ancient Moat… The Picturesque Old Gardens and Orchard are entirely walled and adjoin the moat.

The outbuildings near the house may once have been farmworkers' cottages with dormer windows, and one part was a dairy in the nineteenth century.

Since the Hall ceased to be a farm it has had two famous residents. Dr Calvin Percival Bampfylde Wells, FRAI, PHD, MRCS, LRCP bought the Hall at the beginning of the Second World War and lived there after serving in the Royal Army Medical Corps. He was an outstanding international authority on palaeopathology (the study of diseases in ancient human bones, which can help modern medical research). After his death in 1978 the Hall was bought by David Mellor, who became the most senior judge at Norwich Court Centre from 1998 and, his obituary noted, controlled the court with 'a twinkle in the eye and the voice of quiet reason.'

The Old Hall has changed little since the Victorian photographs and watercolours that still exist from when the Draper family lived there. By then it had been re-roofed with tiles – possibly in the 1880s. Until the 1920s or later, the main entrance was in the south gable-end, where the old doorway remains but new ground-floor windows were added in 1965. Dr Wells also added a porch to the 'new' main entrance and a flat-roofed extension on the south-east end in the mid-1950s. One of the barns has since been altered and made part of the house, with yet another 'main entrance'.

The exact age of the existing house is uncertain. The late 1500s was the time of the 'Great Rebuilding' – England was prosperous and many contemporary writers commented on the amount of building, the beautiful buildings, the vast number of chimneys appearing everywhere and the amount of timber being used. Certainly this house has some particularly fine beams. If there was a house on the moated site at this time, it was probably replaced by a grander late-Elizabethan hall .

Most of the house is timber framed with lath and plaster, and brickwork at the southern end – was this the building work of the 1667 bill? Inside, one unusual beam with a rounded end is in line with the beginning of this brickwork and probably marks the position of the old end-wall of the main house. The bricks of this south end are laid according to Flemish Bond – first used in Britain in the 1630s. This is less strong than English Bond, but easier for shapes and decoration such as the particularly fine 'Dutch gable' added in the seventeenth century. It matches the gable ends of the nearby tithe barn that belonged to the Old Hall. The side overlooking the moat has two wings, one of which contains a staircase and a brick chimney-stack. The other wing has a stepped gable end on either side of a central chimney of various fireplaces and the old ovens in the kitchen. The old

brickwork here is English Bond. Inside, the extensive Regency panelling suggests there was some major renovation and even rebuilding around 1800, when the door onto the front lawn was given its canopy.

Mulbarton Hall

Not to be confused with the Old Hall is Mulbarton Hall, at the south-east corner of the Common. Nikolaus Pevsner (author of *The Buildings of England* series) describes Mulbarton Hall as 'a long, in fact lengthened, white Georgian house behind two splendid cedar trees.' On the 1724 map it is shown with three storeys and a dome. The present owners believe the roof line was lowered and a decorative pediment added soon after it was built. Internally, there are slight differences in floor level, marking nineteenth- and early-twentieth-century extensions.

Residents of the Hall included Philip Stannard, a wealthy cloth merchant, who moved to Mulbarton from his Norwich house for the summer months from around 1750 until his business went spectacularly bankrupt in 1769. The following year it was bought by Richard Parkerson, a baker, for 2,000 guineas (£2,100). According to a newspaper report, he planned to run it as a tavern and open the gardens to the public – but there is no record that he ever did.

Revd Dr Miles Beevor, DD, Rector of Hethel, Vicar of Ketteringham and Rector of Bircham Tofts, 'lived for a considerable time at Mulbarton House, now Mulbarton Hall.' He is listed as a 'freeholder', and therefore a voter, in the Norfolk Poll Books of 1802, 1806 and 1817, and listed as 'resident' in a book of 1829. He married his cousin, Mary Beevor, from Norwich and in 1834 was buried at Hethel.

He is said to be the first person to introduce the Swede Turnip into England… I am told that the village blacksmith who had a feud with him, named his dog 'Miles Beevor' that he might curse him to his heart's content and at the same time declare that no disrespect to the Rector was intended!

(Revd A.R.V. Daubeney, Rector 1931–33)

Mulbarton Hall viewed from the garden, c.1820 – from a lithograph, possibly commissioned by Revd Dr Miles Beevor DD, who was resident at that time.

(CONTRIBUTED BY LINDA STEYNOR)

Philip Stannard of Mulbarton Hall

Around 1750, Mulbarton Hall was acquired by a wealthy cloth merchant from Norwich, Philip Stannard. 'Norwich stuffs' were elaborately woven and colourful material traded throughout England, Europe and beyond. They were usually made to order, often to a tight time schedule, and traders often dealt in sidelines from the countries to which they exported. In January 1753 Philip Stannard wrote to a wine-merchant whose imports he was handling:

As my family and self retire into the country next April until October, and although I come into Town every day, yet having so much business of my own, I dare not venture to engage for more than I receive orders for.

Philip Stannard was born in Bury St Edmunds in 1703, the eldest son of another Philip, a milliner and prosperous merchant. He was apprenticed to a worstead weaver and merchant in the Colegate area of Norwich at the age of 15. When Philip had finished his seven-year apprenticeship in 1726, he became a Freeman of the City of Norwich and set up his own business. Soon afterwards he married Priscilla Crowe in Norwich Cathedral, but sadly both their babies died. He became Sheriff of Norwich in 1747 – the year his father died. After this he fades out of municipal affairs – maybe to 'retire' to Mulbarton.

In Stannard's time, Mulbarton Hall was an elegant house with eight acres of ground and '... stabling for twelve horses, and spacious pleasure gardens, ornamented with statuary and vases, and liberally planted with flowering shrubs and beds of tulips and ranunculus...' In one of his books, Philip Stannard listed 'Foreigners who have been at my House' between 1751 and 1755, including merchants from Venice, Leipzig, Copenhagen, Lübeck, Amsterdam, Zurich, Basle, Frankfurt, Cologne, Stockholm, Weimar, Bremen, Christiania [*now Oslo*] and Lisbon. How many of them stayed at Mulbarton?

Priscilla Stannard died in 1757 at the age of 49. The family memorial in St Giles Church, Norwich, commemorates her 'patient Resignation during a long Series of Afflictions.' In 1762 Philip married Anne Hopson, who was 25 years his junior. In 1763 it was announced, 'Our worthy Mrs Stannard was safely delivered of a son at Mulbarton, to the great joy of all the family and friends.' He was baptised in Mulbarton Church and was named after his father and grandfather – another Philip! In 1765 his sister, Ann, was born and baptised at Mulbarton.

It would be interesting to know if country life suited Philip Stannard too well, and whether he left decisions about his business, Stannard & Taylor, to others. Taylor seems to have been a nephew. A partner named John Taxtor expanded the business enormously, seeking orders throughout Europe as far as Russia and trading with South America and Mexico from 1766. Some of the goods came from other Norwich manufacturers, many were sent 'on spec', and there seems to have been considerable naivety about the problems of direct export and collecting the money.

In 1769 Stannard & Taylor went bankrupt – spectacularly. The firm's total debts were £47,000 – a huge sum in those days, and one of the largest provincial bankruptcies of the century. As a result, all that Stannard owned had to be sold – including Mulbarton Hall, with its fittings, furniture and flowers, all advertised separately in May 1770. After the bankruptcy, Philip Stannard and family lived quietly in Norwich, largely thanks to his wealthy father-in-law. He died in 1777 aged 74.

The front of Mulbarton Hall (facing the Common) before the First World War. This card was posted on 26 February 1914. (PHOTO CONTRIBUTED BY TERRY BURCHELL, FROM PHILIP STANDLEY'S COLLECTION)

Mulbarton Hall – rear view from the garden, dating from before 1920. The white extension on the far left was designed and added in 1907. (CONTRIBUTED BY JULIET AMOS)

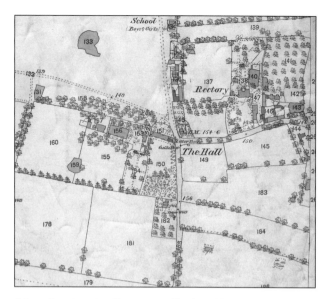

Map showing Mulbarton Hall, the old Rectory and the south-east corner of the Common (with the old school) from 1:2500 County Series, 1881.

(REPRODUCED BY KIND PERMISSION OF THE ORDNANCE SURVEY)

Major-General Charles W. Wingfield, RA and Mrs Emma Dorinda Wingfield probably moved to Mulbarton Hall in 1871. Charles Wingfield died the following year, but his widow continued to live there for over 30 years. Mrs Wingfield is named as owner and occupier in the Poor Rate Book, 1875–76, when the 'Extent' is given as 7 acres 2 rods 22 perches; rateable value £50. Mrs Wingfield died there in 1906, aged 91, and is commemorated in a window at the west end of the church. The village has much to thank Mrs Wingfield for, including the formation of a Nursing Fund, providing much of the funding to build the schoolmaster's house and leaving money for a Parish Hall (often called the Wingfield Hall) to be built. She was also a manager of the school.

Sir Edward Wingfield, nephew of Charles, probably moved to join his aunt at Mulbarton Hall when he retired in 1900 as Permanent Under-Secretary of State for the Colonies. He was knighted in 1899. Certainly he and his wife, Lady Mary Georgina Wingfield, were living there in 1901. He frequently visited Mulbarton School, inspecting work, presenting prizes, paying for a pathway and donating a flagpole. He inherited the Hall and in 1907 added a large extension to the west end, designed by Norwich architects Edward Boardman & Son as staff quarters linked to a dairy and brewhouse. Sir Edward died in 1910, but his widow continued to live there until 1916 or later.

Antony Sargeaunt, Esq., lived in the Hall for only five years before he put it up for auction in September 1927. It was described as:

The charmingly situated Freehold Residence known as Mulbarton Hall, near Norwich with Ornamental gardens, Large Tennis Lawn, Glasshouses, Stabling

and Garages, Small Farmery. Four cottages and gardens and Four Enclosures of Valuable Arable and Pasture Lands.

A distinctive feature was 'Engine House with Electric Light Plant with 8hp Crossley oil engine, dynamo, switch board, 56 large accumulators' – which enabled Mulbarton Hall to enjoy electric light long before the rest of the village!

Mrs Ellen Massingham bought the hall and in 1928 had various alterations made to modernise the house and improve the heating system. A new ground-floor window was fitted at the east end, where the old stoke-hole had been. People remember:

The Hall was the home of Mrs Massingham, whose employees were Messrs Skipper and Warman... She had a grove of fir trees planted to hide the council-houses from her view. When more houses were built, horse-chestnut and willow trees were planted at the end of their gardens to hide them.

Some local girls went into service at the Hall. Margaret White wrote in *Parish News* that 'Violet Bailey (née Barrett), 1911–95, lived all her life in Mulbarton like her mother, her grandmother, and her great-grandmother... On leaving school [she] went into service with the Massingham family at Mulbarton Hall' until she married Robin Bailey. Later, Violet Bailey was head cook at The Grove, first for Scott and then for the East Carleton Cheshire Home, until she retired in 1981.

After Mrs Massingham's death the Hall was back on the market again in 1947, to be auctioned in four lots (main house; cottages in Long Lane, and two pieces of land rented to Mr Jackson of Paddock Farm). Many of the house details are the same as in 1927, though mains electricity had been installed, and all the main rooms had hot-water radiators. The 'delightful Old-World Gardens and Grounds' included a 'shrubbery; Nut-walk; Herbaceous borders and pond' and 'Prolific Kitchen Garden in a high state of cultivation...'

As a result of the 1947 sale the house, plus outbuildings and one cottage, were bought by Norwich City Council for an old people's home. The cottage on the corner of Rectory Lane became the matron's house and a new staff bungalow was built to the west of the hall. Some of the land was later used for Mulbarton First and Middle Schools with their separate playing-fields – much of the First School field is part of the former kitchen garden. The pair of traditional cottages south of the house have been modernised. The story of the fields that became building plots belongs in the final chapter.

Brenda Ford (née Collins) recalls that:

When Mrs Massingham died, the contents of the hall were auctioned and crowds of people came to the sale. The Hall then became a home for old ladies, and these lady residents used to come to church on Sundays.

Evelyn Smith (née Stackyard) continues:

Both my mother, Mrs Gladys Stackyard, and my aunt, Mrs Elsie Stackyard, worked there, along with Mabel Larter, Mrs Agnes Cooke, Mrs Joan Collins, and Mrs Abendroth, who was the cook.

Queenie Wasey worked for the matron:

… for 14 years from the age of 51. There were 28 elderly people – all ladies until the last year or two when we had four men. In fact, there was a man and his wife there for a bit. The rooms were big, mostly with five to a room. Most of them stayed in the Home, but three of the ladies used to dress up and go out round the village, and one lady used to take herself off to Yarmouth by bus! The bungalow was the matron's house, and the under-matron lived in the cottage on the corner of Rectory Lane. Eventually the Council decided that the premises were not very suitable, so all the residents were moved to a residential home in Norwich where they could have their own individual rooms – and I went with them and carried on working there until I had to retire.

The Hall and adjacent bungalow were auctioned again in March 1976 and fetched £34,500. When sold, there was planning consent for change of use to '… residential flats, a students' hostel, boarding house, hotel and country club.' In fact, it became Benton's Antiques for a number of years, and was then sold again in 1984 and once more became a private house.

The Lodge

The Lodge is a fine late-Georgian house to the east of the village, behind a high wall alongside Rectory Lane. It was probably built around 1800, on or near the site of an older building shown on the 1724

Manor map. In 1876, The Lodge was listed as having 12 acres of land and a rateable value of £31.

The original house was basically a square building with a central oval staircase, a portico with four pillars on the south side and a verandah on the west. In 1876 W.H. Hackblock, Esq., asked Norwich architect Edward Boardman to design a large extension. The south front was extended forwards to enlarge the drawing-room and breakfast room, an outer hall added in front of the old lobby, and a semi-circular portico sheltered the front door. A number of new rooms were added on the east side with servants' quarters above. Twentieth-century additions to the house include a modern sun-lounge with swimming pool. Before the indoor pool was built there was an outdoor pool (now a sunken garden) with a gypsy caravan as a changing room!

The house was probably built for Edmund Hooke, barrister, and his wife, Naomi (née Wilson), who also owned Churchman House, St Giles Street, Norwich. The arms of the Hooke family appear on part of the hatchment above the tower arch of Mulbarton Church, where he was buried in 1811, aged 61. His young widow, who married John Story and died aged 53 in the Pyrenees in 1830, was brought home and buried beside her first husband. Edmund and Naomi Hooke had two daughters: Cassandra Wilson Hooke (his heiress), who married William Bellairs in 1822, and Clara Amelia Hooke, who became Mrs J.H.S. Jekyll. Both have memorials in the church.

Cassandra inherited The Lodge and her husband, Sir William Bellairs, is listed as 'owner' in the Tithe Apportionment documents of 1841. Sir William, born on 10 October 1793, joined the Army in 1811 at the age of 17 and died in London on 2 October 1863 in his seventieth year. He is buried in Mulbarton churchyard in a fine granite tomb to the east of the church. According to the inscription, he 'Served in the 15th King's Hussars at Morales, Vitoria, Pyrenees, Pampeluna, Orthez, Tarbes, Toulouse, Quatre Bras, Waterloo.' These are campaigns against Napoleon's armies in Spain and France between 1813 and 1815. His horse was killed under him in the retreat from

The Lodge, front (south-facing) view. In the distance to the right is the roof of the barn of Lodge Farm.

The west-facing façade of The Lodge looks out onto the garden. On the left is the post-war bungalow built for Mrs Trafford's mother.

The tomb of Sir William Bellairs (1793–1863) of The Lodge. The granite gravestone in Mulbarton churchyard is inscribed with the battles of the Napoleonic Wars in which William Bellairs fought.

Quatre Bras and he was wounded at the Battle of Waterloo. He became Sir William Bellairs around 1850. His widow, Lady Bellairs, died on 1 November 1876 at the age of 77 and is commemorated on the same grave. Their son, Captain Edmund Hooke William Bellairs, gained local notoriety when he chaired a committee to discuss enclosing the Common in May 1865. The proposal was strongly opposed (Chapter 2).

The next important owner, William Henry Hackblock (1870s to 1890s), is named as owner and occupier in the Poor Rate book for 1875–76. He also owned Lodge Farm next door. He had The Lodge enlarged in 1876, nearly doubling its size. Mrs Hackblock, a school manager and a frequent visitor to Mulbarton School, is first mentioned in the school log-book as inspecting needlework in 1875. Another entry mentions: 'July 11th 1879: Mrs Hackblock visited the school on Friday afternoon to pay for eight children fees for the quarter.' There are three Hackblock graves in the churchyard: those of Herbert Charles, William Henry and May Hackblock.

Around 1900 The Lodge was the retirement home of General George Nicholas Channer, CB, VC. He was born in India in 1843, survived the Mutiny and served with the Indian Army for more than 40 years. He won his Victoria Cross on 20 December 1875 at Burkit Putus Pass, Malaya, where 'he was the first to jump into the enemy's stockade whilst leading a small party to obtain intelligence of their position and strength.' Later, he served in the 2nd Afghan War and its aftermath, and then went to Assam. Presumably he retired to Mulbarton, but he did not live here for long, and died at Westward Ho! in 1905.

Charles Teesdale is listed as owner in 1904, and Edmund Walter Hanbury Wood in 1922. Then came Mrs Agnew, who lived there until she died in 1943. People particularly remember her chauffeur/ gardener, Mr Blackman, who was a Sunday-school teacher and gave 'magic lantern' shows in the Parish

Hall: 'He wore breeches, boots and buskins when at work.' The Lodge was sold by auction in 1948, along with Lodge Farm and seven cottages. The house was described as 'built of brick, cement rendered and colour washed with slate roof…' with:

… gardens to west and south of property: rose garden; summer house; pleasure lawns with sheltered walks among mature trees, octagonal garden room, partly walled-in kitchen garden with heated greenhouse, well-stocked orchard, plantations, grazing.

It was purchased by Mr and Mrs Trafford, who had a bungalow built in the grounds for Mrs Trafford's Hungarian mother.

From Farmhouse to Great House

A close look at the other 'great houses' of Mulbarton – Lodge Farm, the Old Rectory and the Malthouse – suggests they were once farmhouses that were turned into prestigious 'period' houses by wealthy owners. On the 1841 Tithe Map, Lodge Farm is shown as a narrow house, aligned north-south. This can still be seen today as the older part of the

The front of the Old Rectory, Mulbarton. This shows clearly that the house is in two parts. The east end (right) *is a much older and smaller timber-framed house, which has its own staircase. The main part is a large Georgian extension added to the front of this house in the 1720s by Revd George Gay.* (CONTRIBUTED BY DAVID WRIGHT)

The back of the Old Rectory in the early 1960s, showing the many additions to the original house and the pond with reflections. (PHOTO: DEREK VALIANT)

building, to which a large and much grander extension was added, with a new and more splendid entry made in this south-facing side.

The Old Rectory, home of Mulbarton's Rector until 1976, was built in the 1720s by George Gay, Rector 1721–28, who died in 1728 according to a monument in the chancel of Mulbarton Church. This has a long Latin inscription, part of which translates as:

Calmly he passed away but he did not yield to death until, at his own personal charge, and that a great one, he had built up from its foundations the residence of the Rector. Whosoever thou art who readest this, being the unhappy master of a residence in ruins, be up and doing, bear in mind this praiseworthy piety and do thou likewise.

It is likely that George Gay added a large Georgian extension onto an existing house. Whether this was an earlier Rectory or not we do not know – it is a long way from the church. It was George Gay's successor, Revd John Phillips (Rector 1728–37), who had the tithe barn built in 1731, in a style similar to that of the Long Barn of the Old Hall. The coachman's house was added at the end nearest the road. The Old Rectory was sold by Norwich diocese in 1977 as a 'five-bedroom house', and the orchard as a building plot for Old Rectory Close.

The third large house to be extended from an original farmhouse is The Malthouse, by the south-west corner of Mulbarton Common. In this case, however, a working malthouse was converted into a house (Chapter 7). Its association with the Fairman family is described in Chapter 6. In the 1960s and '70s, Miss Ireland (of the family of Irelands, Estate Agents & Auctioneers) lived in the Malthouse and created a garden of rare and interesting plants. She is remembered for the many parties she held there and for a parrot that lived in the kitchen. The present owners, who bought the house in 1979, have found no fewer than five fireplaces of different ages in the lower part of the house!

The oldest part of the house (the lower part) probably dates from around 1650. It is certainly shown on the 1724 map. The taller part was the malthouse itself, which probably dates from the early-nineteenth century – and astute observers will notice that the two buildings are on a slightly different alignment. In the 1860s there were plans to demolish the malthouse and build a Georgian-style residence in its place. Instead, the building itself was converted into a house, with three new floors and windows.

The farmhouse and former malthouse seem to have been kept as separate houses, with separate gates and entrances and (after 1931) separate electricity meters. The taller house was rented or leased and is called Thorpe House in the 1901 census. Although a mains tap was installed in the kitchen, the property depended on a deep well and an electric

pump for many more years. The house was refurbished in 1953, when the old lath and plaster was removed and walls straightened with cement.

Cottage Homes

The majority of villagers lived in small 'two-up, two-down' cottages built of clay lump or brick. It seems surprising to us today that in 1851, out of 124 dwellings in Mulbarton, only nine were lived in by 'owner occupiers' – of which only three can be described as 'small houses'. The majority were 'tied cottages' belonging to landowners in Mulbarton or neighbouring villages. The rest were rented out by landlords living in Norwich or further afield. In 1891 two pairs of cottages west of the Common were sold by auction on behalf of the executors of James Banham, a Norwich innkeeper. He was probably typical of Norwich businessmen who invested their

The aptly named Holly Cottage in The Rosery, in the late 1920s. It is part hidden by one of the holly trees in the front hedge. Today the ivy has gone, to reveal a plaque (top right) *showing it was built in 1830 by T.G. This cottage was the home of the Stackyard family for many years.* (PHOTO CONTRIBUTED BY EVELYN SMITH, NÉE STACKYARD)

The terrace of brick houses, long known as 'Blakes Cottages' after their original owner, still stand facing the south-east corner of the Common. This photograph, from 1900 or earlier, also shows that bicycles were speeding up journeys within and beyond Mulbarton. The terrace was lengthened around 1990, when a single-storey extension was rebuilt. (CONTRIBUTED BY JULIET AMOS, NÉE LOFTY)

savings in property in and around Norwich that would provide a regular income from rents.

On the west side of the Common is 'Carpenters', formerly 'Common View', which was occupied by a number of carpenters (Chapter 7). It is a good example of a property that was enlarged and improved by its owners as their businesses flourished. Another example is Mill House, with its elegant Georgian front. This, however, is only a façade – quite a narrow frontage added to a much humbler older cottage with a slightly lower floor level.

Many of the brick cottages have survived and been modernised, often by turning 'double-dwellings' into one. Several 'modern' brick houses were built around 1900, including the former Post Office (Chapter 8) and the schoolhouse (now 'Brook House'). Most of the clay-lump cottages have gone, unless they were extended and improved (as was Butler House, opposite the World's End) or rebuilt – as happened to Mr and Mrs Carver's attractively thatched house at the north end of the village after a disastrous fire (Chapter 6).

Chris Mickleburgh lived in one of the clay-lump cottages along Norwich Road. He remembers the rotten floorboards in the bedroom he shared with his young brother before the family was rehoused in St Omer Close in 1936. Bryan Tungate remembers:

In the 1940s we lived in a 'clay-lump' hovel which adjoined the local pub – the 'Tradesman's Arms' [Chapter 3]. It had a living room, small kitchen and three bedrooms which were reached by wooden stairs.

Many cottages were built of clay lump, to which brick outhouses were added, as with this house west of the Common seen here mid-1930s. Hilda Martin (sitting on the motor cycle) went into service in London; Stella Martin worked for Mrs Rowbottom, headmistress of Mulbarton School. (PHOTO CONTRIBUTED BY CLIFFORD ROBINSON)

No electric, only a smoky oil lamp, so we didn't stay up very late at night. No television and our wireless was battery and accumulator powered... At the back of the house was the wash-house where there was a big open copper which had to be filled by bringing up buckets of water from the pump – we didn't have mains water then. When the water was boiled up there was a big stick which was used to keep plunging the clothes into the water. Then it was out of the copper and onto the big mangle which forced the water out of the clothes, by wringing them between two big wooden rollers. This was the hardest job of all and called for all your energy. Me and my brother had to do this together as neither could turn it on our own. There was no 'inside toilet' but down the bottom of the yard we had a lean-to with two buckets in. At night the spiders looked big by the shadows on the wall from our candle. Father and Jack Cooper, our neighbour, had to dig holes at the bottom of the garden and empty the buckets every week.

The brick cottages were not much better: Maurice Norman was born in the cottage that is now next to the Rectory entry. Despite being a brick 'semi', 'We had no electricity or running water. We used the pump beside the pond. The toilet was down the end of the garden.'

Church Cottages

Two pairs of picturesque thatched cottages stood at what is now the front of the current Rectory. They are first mentioned in a terrier (inventory of church property) of 1706 as 'inhabited by 4 poor persons', and by 1725 are described as 'in very bad repair, let to four different tenants at 30s. each, but the rents are collected with difficulty.' They were rented out by the churchwardens to provide income for the church – producing £5.16s.0d. in 1843, rising to £8 by 1879/80 (£2 per cottage). In 1851 the occupiers were Mary Baldry (pauper), Kizia Allen (pauper), William English and five children (widower, ag. lab.), William Dawson (carpenter) and his 70-year-old wife and five grown-up children (ag. labs). Each dwelling had a rateable value of £1.10s.0d., the rates being paid by the owners, with a 25 per cent reduction. The cottages were maintained at church expense – they were re-thatched with straw in 1863–64 by Mr Kirby for just over £9, and re-thatched by him again in 1883–84 for over £11.

Laurence Bailey (born 1920) was brought up in one of the cottages by his grandparents, Mr and Mrs Hemnell (née Beaumont) when his mother died of pneumonia when he was six months old. He remembers:

There were two rooms down and two rooms up. The ceilings were very low and large beams went through from one cottage to another. One of the neighbours had

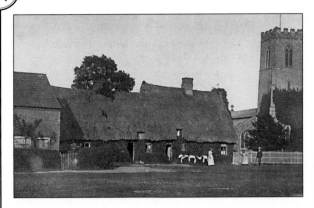

The old Church cottages stood at what is now the entry to the present Mulbarton Rectory. Washing has been put out to dry on the hedge. The brick cottage (left) is where the footballer Monty Norman was born (Chapter 2). This photo probably dates from the early 1900s.
(PHOTO FROM VILLAGE ARCHIVE)

The old Church cottages with (left to right) Jane Blackburn, Mrs Hemnell, Billy Butler with Mrs Blackburn's dog, Peggy. (PHOTO FROM VILLAGE ARCHIVE)

Jane Blackburn (1873–1958) outside the thatched cottages by Mulbarton Church in the early 1930s, holding her grandson, Tony Kent.
(PHOTO FROM VILLAGE ARCHIVE)

Brough and Mary Hemnell outside their thatched cottage in the late 1920s.
(PHOTO CONTRIBUTED BY LAURENCE BAILEY)

Left: Laurence Bailey with his grandmother, Mary Hemnell (née Beaumont) and a visitor in the late 1920s. This photograph shows the structure of clay-lump walls and the thatched roof of the cottages. Beyond is the end-wall of the most southerly brick cottage by the pond (where Monty Norman was born).
(PHOTO CONTRIBUTED BY LAURENCE BAILEY)

Lads on the Common, c.1940. Behind the group are the thatched Church cottages and the church without a clock in its tower. Left to right: H. Chadwick, Stanley Canham, Cliff Allison (pointing), Mr Nicholls, Michael Cooper (in cap), Harold Rix, Jack Connell, Eric Funnell (boy at front), Billy Larter (with cap), Jack Ramsey and, lying at front, Cecil Rix.
(PHOTO CONTRIBUTED BY CLIFF ALLISON)

Sylvia Dack (right) with the family dog, Tessie, and Frances Robinson on the Common in the 1950s. Note the clock added to the church tower and the thatched Church cottages behind. (PHOTO CONTRIBUTED BY ANNE DACK)

The demolition of Church cottages in 1957 or '58 by Bob Mickleburgh and two of his sons. For a decade they had been used as a builder's store. (PHOTO: DENNIS MICKLEBURGH)

a bread oven built into the wall. We had an oven in the brickwork in which my grandmother baked bread – and would sometimes throw on a small cocoa tin full of paraffin, with dire consequences! I'd be sent along to fetch my uncle who lived in a cottage by the pond to get him to come and push the oven back into place and repair the brickwork...!

Their neighbours included the Blackburn family (Oliver Blackburn drove the butcher's van and the fire engine), and Mrs Kedge, who held the church key. In 1933 the Rural District Council wrote to the Rector threatening to impose a demolition order on the cottages:

The Council have no desire to destroy every cottage in the District which happens to be unfit for habitation at present and they are willing to consider the question of a grant towards the cost of reconditioning these cottages if the proposals for the works are likely to result in the provision of reasonable and decent habitation...

A few years later the residents were rehoused in newly built council-houses: Laurence Bailey and the

Hemnells moved to No. 49 St Omer Close. The Church cottages remained standing and during the Second World War the Utting family from Norwich, rehoused there, tidied them up. Miss Utting was a music teacher, and Brenda Ford (née Collins) recalls:

I had piano lessons with Flo. They did not have electricity, so when it got dark Flo would light the hurricane-lamps at either side of the piano to enable pupils to see for the lesson.

When the Uttings moved, the Church cottages were taken over as a builder's store by Bob Mickleburgh and sons. They were demolished around 1958 and the clay lump was used to raise the edge of 'Church pit'. The land on which they were built is now the entrance to the new Rectory.

The Factory Houses

Perhaps most remarkable of all the 'small houses' of Mulbarton was Scott's Terrace, more usually known as the 'factory houses', on Norwich Road. This terrace of five three-storey houses was on land now occupied by the vet's surgery and car park. Former residents remember that the top floor of each was a large room, reached by a winding staircase, which families divided by a curtain or partition.

The *Norwich Mercury*, on 6 March 1830, advertised the sale of 'A substantial newly-erected Building at Mulbarton, in Norfolk, lately used by the said Arthur Beloe as a Silk Factory, with a piece of ground at the back thereof', plus a 'good brick cottage' and 'a double cottage' nearby. Mr Beloe's silk-weaving business had gone bankrupt, and his Norwich house and another factory building were also being sold to pay his debts. The 1832 map of planned improvements to the turnpike marks the buildings as 'the late Manufactory'. It seems that the Mulbarton premises did not sell as a factory, but someone – possibly a Mr Scott – saw their potential for conversion to housing. In the 1851 Poor Rate Book they are owned by William Scott – hence 'Scott's Terrace' – and rented out to five families: No. 1 – Elizabeth Alborough, a widow with four children; No. 2 –William and Sarah Leek; No. 3 – Richard and Hannah Howes and eight children; No. 4 – Charles and Mary Larter and nine children; No. 5 – James and Susan Davey, three children and three lodgers. By 1876 the Poor Rate Book gives the owner as Charles Abednego Betts, but only two of the five cottages were inhabited – by William Beaumont and Charles Baxter. The rateable value was £4 and the residents received a 15 per cent rate reduction.

Bill Alborough, born in Scott's Terrace, discovered that his great-grandfather was living there in 1851:

... 60 or 70 years ago, if you told any Mulbarton local that you lived, or had lived, in The Factory, they would

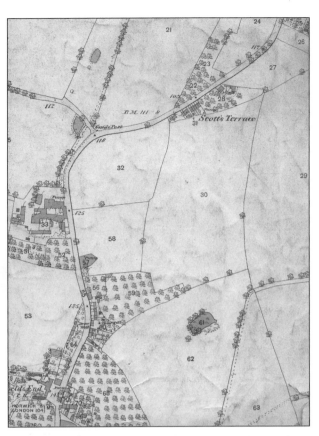

Map of Norwich Road from Paddock Farm to Hill House, showing the location of Scott's Terrace (the 'factory houses'). From the Ordnance Survey 1:2500 County Series 1881.

(Reproduced with permission of the Ordnance Survey)

Donny Abendroth (left) *and Bill Alborough at the back of the 'factory houses' (Scott's Terrace), probably 1933. Note that rainwater is collected from the roof.*

(Photo contributed by Bill Alborough)

have understood. Now, memories of The Factory are fading… My parents moved there in the late 1920s. My father, badly wounded in the First World War and in receipt of a Disability Pension, still managed to hold down a job on a farm. This involved the tied cottage system whereby if you lost your job you lost your house. My parents had already been the victims of this, not because of anything my father did, but because his boss went bankrupt. They were anxious to escape the system and they heard that 3 Scott's Terrace was vacant and was owned by Arthur King, the butcher at Swardeston (where the pet shop is now). My mother went to see Arthur and asked if they could have the house. Amazingly, Arthur didn't even know he owned the house, but his reply was 'If it's mine, Alice, it's yours', a phrase that my mother repeated often and remembered to her dying day.

I was born there in 1931 and I was five when we left. There was no drainage. Water came from a pump; waste water was thrown in the ditch at the bottom of the yard, which had a smell all of its own. (Sometimes, even now, on our cycle trips through French villages whose waste water flows down the side of the road, the memories of that smell come flooding back!) There was a

Left: *Gordon Andrews behind his home in Scott's terrace (the 'factory houses') Mulbarton. Later he moved to St Omer Close (Chapter 11).*

(Photo contributed by Clifford Robinson)

tumbledown shed and a bucket lavatory, the contents of which had to be carried to and buried on the allotment ('The Swamp'). There was always the threat of flooding as the water swept down off the fields behind in heavy rain.

In 1936 St Omer Close was completed and all five families from 'The Factory' were rehoused there. I think they were the Hemnall, Tuddenham, Alborough (mine), Andrews and Wharton families from one to five in that order. The vacant building stood in a dilapidated condition until after the Second World War and we local children used it as an adventure playground and Donny Abendroth kept his rabbits in there. How we didn't have more accidents I don't know, as many floorboards were missing or unsafe. I remember the narrowness of the steps on the staircases, especially on the bends! The building was demolished after the war. The site was firstly the doctor's surgery and is now the vet's.

The Andrews Family lived in the second of the five houses in Scott's Terrace (the 'factory houses'). They pose for a family photo by Tom Nokes on 'the Swamp' – allotment land by Norwich Road. The family were one of the first to be rehoused in St Omer Close. **Left to right, standing:** *Maude (later Mrs Abendroth), Leslie, Harold (father of Rosalind Robinson), Christine (mother of Sylvia Haverson), Russell, Catherine (Kate, later Mrs Canham), Mabel (later Mrs Woolmer);* **sitting:** *James, Gordon and Maria Andrews (parents), Dora (later Mrs Snashfold), Ethel (later Mrs Eastell).*

(Photo contributed by Rosalind Robinson)

CHAPTER 10

Mulbarton in Wartime

The First World War

A Roll of Honour in the church porch lists all the Mulbarton men who served in the First World War. A total of 90 men went to war out of a population of about 480 (1911 census). The 16 who died are highlighted in gold. To begin with, many were exempt because of their involvement with agriculture and allied trades, but as the war dragged on more and more volunteered or were called up.

Events were organised to support the war effort. Mr W.A. Emms of Birchfield Lane received a letter sent on behalf of King George V (dated 7 October 1914) thanking him for a donation of £5.10s.0d. sent to the National Relief Fund from Mulbarton & Swardestone [sic] Brass Band. However, a minute of 5 October 1914 shows that the Parish Council declined to make a contribution. Soon afterwards, the same brass band sent a donation of £3.3s.0d. to the Commission for Relief in Belgium.

The Volunteers

Men joined the local volunteer regiment – a cross between training for possible service and a Home Guard. They held their first church parade at East Carleton on Sunday, 5 September, and the *East Carleton Magazine* reports:

About 20 were present under the command of Squadron Commander R.W. Tuddenham and Sergeant West.

The Roll of Honour from the First World War in the porch of Mulbarton Church – recording all who served, with gold lettering for the 16 who died.

The Squad marched to and fro' Headquarters accompanied by the Mulbarton and Swardeston Band.

But the next report, in January 1916, states:

The Mulbarton and District Platoon of the C Company, 7th Battalion Norfolk Volunteer Regiment has not been able, for various reasons, to do much drill since harvest. The new landlord of the World's End has put his club-room at our disposal, and the platoon hopes to resume regular drill at once.

'Private C.B.P. Ramsay' (the East Carleton Rector) took over as platoon commander, with Sergeant West as platoon sergeant, and called a church parade on:

'Mulbarton Detachment of 'C' Company, 4th Battalion Norfolk Volunteers meet for Drill at Mulbarton on Mondays and Wednesdays at 8 p.m.' The clergyman (second from left) is Revd C.B.P. Ramsay, Rector of East Carleton, who took over as platoon commander. (East Carleton Magazine, July 1915) (CONTRIBUTED BY IRIS FROST)

First World War volunteers march behind the local band – led by Revd C.B.P. Ramsay. (CONTRIBUTED BY IRIS FROST)

The volunteers pose for the camera at the back of the World's End in 1916. Back row (standing) fifth from left: *Fred Middleton (postmaster);* seventh: *Loftus Watling (Bracon Ash);* eighth: *Horace Lofty;* far right: *Fred Stubbings;* middle row (seated): *Charlie Cracknell (Mulbarton shop owner), ?, Sgt West, ?, 'Bowler' Scarff (road sweeper), two unknown;* front row (on grass), second from left: *Harry Hall.*
(PHOTO CONTRIBUTED BY JOHN BETTS)

First World War volunteers – mostly in uniform by now – on parade outside the World's End in 1916.

(PHOTO CONTRIBUTED BY JOHN BETTS)

Monday, Jan. 3rd, at 8 pm, at the above Headquarters, and hopes for a full attendance in order that he may get the enrolment papers in order so that members can receive the Government brassard to wear. Dummy wooden rifles have been ordered for drill purposes, and we hope to put the members into uniform shortly.

We shall be glad of recruits to come to the parade. Recruits required are of four classes:
(1) Young men under military age.
(2) Men of military age who are willing to sign an agreement to join the regular forces, if called upon.
(3) Men who have attested under Lord Derby's group system, and would like to have some preliminary drill.
(4) Men over military age, who would like to 'do their bit'.

The uniforms were received, and more church parades held. Rifle practice was at a rifle range on Lord Linley's land at East Carleton Lodge, in Catbridge Lane. By March 1916:

The Platoon has more men in uniform and is fast becoming efficient. It has done a great deal of important and useful work lately and recruits are still coming in. Volunteers are now recognised under the Volunteer Act of 1863 by which they become an integral part of Home Defence Troops. If mobilised, they would receive the same pay and allowances as their brothers in the regular forces.

The War at Home

Besides the worry for families with men abroad, there were changes to be faced by those who stayed at home. In the Parish Council minutes of 9 July 1914 we read:

Correspondence from Major Allen of 3rd Norfolk Battery RFA asking for use of Common for manoeuvres... Propd by A. Sturman, 2nd by C. Frost that this Council knows no reason why the 3rd Norfolk Battery RFA should not practise for the weekend as required providing that the turf of the Common is not disturbed. Carried unanimously.

In 1915, the 'Defence of the Realm Lighting Order' enforced blackout. Parish Council meetings could no longer be held in the school as the windows were too big to black out, so were moved to the clerk's house

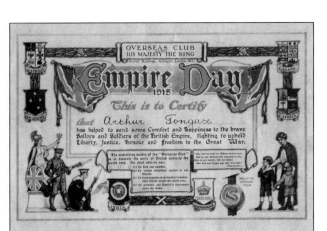

Certificate for Empire Day 1915 – awarded to Arthur 'Tongate' (should be Tungate) for sending 'some Comfort and Happiness to the brave Sailors and Soldiers of the British Empire...'   (CONTRIBUTED BY BRYAN TUNGATE)

War memorial in Mulbarton Church – commemorating the 16 men killed in the First World War, to which a plaque with the names of the seven men who died in the Second World War was added. Photo taken on Remembrance Sunday 2004.   (PHOTO: JILL WRIGHT)

(the schoolhouse) from November to March. With councillors absent on military service, the quorum was reduced to one third of members. By September 1916, only two councillors and the clerk attended the meeting. Early in 1917 the Parish Council agreed to act as a local sub-committee of the Committee of National Service, to get the particulars of fit people not already engaged in national work.

With so many men going off to war, women and children had to take on more work and families had to cope as well as they could. Queenie Wasey (née Dack) told us that her mother died when she was five while her father was away in the trenches, so the children were scattered among various aunts. Charlie Frost's business was carried on by his wife 'with the exception of the execution of Repairs' (Chapter 7). School exemption certificates were issued for farmers who could give work to lads over 12 (the normal school-leaving age being 14), and in January 1916 this was extended to girls who could look after younger children to enable their mothers to work.

The Mulbarton School log-book records two boys and a girl being granted a labour certificate (war duration) in 1916, and a boy who went to work for Mr Hill at Lodge Farm in 1918. There is no other mention of the war in the school log-book – it began during a measles epidemic and ended with the school closed for a few weeks for an influenza epidemic. Armistice Day was marked annually in school after the war.

Those Who Never Returned

The Memorial in Mulbarton Church lists the 16 names of those who died. The following have been traced through the Commonwealth War Graves Commission:

DAWSON, Albert, Private, Norfolk Regiment, 7th Battalion. Died 31 July 1915, aged 20. Buried at Rifle House Cemetery, Comines-Warneton, Hainaut, Belgium. Son of Mr and Mrs J.A. Dawson, Mulbarton.

HUGGINS, Ernest Albert, Corporal, Border Regiment, 7th Battalion. Died 23 April 1917, aged 33. Commemorated on Arras Memorial, Bay 6. Son of Edward and Louisa Huggins of Mulbarton; husband of Lily Florence Huggins of Norwich Road, Mulbarton.

LARTER, Joseph Alfred, Private, Norfolk Regiment, 9th Battalion. Died 15 September 1916, aged 28. Commemorated on Thiepval Memorial, Somme, France. Eldest son of William and Sophia Jane Larter, Swainsthorpe.

MUSKETT, Cecil Frederick, Private, Norfolk Regiment 'A' Company, 1st Battalion. Died 9 October 1917, aged 20. Buried at Hooge Crater Cemetery, Ieper, Belgium. Son of Frederick and Alice C. Muskett of Hill House, Mulbarton.

STACKYARD, William, Private, Norfolk Regiment, 1st/4th Battalion. Died 12 August 1915, aged 21. Commemorated on Helles Memorial, panel 42–44, Gallipoli, Turkey. Son of Walter and Alice Jane Stackyard, The Rosery, Mulbarton.

TOOKE, Bertie, Gunner, Royal Garrison Artillery, 247th Siege Battery. Died 15 July 1918, aged 35. Buried Staglieno Cemetery, Genoa, Italy. Son of Samuel and Betsy Tooke, Mulbarton.

WHARTON, George Bertie, Private, Norfolk Regiment, 8th Battalion. Died 1 July 1916, aged 21. Commemorated on Thiepval Memorial, Pier & Face 1C & 1D, Somme, France. Son of George Henry Wharton, The Wood, Mulbarton.

WOOLTERTON, Percy Harold, probably the Woolterton who was a private in the Dorsetshire Regiment, 1st Battalion. Died 2 May 1915, aged 20. Commemorated on Ypres (Menin Gate) Memorial. Son of Mr A. Woolterton, 4 Church Lane, Eaton.

The other names on the Memorial are: James CARVER; Robert G. CARVER; George F. DAWSON; Henry P. DOUBLEDAY; Albert E. LINCOLN; Ronald PRIEST; Cecil J. RANDALL; William F. STUBBINGS.

Soldiers demobilised after the First World War meet at the back of the World's End, July 1919. The title indicates these men are from Bracon Ash, Hethel and Swardeston, but the group may include some Mulbarton men.

(CONTRIBUTED BY VIC GRAY)

From a contemporary newspaper cutting:

Mulbarton's memorial to her fallen sons was dedicated and unveiled on Sunday afternoon [17 October 1920]. The memorial tablet is fixed on the south wall inside the church and is of Sicilian marble, with Irish green marble mount, all polished. It has a bronze border, with an oakleaf design... The service was conducted by the Rector, the Revd E.E. Ward. The Dean, in his address, said the names engraved on the tablet would last as long as the church lasted. They should all remember, too, those men who returned safely... At the end of the service, wreaths were laid near the tablet by relatives of the fallen... A muffled peal was afterwards rung on the bells.

The British Legion

A branch of the British Legion was formed for Mulbarton and district in 1931. Its first parade was for Armistice Day, 11 November, that year:

... a large congregation at Mulbarton Parish Church for the special service on Armistice Day. Members of the British Legion attended under Mr T. Pearce (Warrant Officer, Conductor Indian Ordnance Department) and the president of the branch, Lieut-Col. R. Boileau [of Ketteringham Hall] was also present...

Members marched from Mulbarton to the East Carleton war memorial and then to East Carleton Church for their first church parade.

Another newspaper cutting, dated 3 April 1932 reports:

A special service was held at the Mulbarton parish church on Sunday afternoon, for the purpose of dedicating the new banner of the Mulbarton and District Branch of the British Legion. The branch, which was only formed last year, is rapidly gaining strength. The company... headed by the Wymondham British Legion Band, marched to the church...

At the head of the local branch were: Colonel Boileau, President; Mr T. Pearce, Secretary... On leaving the church the Legion, headed by the band, paraded round the Common and back to the Headquarters, the World's End Hotel...

The banner is the much-repaired standard now 'laid up' in Mulbarton Church.

Mulbarton and District British Legion became an active branch – another newspaper report of 2 March 1934 describes how:

The Mulbarton branch of the British Legion entertained some 50 of the wives and children of members at the World's End Clubroom on Friday. After a tea the company were entertained and amused by a sketch... Games were organised...

Only five-and-a-half years later those children were facing war for themselves...

Mulbarton & District British Legion proudly display their new standard at the World's End, 1932.

(CONTRIBUTED BY BILL ALBOROUGH)

The Mulbarton Home Guard on the Common in front of the remains of the mill. The group was photographed before the men were disbanded in late 1944. The following are present: Otto Abendroth, Ted Aggas, Leslie Andrews, Bob Bailey, George Barrett, D. Bennington, Louie Bennington, George Bosten, 'Pots' Brighton, Harry Carver, Jack Cooper, Ted Copeman, Tom Cotton, L. Cross, Toby Cullum, Russell Dent, Ted Farrow, C. Hooney, Fred Jackson, A. Jenkins, Reggie Ladbrooke, Billy Larter, Horace Lofty, Tony McKelvey, Jimmy Mackerell, Ted Nelson, W. Rose, Tony Rowbottom, Don Skipper, Tom Smith, Fred Wasey, Jimmy Whurr, George Wick, Leslie Woods, Pat Wymer plus three others.

(CONTRIBUTED BY ENID FOX)

The Second World War:
Memories of a Village at War

Everyone was directly affected by the Second World War with its air raids, evacuees, rationing and the proliferation of air bases in East Anglia. Preparations began early – a meeting to recruit air-raid wardens was held at the World's End in July 1938. Gas masks were demonstrated and issued – Dorothy Tungate remembers that 'just before the war the Parish (Wingfield) Hall was used to make up gas masks, and babies' masks that the child used to lie completely inside with a plastic type front...' Her baby son, Bryan, was used for a demonstration and hated it!

People have clear memories of events in and around Mulbarton during the war. Bill Alborough:

I well remember the tones of the Prime Minister of the time, Mr Neville Chamberlain, when he uttered that chilling phrase '... I have to tell you that this country is at war with Germany.' It was September 1939 and I was nine. Rationing started, sweets disappeared, we started saving metal, people built makeshift air-raid shelters, gas masks were issued and, strangely enough, at Mulbarton School, we started to learn the National Anthems of the Allies. I remember learning La Marseillaise word perfect. We hadn't a clue what the words meant, but to this day I know the anthem better than many French school children.

Soldiers started to appear in the village. They were billeted at nearby big country houses which had been commandeered... With the threat of invasion came various precautions. The Home Guard exercised regularly at weekends. Old wagons were parked at

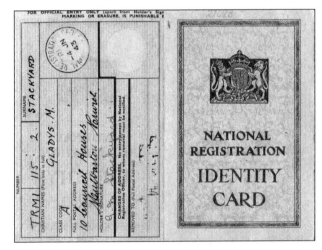

The cover and inside of a Second World War identity card belonging to Gladys Stackyard of No. 10 Council Houses, Mulbarton (now Long Lane).

(CONTRIBUTED BY EVELYN SMITH, NÉE STACKYARD)

intervals on the common to prevent gliders landing. I was told that the remains of the mill were demolished so as not to provide a landmark for gliders. Huge Army lorries were tested by being driven into the pond near Frost's garage and then climbed up the steep bank on to the common. The sky was always full of the aircraft we now associate with the early days of the war...

At the Parish Council meeting on 18 July 1940:

Clerk read a letter from RDC re Prevention of Invasion. The centre portion of the Common only to be put out of commission with suggestions as to the most efficient means of rendering them dangerous to aircraft. The

Watling's vans parked on the Common, 1940. About 40 lorries were brought to Mulbarton from Surrey Street, Norwich, every evening during most of the Second World War to ensure they were safe from being bombed in the city. One lorry returned with all the men and brought them out next morning. In the centre, in the tall black hat, is Geoffrey Watling, director; next right are Charlie Watling and Frank Watling. Seated second from left on front row: Jack Grady.

(PHOTO CONTRIBUTED BY JACK GRADY)

Chairman reported he had been in conversation with Col. Beck on the question... and he advised the Council to await instructions from the military... Clerk instructed to write to RDC for permission to place a Bus on the Common to be used as a Guard Room for the Local Volunteer Defence Corps [renamed the Home Guard] providing the Military would bear the expense of moving the old Bus to the required position.

Bill Alborough remembers the Norwich blitz and the many people who left the city for the relative safety of the countryside each night:

From Mulbarton you could hear the thud of the bombs and see the glow in the sky from the fires. People came from Norwich to the country to escape the devastation of their homes. Mulbarton Chapel housed families for a while. We housed two families in our house. One man was a very good darts player and I played darts with him for hours.

Tony Kent remembered bombs over Mulbarton:

During the war, a German aircraft making a run from the Norwich air defences dropped a stick of bombs across the farmyard in Rectory Lane. One dropped in the horse yard, one in the pond and the rest across a meadow. No one was hurt, but as the bombs exploded a young colt was born. He was registered with the Suffolk Horse Society as 'Mulbarton Blitzkreig'. How apt that was! He was completely untrainable and eventually had to be disposed of.

Mrs Tooke can point out the remains of the bomb crater quite near her house on Shotesham Road. Although filled in now, there is still a circle where crops do not grow properly, caused, she believes, by the remains of phosphor. This was probably the night of 18–19 March 1943, when three 'firepots', two high explosive bombs and two ABB500s are recorded

as falling in Mulbarton parish.

During the war, Mulbarton acquired a fire engine for the district, garaged at the Old Hall. Oliver ('Crom') Blackburn became station officer when R. Hunt retired through ill-health. Others involved included Mr Skipper, Stanley Hammond and Peter Dawson. The vehicle was a light fire engine, with a Rolls-Royce engine and a light pump, but the only activity people can remember now is that it attended a chip-shop fire in a wooden hut in Wood Lane, Swardeston! It still existed long after the war – some people tried it out around 1960: it still worked, but water went everywhere except out of the hosepipe!

Brenda Ford (née Collins) remembers:

Mulbarton did not have any bombs fall on it as such to cause damage, but we could see and hear the air raids taking place on Norwich and hear the guns firing at enemy planes. My mother's family were bombed out in Norwich and came to live with us in our small bungalow, along with a land girl who worked for Mr Betts at Bracon Ash. Goodness knows where we all slept, but it was wartime and we managed.

Her neighbour, Gerald Collins (no relation), remembers his aunt and uncle from Earlham staying overnight: 'They biked over from Norwich all through the blitz.'

Evelyn Smith (née Stackyard) remembers the evacuees:

During the war years, my mother had evacuees. First we had a family from Bethnal Green – their name was Callaghan and there was a mother and two boys. In the latter part of the war we had the Jay family from Norwich: mother, two boys and a baby. I think most people had evacuees if they had room. My father was in the Army during the war, but there was still my mother, brother and myself in a three-bedroom house, so goodness knows where we all slept!

The school log-book reflects the disruptions of the sudden arrival and departure of evacuees:

1939: Sept. 11th – School reopened today after harvest Holidays. 11 London County Council Evacuated Children; 2 Private Evacuated Children admitted; 2 new children from other areas.

Sept. 18th – 2 children returned to London. 2 girls admitted from Aldershot Barracks School.

Oct. 2nd – 7 LCC children returned home this week. 7 children have been trans. from School register to Evacuees list – These are 1 from Portsmouth and 6 from Aldershot.

The children themselves remember: 'The London children were very different to us and thought they had come to a real backwater'!

Care was taken over children's health and welfare in the Second World War, with double milk rations, cod liver oil, Parishes Food Supplement and Virol given to those thought to need it. Children were taken to the Parish Hall for first-aid lessons and to see Ministry of Information films, and they contributed to 'Warship Week', 'Wings for Victory', and other collections.

Chris Mickleburgh remembers finding masses of tin foil all over the Common after a night of raids – dropped by German planes to try to confuse radar – and going from door to door with other children after school to collect rubbish to be recycled for the war effort. This was stored in some old huts between the butcher's and the school. The local Home Guard successfully thwarted a (mock) invasion of Norwich by putting hurdles across the roads at each end of the Common. It was the day the World's End (their HQ) had a delivery; his story is that 'after the celebration, one of the officers spent much of that night on the Common penned in by the hurdles by his men, who then staggered home!'

The Children's War

Many children did not see their fathers for much of the duration of the war. Brenda Ford (née Collins):

My father had been a regular soldier in his young life and when he left the Army he went to work for Peter Finch at 'Woodlands' (Long Lane) but remained a member of the Territorial Army, so when the war was imminent he was called up and we saw very little of him for the next six years... It was quite an exciting time for children as there was a lot going on around us and, although we didn't understand fully what it meant, there was something interesting happening a lot of the time...

Boys played at being soldiers and formed themselves into their own corps. Bill Alborough and Peter Haverson remember the 'Royal St Omer Close

'*The Royal St. Omer Close Corps' protecting Mulbarton in 1941! The group was organised by lads living in St Omer Close during the Second World War, who borrowed their dads' equipment or made their own.* Left to right, back row: *Bill Alborough, Donny Abendroth, Peter Haverson, Rex Mickleburgh;* middle row: *John Tuddenham, Chris Mickleburgh, Barry Dent, Dennis Mickleburgh;* front row: *Bernard Rayner, Colin Spoor, Bryant Mickleburgh, Lionel Robinson.*

(PHOTO CONTRIBUTED BY BILL ALBOROUGH)

Corps'. Their tin hats really were made of tin, with sharp edges that their mothers covered with tape. They crept along ditches to raid the lads from The Rosery, and once 'attacked' Flordon.

Italian prisoners of war came to work on local farms and loved to talk to children. Clifford Robinson remembers watching them, in their distinctive uniform with a large circle on the back, carve items during their lunch break in one of the sheds at Paddock Farm. 'If they chatted up the local girls at dances when the Americans were around there was trouble, though.'

At the local school, air-raid precautions were primitive. There was no local siren – people listened out for planes and for the wailing of the Norwich sirens:

Some of my earliest memories are of going to school in 1944 when I reached the grand 'old' age of five. Every time any sound of an aeroplane came into hearing we all had to dive under the desks; this would have been no good if a bomb came down on us. [There was a deep ditch running from the schoolhouse to Hall Farm barn and this was the school air-raid shelter.] *The children cut pieces of cardboard, covered them with the inevitable wallpaper, and sat on them in the ditch. Most were hoping for a bit of excitement. There was some – one afternoon a German aircraft running the defences of Norwich flew low over the school and one of the crew was seen to wave.*

Bryan Tungate

But there was fear, too. After the fall of France, 'I remember feeling very depressed and scared at the thought that the Germans were now 22 miles across the Channel from us' (Bill Alborough).

On one or two nights dogfights took place in the skies above our part of the world and unfortunately there were one or two nasty crashes when pilots were killed and us children were kept well away from the crash sites.

Brenda Ford

Crash Landing

The most vivid memory is of a Stirling bomber from RAF Marham (218 Squadron) limping back from a raid on Stuttgart, Germany, on the night of 4 May 1942 that crash-landed in a field south of Cuckoofield Lane – just beyond what is now the Mulberry Gardens estate. Gerald Collins was about ten at the time, and his father was head gardener at Woodlands, Long Lane.

At about 5 o'clock in the morning I was woken by the sound of aircraft engines. It circled around then there was a loud bang and the engines stopped. My father and uncle went outside carrying a shotgun and a torch as they did not know if it was an English or a German aircraft that had crashed. In the darkness they heard a voice shouting 'We are English! Don't shoot!' and the torch soon picked out the roundels of an RAF aircraft. They then helped three of the crew back to our house, the other crew members were taken to Woodlands.

As the Stirling landed, it hit a tree, broke a wing, demolished a chicken hutch and ended up in a ditch with its back broken. Fortunately there were no bombs on board, but some flares caught fire – 'father tried to stamp them out, but they were phosphor and impossible to put out and stuck to his boots. Very dangerous!' The pilots were uninjured but the rear gunner's arm was badly hurt. Gerald's mother ripped up sheets as bandages and heated up water to help him. They only had oil lamps then. Some crew went to the main house, where emergency services were called. 'The plane was under guard for two weeks and mother took drinks out to the police on duty there'. It was then dismantled and taken back to RAF Marham on huge 'Queen Mary' transport lorries 'which nearly didn't get up the loke to the crash site!'

There were other crashes nearby: John Tuddenham remembers a B24 Liberator crashing on Mr Cross's land near The Vale, Swainsthorpe, and when two Thunderbolts from RAF Bodney collided, the crew and their parachutes came down in the area. Brenda Ford remembers:

One morning we found a parachute in a ditch along the lane and were quite excited about it. Several parachutes were found during the course of the war but we never knew why they were there or if anybody had landed by

them. The village policeman would come and collect them and that was the last we heard...

Parachute silk was a prized find – one lady made three pairs of knickers for each of her daughters! Another prize was Perspex – even small pieces could be carved into rings and pendants.

The American 'Invasion'

Bill Alborough remembers:

In World War Two, 122 airfields were constructed for the USAAF – mostly in East Anglia. Our nearest was Hethel, only a mile away. It was started in 1941 and completed in late 1942. I was involved with its construction! I was 11 at the time and used to travel with Bert Bailey, a neighbour of ours, in his Bedford lorry to collect sand and gravel to take to Hethel airfield to make the runways.

There were some comings and goings by American aircrew as early as November 1942 but the first permanent residents came in June 1943 when the 389th Bomber Group arrived with B24 Liberators. Their first wartime mission took place on 7 September 1943. I well remember watching them from Mulbarton School taking off for raids and forming their tight formations before setting off for their target, mainly in Germany. This would be about 10a.m. as the Americans were responsible for daylight raids and the RAF for the night raids. After school we would sometimes go to Hethel and watch the aircraft landing from a nearby road. We now know, from history, how hazardous these daylight raids were, but even then we knew how dangerous it was by the sight of some of the damaged aircraft staggering back. If an aircraft had injured crew on board it would fire a cartridge before landing.

These well-dressed and relatively rich servicemen

Mulbarton lads on a visit to the 389th Bomb Group at the nearby USAAF base. Left to right: John Larter, Barry Dent and Peter Haverson beneath a B24 bomber on Hethel aerodrome. (PHOTO CONTRIBUTED BY PETER HAVERSON)

Local people remember the US airmen from nearby Hethel: 'Their uniforms were good quality; they wore ties and shoes and had lots of money.' Joining the landlord, Mr W.H. (Billy) Swift at the back of the World's End (above) and in the bar (below) are Staff-Sgt. Jimmy Roland, Sgt. Gerry Opitz (both photographers with 564th Squadron) and Cpl. Ernie Novak (48th Station Complement Medic.). Dated 'October 1943'. (PHOTOS CONTRIBUTED BY MRS J. SWIFT)

US airmen from the Hethel air base (389th Bomb Group) with local residents outside the World's End, probably October 1943. Left to right: The GI who married, second from left, Betty Nicholls (daughter of Mrs Nicholls who organised the weekly dances), another GI from Hethel, Mr W.H. (Billy) Swift (landlord), Charlie Elvin (ploughman and watch-mender), Bertie Breeze, Mrs Swift and another Hethel GI. (PHOTO CONTRIBUTED BY MRS J. SWIFT)

were soon a regular sight in our pubs and at dances. They were looked on with a certain amount of envy, of course... They were generous to us locals and the expression 'Got any gum, chum?' was common. Most of my friends collected American gum wrappers, so to be different I collected 'candy' wrappers. Needless to say, this was a very romantic period in the life of Mulbarton: most girls of eligible age had an American boyfriend!

Evelyn Smith remembers the impact the Americans made on local children:

The Americans based at Hethel were a familiar sight in the village... They gave us schoolchildren Christmas parties. We were collected in an Army truck; we were all given a present, and that's where I had my first taste of ice-cream.

John Larter, Barry Dent and Peter Haverson outside one of the huts at Hethel camp – note the bicycles, many of which were bought by American airmen from Frost's garage, Mulbarton. (PHOTO CONTRIBUTED BY PETER HAVERSON)

Brenda Ford remembers the dances:

Social life in the village continued in spite of the war and dances were held in the Village Hall. Although I was very young I remember the band where Flo Utting, who lived in one of the thatched Church cottages, played the piano.

These Saturday night dances were organised by Mrs Harriet Nicholls in the Wingfield Hall and Mulbarton

Memorial in Hethel churchyard to the 389th Bombardment Group, who were stationed at nearby Hethel USAAF base.

was introduced to 'jitterbugging'! Later her only daughter went out to America to marry a US airman. The dances and both pubs were patronised by the Americans from Hethel and New Zealand soldiers based at Keswick.

The World's End was soon overwhelmed and was frequently out of beer. I remember, after a hard day in the harvest fields and dying for a drink, my father complaining, 'The Yanks have drunk the pub dry!'

Bill Alborough

Another lad who once lived in St Omer Close remembers:

The Americans used to cycle over to the World's End. Some lads I knew would take the valves out of the tyres, then when they came out and found their tyres flat would appear and offer help – only to replace the valves and pump the tyres up again. There was usually a good tip for such mischief! Charlie Frost provided a taxi service and sold a lot of bikes! At the end of the war, he bought back some of those bikes, repaired them and sold them second-hand.

Several local ladies got work in the NAAFI and Red Cross depot at Hethel. There was a continuous flow of US military vehicles through Mulbarton. People remember an accident near the Tradesmen's Arms when an ambulance from Hethel base came over Mulbarton Bridge too quickly, missed the corner and crashed.

In May 1945 the European War ended and the Americans left. It all seemed very sudden. I went to

Hethel just before. We were allowed on the base and I was given a pair of boots which I treasured. I tried to make off with some sheets but a Military Policeman with a gun told me to put them back and I didn't argue! My father bought a bike from Mr Frost which had been sold back by a GI.

Bill Alborough

'We Shall Remember Them'

The memorial in the church lists the seven names of those who died in the Second World War:

BURFIELD, Bernard S. Son of Dr Burfield of Kenningham Hall.
KEDGE, Clifford Arthur, Private, Norfolk Regiment, 4th Battalion. Died 13 October 1943, aged 24. Buried in Chungkai War Cemetery, Thailand.
LAKE, Arthur William, Sergeant (W.Op/Air Gunner), RAF Volunteer Reserve, 191 Squadron. Died 3 October 1943, aged 22. Buried Karachi War Cemetery. Son of William and Blanch Mary Lake; husband of Myrtle Christina Lake of Fundenhall.
MIDDLETON, Geoffrey Alfred Frederick, Sapper, Royal Engineers, 248 Field Company. Died 28 May 1940, aged 34. Commemorated on Dunkirk Memorial. Son of Frederick William and Rose Ellen Middleton; husband of Audrey Helen Middleton of Mulbarton. [A bell in Mulbarton tower was given in Geoffrey Middleton's memory – Chapter 5.]
PARKER, George.
REYNOLDS, Jonathan Charles, probably the Gunner, Royal Artillery, East African Artillery, 301 Field Regiment, who died 12 February 1944, aged 30. Commemorated on East African Memorial, Nairobi War Cemetery. Son of Leonard and Harriet Reynolds; husband of Betty Reynolds.
ROWBOTTOM, Anthony. Eldest son of Mrs Rowbottom, head teacher of Mulbarton School, who died of a tropical disease in South Asia.

A memorial tablet was added under the existing war memorial in church and a clock for the tower was paid for by subscription. Both were dedicated by the Bishop of Norwich on Sunday, 8 October 1950 at 3p.m., assisted by the Rector, Revd A. St John Heard. According to a news report:

A Colour Party of the British Legion followed the choir to the singing of 'Soldiers of Christ arise…' Psalms 121 and 122 and the Nunc Dimittis were sung. The lesson was 1 Peter 5 vv.6–11. Other hymns were 'The radiant morn hath passed away' and 'O God our help in ages past', and the Anthem was 'The souls of the righteous are in the hand of God'. Last Post and Reveille were sounded at the dedication.

Membership of the Royal British Legion was boosted in the post-war years by those who returned – over 80 members would march to church for the

Mulbarton Church clock is the village war memorial, installed by public subscription after the Second World War.

Remembrance Sunday service in the 1950s, and there were regular meetings and sporting events at the World's End. Len Dack's 42 years of service in the British Legion was marked by a gold badge in 1964 and an invitation to a Buckingham Palace garden party in 1974. The Mulbarton and District branch still meets regularly in the Social Club.

One Who Returned

The Distinguished Conduct Medal, second only to the Victoria Cross, was awarded to Regimental Sergeant Major 'Bill' Haverson, who served with the Royal Norfolk Regiment. The Haverson family moved to Mulbarton in 1940 and all the children went to Mulbarton School. Bill Haverson had already seen service in the First World War, and between the wars had served in India, Gibraltar and at Aldershot.

The 'Norfolks' were in France at the very start of the Second World War and Bill Haverson was awarded the DCM in 1940 for holding Aire Bridge on La Basse Canal in Northern France to allow survivors to escape during the retreat to Dunkirk. Bill became Regimental Sergeant Major and trained fresh troops for the D-Day invasion in June 1944. People remember him cycling from his home (one of the brick cottages in Norwich Road) to Britannia Barracks in Norwich.

After the war, Bill left the Army to become Mulbarton's postman for 17 years. He was also a school governor, parish councillor, secretary of the British Legion and was a leading light, with Bob

Mickleburgh and others, in raising money for the war memorial clock in the church tower. He was also the local poppy day organiser.

Bill Alborough comments: 'Always the disciplinarian, as befits an RSM, the rows of seeds in his garden were immaculately straight. The story goes that he slept "to attention"!' Mrs Haverson died in 1985 and Bill spent his last years in Wymondham, where he died on 17 December 1991 in his 93rd year.

After the Victory

Chris Mickleburgh remembers getting two days' paid holiday just after he started work – for VE Day. There was a huge bonfire on the Common and somehow Charlie Frost managed to produce some 'Standard' fireworks for sale, despite the fact that fireworks were not made nor were available during the war!

Bill Alborough remembers:

In May 1945 the war was over for us and we were allowed to burn the wagons on the common. I have a memory of visiting the fires the next morning and the huge hubs of the wheels were still glowing. The Americans left Hethel in what seemed like a matter of days. Sweets gradually appeared in Cracknell's shop, but not for long! If we couldn't get sweets, sometimes liquorice root was a passable substitute.

Despite the fact that we had supposedly won the war, we then had what seemed like an endless period of austerity and food items took an age to come off rationing. We realised this was the only fair way of doing things and accepted it. It was 1963 before St Stephen's Street in Norwich, where my mother used to do her shopping, was rebuilt.

The darts team of the Mulbarton branch of the Royal British Legion in the World's End. They were league winners 1973–74 and 1974–75. Left to right, standing: David Ireland, Brian Knights, Michael Cooper, Ronnie Barrett, Jimmy Thurston; seated: Bert Chapman, Lenny Dack, Clifford Allison (holding cup), Jimmy Abendroth.

(PHOTO CONTRIBUTED BY CLIFF ALLISON)

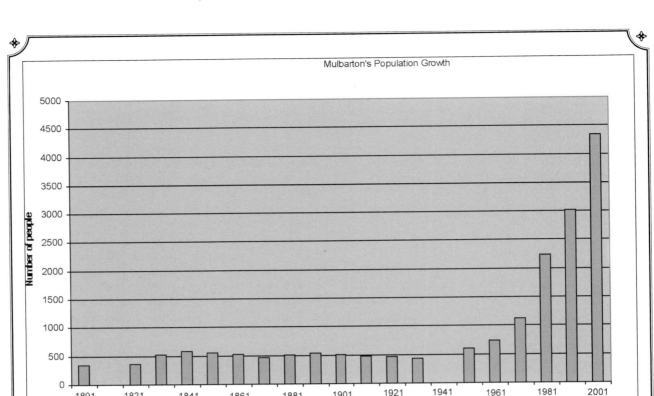

The number of people in Mulbarton remained almost the same through the nineteenth century, and fell slightly from 1901–31. The rapid growth came after 1971.

Birchfield Lane runs between the two hedges. On the far left is the end of Mr Emms's clay-lump cottage, with his orchard to the right. Spring 1959.

(PHOTO: DEREK VALIANT)

Left: Birchfield Lane in the snow, winter 1958–59, looking southwards from near the Common, when it was a narrow lane with fields on either side. Land on the left is now the school field. On the right is now the entry to the Post Office and shop.

(PHOTO: DEREK VALIANT)

CHAPTER 11

A Village that Grew and Grew

It is a remarkable fact that the population of Mulbarton remained steady until 50 years ago. The 1841 census records 582 people – almost the same as the 1951 census (598 people). Then came a period of rapid growth, when the population almost doubled from 1951 to 1971, and nearly doubled again between 1971 and 1981. The various Ordnance Survey maps of the twentieth century that include Mulbarton show how the area covered by housing began to grow slowly in the 1920s as old cottages were replaced by modern houses, then grew rapidly from the 1960s as more and more fields were covered with houses. We will begin with the story of one road to learn how Mulbarton was able to grow.

Birchfield Lane

The 1724 map of the manor of Mulbarton marks 'Burch Field Way' running south from the Common to the boundary with the parish of Bracon Ash. There were no buildings along the lane. The land on either side was mostly divided into long narrow strips, and some was rented out by the church as 'glebe land' to pay the Rector's income. Near the Common, land to the east belonged to Mulbarton Hall, and small fields to the west to J. Turner. Further south was the Nether Gate Furlong, and then the Second Cuckoofield: by 1841 this land was part of Malthouse farm.

The smaller-scale maps by Faden (1797) and Bryant (1826) show the lane but there are still no buildings. The next detailed map of the area is the Tithe Award map of 1841. This shows one house in the lane – a smallholding owned and occupied by John Blake, apparently on two fields once owned by J. Turner. By 1851, John Blake (aged 51) was a farmer of 30 acres, employing one man. He lived with his wife, Mary, and his daughter, Martha. He also rented several acres of glebe land from the Rector. Mary Blake continued to run the farm as a widow in 1871 with the help of her daughter and son-in-law, James and Martha Cole. The 1:2500 Ordnance Survey map of 1882 names the road 'Coles Lane'. However, by the 1881 census the property seems to be owned by Samuel Gowing, pork butcher, and in 1901 by James Barrett, market gardener. His housekeeper, 76-year-old Rossetta Emms, saw the start of the Emms family connection with this house and market garden – finally sold after the death of Billy Emms in 1969 (Chapter 6). The family were so much part of the lane that older residents knew it as 'Emms Lane'.

The opportunity for other development in Birchfield Lane came when particular fields were sold when estates were auctioned, and when the glebe land was sold by the diocese in 1919. Some land between the old smithy and Birchfield Lane was bought by the blacksmith when land owned by the Stewards of East Carleton Manor was auctioned in 1920. After the sale of Mulbarton Hall in 1927, some of its farmland continued to be rented out to the tenants of Paddock Farm. One narrow strip became The Dell – where newspapers were sold in the late 1930s and which is now the Post Office and One-Stop shop (Chapter 8). When the dairy farm was sold in 1932 (Chapter 6), Mr Emms bought Common Field Pightle and 'Captain' Carver bought Birchfield Pightle and built Birchfield House facing the Common at the corner of the lane. Relatives of Captain Carver and his wife built houses on the south side of the Common, and recent infill has resulted in a number of new bungalows beside the Common and in Birchfield Lane.

Further south along Birchfield Lane, Mr Robertson, a retired groom from 'Woodlands', Long Lane, bought a field on the west side in the 1920s and built a bungalow in one corner (now No.16). Some 40 years later the next owner sold this field to Norfolk Garden Estates Ltd, and Mickleburgh & Rutland built the 40 bungalows of Birchfield Gardens. The adjoining field, at the south end of Birchfield Lane, was bought by Forehoe and Henstead Rural District Council in 1932 for further council-housing. The Parish Council minutes for September 1932 record:

After considerable difficulty the RDC were successful in obtaining Mr A.W. Fairman's land in Birchfield Lane, nearly six acres. Mr Lake prop., Mr Beare secd., 'That the Clerk be instructed to write and ask that the building of the houses be commenced at once, and that when built they should be let to Mulbarton people.' Carried.

Two terraces, each with four single-storey dwellings, were built on the land east of the road – with a shared pump – and all these were rented out by 1935. Some tenants came from the condemned thatched cottages in front of the church (Chapter 9). So by the beginning of the Second World War, Birchfield Lane had a few houses among the farmland, and a council-owned cluster at the far south end.

After the war houses were needed to meet a desperate shortage. Forehoe & Henstead built prefabricated 'Airey Houses' on the vacant plot of

Old maps show Birchfield Lane continuing south into Bracon Ash parish, and it was the parish boundary for a short distance. This view north shows the beginning of the southwards track that has been obliterated by the Mulberry Gardens development. In the background are bungalows built by Henstead Rural District Council for older people on the east side (right) of Birchfield Lane around 1936, and on the left are the 'Airey Houses' built in 1949. Here the Wright family enjoys a snowy walk in January 1978. (PHOTO: JILL WRIGHT)

Birchfield Lane building site in 1958. The caravan and shed belongs to Mr and Mrs Stevens, who were building their 'Cedar Bungalow' on this site. On the left is the bungalow of Mr Harrod senr (The Dell) – now the site of the Post Office and shop. There is a clear view west to Forge Cottage and on the right are the roofs of some bungalows facing the Common.

(PHOTO CONTRIBUTED BY MR AND MRS A. STEVENS)

Demolition of the Airey Houses in Birchfield Lane in 1986. (PHOTO: DAVID WRIGHT)

Replacing the Airey Houses in Birchfield Lane with a new type of prefabricated home which was loaded onto the same foundations and part-clad with brick, 1986.

(PHOTO: DAVID WRIGHT)

Harvesting the field that is now Lakes Avenue, summer 1958 or 1959. In the background is a building and the well belonging to Mr Emms (market-gardener and band leader). (PHOTO: DEREK VALIANT)

land west of Birchfield Lane, which they had purchased for housing almost 20 years earlier. A note in the Parish Council minutes of May 1949 explains that 'New council-houses not yet occupied as sewerage not completed.' The first residents moved in soon afterwards, among them Maurice Norman, who later played football for Norwich City, Tottenham Hotspur and England (Chapter 2). These distinctive concrete houses lasted some 35 years, and in 1985–86 the residents were gradually moved into temporary accommodation while their houses were replaced with a new style of prefabricated dwelling on the same foundations – and hence with the same large gardens.

The next big opportunity to acquire fields in the area came when Mulbarton Hall was sold in 1947. Mr Lincoln bought Lot 4, advertised as adjacent to 'Brickfield Lane' [sic]. He built a bungalow for himself on one strip (now No. 24, Crosstyx), and later sold it and built a larger home in another corner of his field (No. 18). Across the road, the Stevens built their cedar bungalow (No. 47) with their own hands on a strip of land bought from the now-retired blacksmith. The semi-detached pair of houses in the style of the council-houses (Nos 25 and 27) were built for the Larter brothers on land bought around 1950 from Mr Emms.

The housing boom meant a rapid rise in land prices once the planners allowed housing within the 'village envelope' and one by one the fields were sold. Mr Lincoln's field was cultivated until it was sold in around 1960 and developed by Sendall Brothers of Norwich for the first 'one-field' estate to be built, Lakes Avenue – No. 6 cost £1,175 in 1964! But this 'open-plan' development had big problems with drainage and sewerage: septic tanks frequently flooded into the road. At the 1965 annual parish meeting, 'Inadequate cesspools and flooding in Lakes Avenue' was the main topic, and a special meeting was arranged with the relevant authorities, which resulted in free emptying every two weeks. Larger pipes were installed for the former stream that crossed the lane – which has flooded a number of times since due to garden rubbish blocking the course of the ditch. The building of Birchfield Gardens has already been mentioned; on the opposite side of the lane was Southern Reach.

Billy Emms's house and land was sold in 1969. George Whitmore demolished the clay-lump cottage and had a modern bungalow built (now No. 39) and for a time continued growing flowers, fruit and vegetables there. Then the land was sold for bungalows in Birchfield Lane, with Tudor Way and Brindle Drive behind. When Mr Larter sold his field in the 1970s for two pairs of linked bungalows – one pair facing Birchfield Lane (Nos 29 and 31), the other at the end of Tudor Way, the infill was complete. Walk along Birchfield Lane today and it is still possible to see the old field boundaries as hedges or ditches and

to look at the housing styles and guess how farmland changed to housing in a little over half a century. But look south from the junction with Cuckoofield Lane and the old lane no longer continues into Bracon Ash parish. Early plans preserved it as a cycle track and pedestrian route, but revised plans for the new Mulberry Gardens estate obliterated the ancient lane that had existed for centuries.

'Homes for Heroes'

There is a prominent date '1921' on some houses in Long Lane. As far back as 1914, the Mulbarton Parish Council minutes record: 'in the opinion of this council, some houses are required for the working classes: six houses to be asked for this purpose.'

After the First World War, the 'Homes for Heroes' policy was implemented, and the first council-houses were built in many villages. In 1920, however, the Parish Council was not fully satisfied: the clerk was instructed to write protesting against

'Homes for Heroes': two of the first houses to be built in Mulbarton by Henstead Rural District Council in 1921. The pump that served the houses in Long Lane is a reminder that these substantial brick houses had few services – but were far better than the tied cottages from which the first residents moved.

After much pressure from the Parish Council, further council-houses were built in Long Lane and Cuckoofield Lane. The first to be built are boldly dated 1931.

Nurse Sexton, district nurse, beside the door of her council-house in Long Lane (then No. 9, now No. 26). Behind her house (extreme right) *are the fields that later became Birchfield Gardens.* (PHOTO CONTRIBUTED BY EVELYN SMITH)

the 'unsuitability' of the site of the proposed houses. Was that the Long Lane site? If so, why was it unsuitable? By 1921 the first residents were able to move in.

Soon afterwards, five pairs of houses were built around the corner in Cuckoofield Lane. It is said that Mrs Massingham of Mulbarton Hall demanded that a screen of trees be planted to hide the washing (Chapter 9). When first built, a pump supplied water for each group of houses. One pump can still be seen in Long Lane, but the hedged enclosure for the pump in Cuckoofield Lane is now part of a garden. The houses had no electricity, and when they were connected to the electricity grid in the 1930s, they had surface wiring that eventually had to be renewed. They were a long way from a shop until Mr Larter opened one in a shed in his garden (Chapter 8), but they had huge gardens, where people could grow much of the food they needed.

By 1930 the Parish Council was dissatisfied again:

A discussion arose as to the desirability of building houses for Mulbarton people in Mulbarton parish instead of, as is now being done, building houses in Swardeston or Bracon Ash, and sending Mulbarton people out of the parish to live.

In 1931 their protests were stronger: 'strongly protest against the policy of building houses in neighbouring parishes and placing Mulbarton people in them, so taking them away from their own parish, often

against their wishes.' The prominent '1931' on another pair of houses in Long Lane shows that the answer was about to be built.

In 1933–34 more houses were built in Long Lane, and two pairs were added either side of the Cuckoofield Lane row. These had a limited number of electric points and lights installed – with proper wiring, but no running water or drainage. Evelyn Smith remembers:

I was born at No. 10 (now No. 28) Long Lane. I still have the letter addressed to my late father, Mr Stackyard, from Henstead RDC offering him the tenancy when the house was new. It is dated 28 March 1934, with a rent of 3s.6d. per week (now 17½p) plus rates.

Soon afterwards, the bungalows already mentioned in the story of Birchfield Lane were built, and the house numbers continued round the corner.

Brenda Ford (née Collins) writes:

I had friends who lived in the council-houses at Mulbarton. In those days they got their water from a pump halfway along the road. It seems ridiculous now, but they had to carry all the water they used in buckets from this pump to their houses. We were little better off as we lived in a tied cottage, but we did have a tap...

St Omer Close

The nine pairs of semi-detached houses in St Omer Close, in the north of the village, were the next to be built. Forehoe & Henstead Rural District Council bought the orchard inherited by Maggie Robinson (née Rix) from her father, and offered to rehouse her and her family rent-free for as long as she lived.

Clearing the overgrown orchard land that became the site for St Omer Close, probably early 1930s. The man in the picture may be Charles Mickleburgh, gardener at Dunston Hall and father of Charles Robert ('Bob') Mickleburgh, who came over to Mulbarton to help Mrs Robinson on her land. (PHOTO CONTRIBUTED BY BILL ALBOROUGH)

Gordon Andrews in the garden of his new home in St Omer Close soon after he moved from Scott's Terrace (the 'factory houses') in 1936. The early council-houses had large gardens where tenants produced much of the food they needed. (PHOTO CONTRIBUTED BY CLIFFORD ROBINSON)

Lillian Mickleburgh (née Robinson) outside the family home at No. 37 St Omer Close, about 1955. Her mother had lived next-door at No. 38, where she ran a small shop.
(PHOTO CONTRIBUTED BY PETER MICKLEBURGH)

In June 1935 she moved from her clay-lump cottage on the main road to No. 38, where she reopened her shop in the front room. Less than three years later, Mrs Robinson died.

Bill Alborough remembers that they were:

... very basic houses with no running water or drainage. Water had to be collected from a central pump and all night soil had to be buried in the garden. Electric

fittings were sparse: one power point in the 'back room' and three lights – one in the back room, one in the front room (parlour) and one in the front bedroom. The roofs had Norfolk reed under tiles but powdery snow came into the roof space with the inevitable problems when the thaw arrived! The 'back room' served as kitchen, dining-room and bathroom. It contained a wall oven and cast-iron copper, both separately fired, either side of the central open fire. There was a pantry off the back room, an outside privy and storage under the stairs which served as an air-raid shelter in the Second World War.

Alice Alborough (Bill's mother), who lived at No. 48, remembered moving in on 11 November 1936, when the rent was 8s.6d. (43p) a fortnight. Bill Alborough writes that:

... despite the seemingly primitive conditions I got the impression that my parents thought it was a vast improvement on where they had been living. That was in Scott's Terrace – a row of five three-storey houses on the site of what is now the vet's [Chapter 9].

Over the years improvements were made: running water was provided and the electrics extended. Night-soil collection was requested by the Parish Council for the whole village in 1948, repeated in 1955 and finally 'the honey cart' began its rounds in 1957. In the mid-1970s extensions were built to provide a separate bathroom and, to prove that civilisation really had arrived, an inside flush lavatory was fitted! Later the roofs were refurbished and replacement windows fitted.

Before the Post Office renumbered many Mulbarton houses, the council-houses were numbered consecutively from Long Lane, along part of Cuckoofield Lane, to the most northerly council bungalow in Birchfield Lane (No. 36). Houses in St Omer Close were (and still are) numbered 37–54. The house opposite No. 36 Birchfield Lane began the sequence again – at No. 55 – which then continued into the rest of Cuckoofield Lane. This road still has a significant gap in its house numbers – interesting for historians, but hopeless for delivery drivers!

Tackling the Housing Crisis

After the Second World War there was a desperate shortage of housing. The first to be built by the Rural District Council were the 'Airey Houses' mentioned above. Then the Council obtained more land bordering Cuckoofield Land by compulsory purchase, to build a mixture of brick bungalows and houses. Many of the first people in these houses were moved out of 'temporary' accommodation at the former Hethel Airbase, and the Parish Council protested that the new houses were not being let to Mulbarton families. Barbara Gent was one of the first

A new home on the old Hethel air base, after the USAAF moved out. The Wilson/Gent families were the first to move into one of the base houses being adapted by Henstead Rural District Council. At first, everyone lived in the nearer end of the hut, then Derek and Barbara Gent moved into the other end of the 'semi'.

(PHOTO CONTRIBUTED BY BARBARA GENT)

The Gent and Wilson families transformed their semis at the old Hethel air base to make them into cosy homes with cottage gardens. They lived here until they were allocated newly built houses in Cuckoofield Lane.

(PHOTO CONTRIBUTED BY BARBARA GENT)

and remembers both the camp and the move to Cuckoofield Lane very well:

My parents' name was Wilson – my father was called 'Tug'. We were the very first to be allocated a hut on Hethel Camp. [After her father lost his job as a gardener at Saxlingham and thus lost his tied cottage, they moved, with all their belongings, on a couple of flat-bed lorries lent by her husband's firm...]. It was called Eastwood Site. There was a cold water tap in the kitchen, a flush toilet, one fireplace but no other heating. The old 'Guard Hut' had a stove with a chimney running through the middle, and it was in here that we did the washing, heating pails of water on top of the stove, washing the clothes in a bath and on the old scrub dolly board. We also had our weekly bath in there, in the old tin bath – very cold and draughty, so it

Cuckoofield Lane in the early 1950s. The houses on the north side (left) had recently been built by Henstead Rural District Council on land obtained from Mr Fairman. The final phase of council-housing, on the south side (right), has not yet been built. In the traffic-free road are (front to back) Kathleen Gent and Rowena Brown in toy car; Mr Crane and dog. (PHOTO CONTRIBUTED BY BARBARA GENT)

was in and out very quickly. But we didn't grumble – we were happy and it was home.

Tradesmen got word that we were there, and other families moved in as the huts were made ready. Mr Rushbrook came round with milk; a fish and chip van came twice a week; Mr Eastell of Swardeston came with fruit and veg. in his van, Leslie Swingler was our 'Postie', so we did not want for much. Eventually there was a little shop selling groceries and stamps. We had a school, a chapel, a surgery... We lived there five years – my two daughters were born there.

On the morning of my second daughter being born we had a letter from the Council to say we had been allocated a house in Cuckoofield Lane – the first to be built. There were lots of families from Hethel Camp moving in as the others were completed. We often spoke of the happy days there – that was 56 years ago, and some of us are still here in Cuckoofield!

From 1959, a mixture of one- and two-storey homes were built for the District Council by Mickleburgh & Rutland, a Mulbarton building firm, on the opposite (south) side of Cuckoofield Lane, and the tenants moved in from 1960. The density of housing was higher and the gardens much smaller than the pre-war council-houses but big by today's standards.

A small shop was included in No. 127 (Chapter 8). At the time of writing any council-houses that are not privately owned have been transferred to a Housing Association, and the new housing development has to include some 'affordable housing'.

The 'Village Envelope'

Why did Mulbarton grow when many neighbouring villages stayed small? The answer was mainly in the hands of the planners. Following the Town and Country Planning Act, 1947, all new buildings had to be permitted by the local authority and all local authorities had to prepare a development plan for their local area. Shortages of building materials restricted building at first, and then, in our area, most new homes were built by the local authorities themselves. With pressure increasing for private housing, in the 1950s planners began to map 'village envelopes'. Their purpose was 'to protect the rural character and charm of the County of Norfolk'. In a GCE A-level study of village growth south of Norwich, Rachel Noonan (née Wright) explained:

These envelopes were drawn around existing housing and recognised an area in which the village could

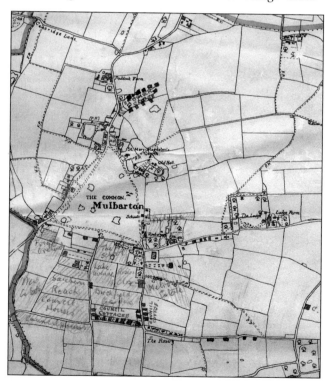

Part of the map produced for the parish by O. Chapman, Surveyor (on a scale of 6 inches to 1 mile) showing most of the village. The 1930s housing has been added in an unknown hand (including St Omer Close on the old orchard). In the southern part of the village, fields that were sold one by one for new housing development are shaded and labelled.

(Reproduced with permission of the Ordnance Survey)

develop... Single-field developments took place within the envelope. Thus the shape of the envelope appears to provide the key [to reasons for village growth].

Mulbarton had its old village centre along the Norwich Road and outlying areas with cottages in the south-west corner of the Common and along Rectory Lane and The Rosery. The planners allowed some infill between existing housing, hence the 'ribbon development' along these roads and around part of the Common. Some of these new houses replaced near-derelict cottages, others were originally built for grown-up children on part of the large plots around their parents' homes. The other large area of housing was Council-owned along Long Lane and Cuckoofield Lane. The 'sandwich' of land between the south side of the Common and Cuckoofield Lane was included within the 'village envelope' and made available for housing development if land owners wished to sell. They did – so the 'single-field developments' off Birchfield Lane took place.

The 1960s housing boom put the planners under pressure both to allow further building in each local authority area and to keep the character of older parts of villages by defining conservation areas. The 'Mulbarton Village Plan', approved in 1973, allowed for housing expansion to the west, east and south of the 'village envelope'. The era of large housing estates had begun.

Moving into Mulbarton

The process by which land between the Common and Cuckoofield Lane became built up has already been described, but what was it like to move into these new roads in an old village? Jane Burgess moved into a new bungalow in Birchfield Gardens in 1963 and in the 1990s she wrote about her family's experiences in *Parish News*, which she edited for over 30 years:

We moved to a bungalow on the Birchfield Gardens estate. The 'estate' was in fact one road, formerly two fields divided by a ditch... The day we moved in was wet, and as a made-up drive was not included in the bungalow's price (£2,350), we had to borrow deals from the local building site to help keep us and our furniture, etc. out of the wet clay! By lunch time we were all rather thirsty and decided to patronise the local Tradesman's Arms (where we were called 'furrinners', and needless to say we did not call there again!)

We settled in with our new neighbours, and soon the next generation started arriving, keeping the local midwife very busy. One thing we discovered was the fact that a modern septic tank did not work in the clay – particularly when it rained a lot. Having had the council empty the tank once, this became a continuous job and nightmare for many of us. Neighbouring Lakes

Jim Rump on a friend's bike on the building site at the far end of Southern Reach in 1973, looking north-east towards Mr Harrod's house (The Dell) and Post Office stores and other houses in Birchfield Lane. This land is now the site of Southern Reach, Tudor Way and Brindle Drive. (Photo: James and Pat Rump)

Avenue was aptly named at this time! Our second daughter really enjoyed the visit from the council wagon and used to 'help' carry the pipes – in fact it was the high spot of her week. It was a great day when we all had mains drainage [installed in 1968/69]*!*

On the other side of Birchfield Lane, a builder from Costessey gradually developed another field, selling each plot and building chalets or bungalows to order. Jane Burrell was one of the first to move in to Southern Reach:

I came to live in the village in 1966 when I bought a plot of land in the area which became Southern Reach, from Eric Kett, builder, who had bought it from Mr F. Mann. The plot was approximately 165ft x 38 ft and cost £570. When the house was being built there was a lark's nest in the garden, and in the long grass neighbouring the house I found a harvest mouse's nest. A barn owl quartered the field at twilight. Water was laid on at completion but at that time sewage was disposed of through a septic tank which was emptied at intervals by a tanker. Mains sewage arrived in 1969, and the pipe was laid through the bottom of the garden instead of under the road as the site plan had suggested. Until the road was surfaced in 1970 there was only a muddy track leading to Birchfield Lane – we lived in wellies – and visitors always removed footwear at the door. Longstanding friends who visit tend to do the same now!

The far end of Southern Reach was developed later and Pat Rump remembers:

... an orchard full of apple trees with masses of mistletoe. They chopped the trees down just before Christmas and

offered bunches of mistletoe to everyone in the road. There was a brick shortage at the time and the builders asked local residents to keep an eye on the site and note the registration of cars and lorries coming onto the site to nick bricks.

A Village Designated for Growth

In April 1976, Norfolk County Council published its County Structure Plan – Draft Written Statement for Consultation. Norfolk's population was growing rapidly, due to families moving out of London and the south-east and the county's popularity as a place for retirement. King's Lynn and Thetford had absorbed many newcomers in the 1960s, but the planners were looking for new areas suitable for population growth. These were to be accessible to employment and services but not on high-quality farmland. The greatest demand for new housing was in the Norwich area. New suburbs were planned to the west (Bowthorpe) and north (Thorpe Marriott), but a number of villages in a six to eight mile radius of the city centre were also designated growth areas. These were Brundall in the east; Spixworth and Horsford in the north; Hethersett and Mulbarton in the south – plus some further development in

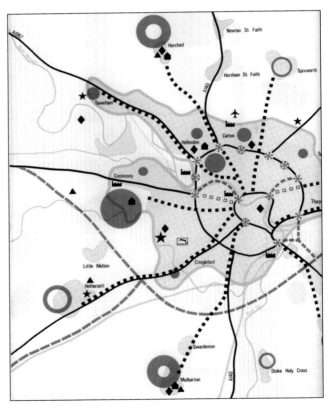

Norfolk Structure Plan for the Norwich Area, from the Consultative Draft Written Statement, 1974, showing the planned growth south and west of Norwich at Mulbarton, Hethersett, Bowthorpe, Taverham and Horsford.

(Reproduced with permission of the Planning Department, Norfolk County Council)

Royal opening of Hanover Gardens by Princess Alexandra in November 1975. Left to right: Mrs Tunney (widow of the church verger), Mrs Wharton (born Bracon Ash), Princess Alexandra. This is one of many sheltered housing schemes in Britain built and managed by the Hanover Housing Association

(PHOTO: EVENING NEWS, REPRODUCED BY KIND PERMISSION OF ARCHANT PHOTOGRAPHIC)

villages that had grown rapidly in the 1960s, such as Poringland and Stoke Holy Cross.

Mulbarton already had a new school, a regular bus service into Norwich and a generous supply of public open space (the Common). Some 30 hectares of land had already been allocated for 750 dwellings up to 1975. Now the planners considered it a suitable location for a further 1,900 dwellings (including council-housing) on 78 hectares of land. Only Horsford was designated as an equally huge growth area:

Horsford and Mulbarton have been selected as a result of a comprehensive analysis of the possible areas for housing development and on the basis of public comment on alternative locations... Development at Mulbarton will take place on land of medium and low value for agriculture and will not involve major infra-structural investment. It also presents less transporta-tion difficulties than any other location...

If the planners' policy went ahead, Mulbarton's population would rise from 1,200 (1975) to 8,300!

Developers were no doubt delighted, but the 'consultation' that followed led to the proposals being reviewed, adapted and changed. Some proposed development was moved to market towns such as Wymondham, with existing shops and services. Apart from small infills such as Old Rectory Close, no new land in Mulbarton was allocated for housing.

Developing the New Estates

Mulrose Park (the Bluebell Road/Gowing Road area) was built by Colroy Homes from 1974 onwards, and described as 'a beautifully designed development of detached houses and bungalows – all with garages or garage space...' In 1976, prices ranged from £9,575 to £10,850. The early residents formed the 'Mulrose Park Residents' Association' and this anonymous poem from News Letter No.1, May 1978, shows that moving in was not all plain sailing:

Home Sweet Home
What problems we all give ourselves,
When we think of moving house.
Where shall we live? How large a place
For husband, kids and spouse?

Mulrose Park – by Colroy Homes
Would seem the place of dreams;
But 'Oh dear me' – illusion shattered –
Can't you hear the shouts and screams!

There's problems with solicitors,
Things we all can tell:
Agents' and surveyors' fees,
Completion dates as well.

One by one we all move in,
New neighbours, friends as well.
Removal vans and hire trucks –
It's sheer and utter hell!

The colour of the curtains,
Beige or pink – or green.
There are many other problems
At present unforeseen.

The plotting of the garden,
Crazy paving to be laid,
A fruit tree here and rose bed there.
Why aren't they ready-made?

I'm sick to death of all the fuss,
And I write this verse to tell
If I decide to move again
I will – to a hotel.

At the same time in the 1970s, the Lark Rise area was being built by another developer on land sold by Cyril Fairman of Malthouse Farm (Chapter 6). This is the 'birds' estate, as the road names show. When the housing boom began to decline, Wilcon Homes took over the site (start price £24,500 for a two-bedroomed semi in 1985). The third new estate, south of Cuckoofield Lane, was built between 1979 and 1983. Catmere Herne and related roads were given the names of animals or some of the old field names of Mulbarton (Chapter 6).

Aerial view of Mulbarton at the beginning of the big expansion, looking towards the school and Common. In the right foreground, Bluebell Road and Gowing Road are under construction, 1975.

(PHOTO: DAVID AND JILL WRIGHT)

Aerial view of Mulbarton looking west above Cuckoofield Lane (left) *and Southern Reach* (right) *in 1975.* **Top right** *is the beginning of the Lark Rise estate, with Nightingale and Kestrel Closes almost complete. The field on the left will become Catmere Herne.*

(PHOTO: DAVID AND JILL WRIGHT)

Harvesting the field south of Cuckoofield Lane in 1976 – now the Mulberry Gardens estate. (PHOTO: DAVID WRIGHT)

Watching the harvest from one of the Cuckoofield Lane houses in September 1988. This field is now the Mulberry Gardens estate. (PHOTO: EVELYN SMITH)

Field names were also chosen for Mulberry Gardens, the large new development of the new millennium being built by Hopkins Homes south of Cuckoofield Lane. There were many protests when plans appeared for about 400 homes on this green-field site, but it had long been designated for housing. In 1973 a letter was read to the annual meeting about:

Residential Development – Cuckoofield Lane: A letter from the Forehoe & Henstead RDC dated April 10th confirmed that planning permission had been granted for phase 1 of this development, comprising some fifty dwellings immediately adjoining Cuckoofield Lane; the remainder of the development to be the subject of further planning applications.

This permission seems to have been for Hanover Gardens, a sheltered housing complex for retired people built in one corner of the Cuckoofield Lane site. When the Parish Council sought clarification, the County Planning Officer came and told them, 'the District Council have accepted the principle of development on this site, but it was unlikely that work would be started before two to four years.' Councillors asked for the school to be enlarged, road improvements, and a speed limit!

The District Council already owned most of the land, which was rented to a local farmer. The final development brief was published in 1998, and plans by Hopkins Homes were accepted in 2000. Mulberry Gardens is a major development of around 400 houses (of which 34 are 'affordable homes') plus sites for a shop and play areas. The developers built a huge underground holding tank for run-off water, which is piped to the stream at the Cuckoofield Lane bridge, and they had to contribute to road improvements and community facilities. The District Council used a small part of the money from the land sale to buy The Meadows, which were handed over to the Parish in 2005 as additional open space.

The book ends here – but the story goes on. From now on, history is made by us.

The next generation: *children from Mulbarton First School with their teacher, Mrs Beverley Theobold, admire the tree they planted at Mulberry Gardens as construction began in 2003.*

(PHOTO: EVELYN SMITH)

Subscribers

Bill Alborough, Fairford, Gloucestershire

Mrs Joyce Alexander (née Fairman), Milford on Sea, Hamsphire

Clifford L. Allison, Mulbarton, Norfolk

Peter B. Amies, Mulbarton, Norfolk

Mr and Mrs H.L. Andrews, Taverham, Norfolk

Laurence and Lesley Appleton, 25 years at Pheasant Close, Mulbarton

Jan, Dave and Eleanor August, Mulbarton

The Bailey Family, Mulbarton, Norfolk

L.W. Bailey, lived with grandmother, Mrs Hemnall, Thatched Cottages, Mulbarton

Christine Baldwin, Mulbarton

D. Barker, Rye House, Mulbarton

Mr Garry, and Mr and Mrs David Barker, Mulbarton, Norfolk

Mr Glyn Barrett, Mulbarton, Norfolk

Jane M. and Ronald V. Barrett, Mulbarton, Norfolk

Mr Mark Barrett, Mulbarton, Norfolk

John and Mavis Bastin, Dedham, Essex

Mr and Mrs M. Bayly, Mulbarton

Eileen Bell, Mulbarton, Norfolk

Margaret Best (née Tungate)

Mr Brian R. Bird, Mulbarton, Norfolk

Joanna Bird (formerly Hinchley), Mulbarton 1976–1986. Now Taverham

Carole Blackburn, Mulbarton, Norfolk

Patrick and Margaret Bobbin, Swardeston, Norfolk

Carl K. Bradley

Dr Andrew Briggs PhD Bsc

Terry Briggs, East Dereham

The Brooks Family

Mrs Margaret M. Brown (née Cross), Mulbarton

Leslie and Dorothy Buck, Mulbarton

Dr Christine Buckton

The Burgess Family, Mulbarton, Norfolk

The Burrell Family, Mulbarton

Alan, Louise Burrows, Mulbarton, Norwich

Craig J. Burrows, Mulbarton, Norfolk

Julie Burrows, Mulbarton, Norfolk

Paul J. Burrows, Mulbarton, Norfolk

Ida Cappuccio, Cuckoofield Lane, Mulbarton

Joy Carroll (née Cooper), Melksham, Wiltshire

Chris and Marina Carter, Mulbarton, Norfolk

Darren Carter, Mulbarton

Kristian Carter, Mulbarton

Barry J. Carver, Shotesham-All-Saints

Richard A. Carver, Mulbarton, Norfolk

Susan Carver, Mulbarton, Norfolk

Joan (née Smith) and Horace Chadwick

Richard Chamberlain, Bracon Ash, Norfolk

Ron Chamberlain, Mulbarton, Norfolk

N., J., A., J. and D. Christian

David Churchyard, Swardeston, Norfolk

Mike and Val Claxton, Cononley, North Yorkshire

Angela Clay, Mulbarton

Mr and Mrs R.S. Clayton

Martin and Elizabeth Cliffe, The Malt House, Mulbarton

Andrew and Emma Cliffe,

Tristan Cliffe

Michael Coates, Hethel

Daphne P. Collins (née Howard), Swainsthorpe, Norfolk

Neil Condron, Village resident 1979–2003

Mike Cook, Mulbarton

Simon (Eddy) Cook, Tasburgh

Stephen Cook, Wreningham

Barbie Cooper, Mulbarton, Norfolk

Louis J. Cooper, Wymondham, Norfolk

Dot Copland (née Scarfe), Stoke Holy Cross

Julian and Margaret Corps, Mulbarton, Norfolk

S.M. Cripps, Thorpe St Andrew, Norwich

Mr F. Cullum, The Wood, Mulbarton, Norfolk

Malcolm and Maurie Dales, Shrub Cottage, Mulbarton

Mrs E.M. Dawson

Jo A. Daynes, Mulbarton, Norfolk

Barry A. Dent, Swardeston

Mr Arthur William Devereux, Hethel, Norfolk

Anita J. Dickerson (née Rump), Mulbarton, Norfolk

Tim Drake, Mulbarton, Norfolk

Mike and Jenny Duffin, Mulbarton, Norfolk

Dawn E. Durrant (née Frost), Wymondham, Norfolk

Jonathan M. Dye, Mulbarton, Norfolk

Matthew G. Dye, Mulbarton, Norfolk

Mr M. Dye, Mulbarton, Norfolk

Irene S. Eagle

Judith Fairclough, Mill House, Mulbarton

Ingrid Fairman, Ketteringham, Norfolk

A. and S. Filmer,

Donald Fisher, Mulbarton, Norfolk

Donald J. Flatman, Mulbarton, Norfolk

Joy Flatman

Michaela Flatman

Stephen Flatman

Mrs Brenda Ford (née Collins), Claxton, Norfolk

Mr and Mrs A. Fox, Mulbarton

Iris K. Frost, Mulbarton, Norfolk

Nigel D. Frost, Fundenhall, Norfolk

Pat M. and Roy K. Frost, Mulbarton, Norfolk

Irene and George, Trevor and Janice Gardiner,
   Mulbarton, Norfolk
Mr Kevin R. and Mrs Shirley Godfrey, Mulbarton
Ross and Rosanna Gowing, Mulbarton, Norfolk
Heather Greaves, Mulbarton
Michael J. and Muriel F. Green, Mulbarton, Norfolk
Mrs Julia Greene (née Mickleburgh), Mulbarton,
   Norfolk
Gloria Grimes, Mulbarton
Julia Groves, Hellesdon, Norfolk
Mr Richard Haines
Mr and Mrs A. Hammond, Mulbarton
Mr and Mrs Daniel Hammond, Mulbarton, Norfolk
Mr and Mrs K. Hammond, Lakenham, Norwich
Rosemary Hanson, Mulbarton, Norfolk
Peter Hardingham, Mulbarton, Norfolk
John S. Hardman, Mulbarton, Norwich
Colin E. Haverson
Sylvia Haverson (in memory of) Peter Haverson
Michael J.M. Hensey, Mulbarton
John, Edna, Jayne and Daniel Hewitt
Joan and Paul Hewitt, Mulbarton
Ron and Dianne Hinchley, formerly Brindle Drive,
   Mulbarton, 1974-1986. Now in Ashwellthorpe
David Hornsby, Cultus Lake, Canada
David Hornsby, former Mulbarton School pupil,
   emigrated to Canada 1956
Jean (née Smith) and Michael Hornsby,
Terry Horsman, Mulbarton, Norfolk
M.A. and J.E. Howard, Mulbarton, Norfolk
Mr and Mrs E. Howe, Norwich, Norfolk
Andrew Huggins, Taverham, Norfolk
Malcolm Huggins, Norwich, Norfolk
Simon Huggins, Reedham, Norfolk
Mrs Margaret R. Hurt, Mulbarton, Norfolk
David and Barbara Ireland, Mulbarton
Bridget M. Jackson (née Finch), Mulbarton, Norfolk
Mr and Mrs William Jackson and Family, Norwich,
   Norfolk
Tony and Jane, Alex and Sarah James
Louie and Sid Jones, Forge Orchards 1986–2005
   (In loving memory). Sidney C. Jones, Surrey
Malcolm and Valerie Jones, Bracon Ash, Norwich
Zoe and Gerry Kelly, Mulbarton, Norfolk
Karen Kent, Swardeston, Norfolk
Paul and Jenny Kirby,
Lacey-Hastings, Mulbarton, Norfolk
Mrs C. and Mr D. Ladbrooke
Simon D. Ladbrooke, Mulbarton, Norfolk
Mr Jim Lake, Lowestoft, Suffolk
Mike Lambert, Mulbarton
The Lambert Family, Mulbarton
Joe Larter, Hapton
Dr Andrew Leaman, Mulbarton G.P. 1974–2006
Dr N.G.M. Legg, Bracon Ash
Fiona and Ben Lettice, Mulbarton, Norfolk
Mr and Mrs T. Leverett, Flordon, Norfolk
Karl Leverett, Long Stratton, Norfolk

Mark Leverett, Wymondham, Norfolk
Mr Kenneth J. Lewis, Mulbarton, Norfolk
Julie, Bill, James and Andrew Lincoln
Peter Lincoln, Dairy Farm, Mulbarton
Peter and Sheila Lockhart, Mulbarton 1959–1980
Diane and Danny Lonergan, Mulbarton
The Loughborough Family, Southern Reach,
   Mulbarton
David and Carol Markham, Mulbarton, Norfolk
Susan Masters, Tasburgh, Norfolk
Marian L. Mattholie (née Rump), Wymondham,
   Norfolk
Kirstie Maughan, Mulbarton
Tony Maughan, Wymondham
Margaret McKelvey Jones, Las Vegas, Nevada, USA
Steve Mendham and Penny
Dennis and Norma Mickleburgh
Jenny Mickleburgh, Norwich
Mr Peter Mickleburgh, Mulbarton, Norfolk
Rex E. Mickleburgh (in memory of), Mulbarton
John and Kathryn Moore, Hill House, Mulbarton
Basil John Moore, Mulbarton, Norfolk
George H. Moore, Mulbarton, Norfolk
Leonard and Hilda Moore, Mulbarton, Norfolk
Doreen M. Morgan, Mulbarton, Norfolk
Mulbarton First School
Mulbarton Middle School
Mulbarton MOT and Repair Centre, Mulbarton
David Myhill, Scarning, Dereham, Norfolk
Emma Myhill, Hethel, Norfolk
New Pin Cleaning, Jeanette
Rachel Noonan (née Wright) and family, Norwich
Louise Nunn, Thorpe Hamlet, Norfolk
Barbara Oakley, Swardeston, Norfolk
Barbara Otty, Hingham, Norfolk
Julie Otty, Tasburgh, Norfolk
Michael B. Parfitt, Swardeston
Vera M. Parr (née Carver), Norwich
Mr and Mrs F. Peed, Ferara Cattery, Swardeston,
   Norfolk
Richard Pilch (Driving Tuition), Mulbarton,
   Norfolk
The Pincher Family
Alan Pledger, Mulbarton, Norfolk
Michael Pocklington, Mulbarton, Norfolk
Mr and Mrs C. Pollard, Molescroft, Beverley,
   East Yorkshire
Mr D. Pollard, Mulbarton, Norfolk
Mrs Susan Pollok, Norwich
The Poole Family, Mulbarton
Raymond, Shirley and Charlotte Prain, Mulbarton,
   Norfolk
Martyn, Julie and Elena Pretty, Mulbarton, Norfolk
Mr William E. Purdy, Mulbarton, Norfolk
Mrs Pauline Quinton (née Haverson), Norwich,
   Norfolk
Joan and Stan Ramsey, Warwick
Keith R. Randell, Swainsthorpe, Norfolk

Richard, Amanda, Zoe and Laura Reeve, Gowing Road, Mulbarton
Olive Riches, daughter of Oliver (Crom) Blackburn
Paul Riches, grandson of Oliver (Crom) Blackburn
Peter Riches, grandson of Oliver (Crom) Blackburn
Mr Robert Riches, Cuckoofield Lane, Mulbarton
Mr Leslie Rix, Mulbarton
Lionel J. Robinson, Swardeston, Norfolk
Mr and Mrs Clifford Robinson, Taverham, Norwich, Norfolk
Diane Robinson, Mulbarton, Norwich, Norfolk
Pat and Jim Rump, Mulbarton, Norfolk
Colin and Beryl Rumsby, Mulbarton
Russells Chippy, Mulbarton
Martin, Tracey, Jack and Tom Salisbury, Mulbarton
The Samson Family, Birchfield House, Mulbarton
Jenifer Seaman (née Barret)
Derek Seath, Mulbarton, Norfolk
Chris, Julie, Hannah and Will Serrell, Mulbarton, Norfolk
John Shaw and Family, Birchfield Gardens, Mulbarton
Mr and Mrs G. Siree, Swardeston, Norfolk
Mr and Mrs P. Siree, Dereham, Norfolk
Herbert and Valerie Slaughter, Mulbarton, Norfolk
David, Lisa, Ashley and Olivia Smith, Mulbarton, Norfolk
Evelyn Smith (née Stackyard), Mulbarton, Norfolk
Tony Smith (in memory of)., Grant Smith
Ron, Kath, Gillian and Philip Smith and their families
Keith and Sally Sowter, Mulbarton, Norfolk
Major Gordon and Mrs Daphne Spalding, Mulbarton
Mr Aurthur R., Mrs Iris M., Mrs Margaret A.E. Sparke, Mulbarton, Norfolk
Keith and Margaret Sparkes, Mulbarton, Norfolk
The Stevens Family, Mulbarton, Norfolk
J. Straford, Gordon Square, Norwich
Bevis, Lucy, Caitlin and Hannah Sydney, Coromandel, Norwich Road

Pam and Mike Tancock and Jonathan and Lisa Rudd, Mulbarton, Norfolk
Patrick, Bev, Jo, Sarah and Sam Theobald, Mulbarton
David and Elsie Thomas, Mulbarton, Norfolk
John and Christine Thurston, Mulbarton
The Towler and Brewington Families, Mulbarton
Mr Anthony Trafford, Thickthorn, Norwich
Bryan Tungate
Charles and Dorothy Tungate
Dorothy Tungate
Robin Tungate
Robin V.R. Tungate, Sprowston, Norfolk
Elizabeth and the late Derek Valiant, Mulbarton
Village ADJ, Mulbarton
Mike Wadsley and Maurice Wadsley
Joyce Walden, Stowmarket, Suffolk
John F.W. Walling, Newton Abbot, Devon
Mr and Mrs Patrick Ward, Ward Construction, Wreningham, Norfolk
Miss Helen L. Waring, Mulbarton, Norfolk
Mrs G. Waterton, Mulbarton, Norfolk
Mr and Mrs Watkinson (Steward)
Darren Webster, Swainsthorpe, Norfolk
Paul Webster, Swainsthorpe, Norfolk
Dennis and Heather Wells, Mulbarton, Norfolk
The Weyer Family, Mulbarton
The Wheeler Family, Mulbarton, Norfolk
Viv, Ian and Olivia Wickham
Joan Widgery
Stephen Wilde, Hainford
Brian Wilde, Hethersett
M. Wilde (née Scarfe), Mulbarton
David Wilkins, Mulbarton, Norfolk
Rachel Wilkins, Mulbarton, Norfolk
Mr and Mrs E. Willer, Taverham, Norfolk
Sylvia Wills (née Cooper), Poole, Dorset
Mr and Mrs Michael Wooldridge, Thurton, Norfolk
Mr and Mrs A. Wright, Mulbarton, Norfolk
Steven Wright, now Lancaster
Charles and Brenda Yallop, Mulbarton